36480000005639

SELLING
········
THE
········
STORY

Selling The Story
The Layman's Guide to Collecting and Communicating Demographic Information

by William Dunn

AMERICAN
DEMOGRAPHICS BOOKS.

A Division of American Demographics, Inc.
127 West State Street, Ithaca, NY 14850
Telephone: 607-273-6343

Publisher	Richard A. Wright
Executive Editor	Diane Crispell
Associate Publisher	James Madden
Assistant Editors	Kathleen Brandenburg, Mary Colella

ISBN 0-936889-14-4
Library of Congress Catalog Number 91-058811

Cataloging In Publication Data
Dunn, William, 1946–
Selling the story

ISBN 0-936889-14-4
Printed in the United States of America

Designed and composited by Stephen Masiclat
Charts compiled and designed by Richard Siegel

For Mom and Dad and Krisha
With Love and Thanks

Acknowledgments

This book could not have been written without the help of numerous people. I'd like to thank them.

Bill Giles and Lionel Linder, my editors at *The Detroit News*, first assigned me to cover demographics and taught me much of what I know about the fascinating subject.

The highly professional staff of the Census Bureau has always been cooperative and instructive, especially Dr. Barbara Everitt Bryant, bureau director.

Over the years, certain individuals have been especially helpful and encouraging: Neal B. Freeman, the late Joseph Willicombe, the late Jim Bishop, John P. Reilly, Francis X. Fay, August Gribbin, and Ron Goulart.

Computer expert and friend Richard Siegel, of Richard Siegel & Associates, Cranford, New Jersey, provided invaluable computer assistance, and designed the charts and graphs.

And, from American Demographics Books, Peter Francese, Dick Wright, and my editor Diane Crispell were unstinting in their support.

Table of Contents

Part I: The Trends

Author's Note

The new editor-in-chief wanted to see me right away. There had been talk of a shakeup in the newsroom. Once inside the boss's oak-panelled office, he let me have it.

"I have a new assignment for you," he said, with a pause. Then he added: "Demographics." He waited for my reaction.

I stared back blankly, not exactly sure what "demographics" meant or what the editor had in mind. He quickly explained that he wanted me to cover population trends—things like mortality, longevity, mobility, and fertility.

"Huh? What is this guy talking about," I wondered to myself, as I vacantly nodded my head in agreement. It sounded like the reporter's equivalent of Siberia, worse than a lifetime of writing obituaries or covering zoning meetings. Population trends sounded pretty boring to me. Perhaps he expected me to crank out unread stories about global population bombs and Third World contraception.

This was bad news indeed for this newshound, who had been happily chasing fire trucks, politicians, and assorted criminals around town for news, as well as the occasional stray dog floating down the Detroit River on winter ice floes.

Of course, I was but one of a score of general assignment reporters and rewritemen, stuck in a comfortable rut, struggling to distinguish myself from the others and break away from the pack. That was long ago, in 1977, when I was little more than a rookie reporter at the *Detroit News*, then the country's fifth largest daily and biggest afternoon paper.

I resisted and struggled with the demographics beat at first, batting out some dreadful stories, top-heavy with statistics. For a while, I felt like William Boot, the hapless protagonist in *Scoop*, Evelyn Waugh's satire of the newspaper world. Boot, a second-string nature columnist for the *London Beast*, is suddenly and inexplicably named war correspondent, a plumb assignment. Lord Copper, publisher of the *Beast*, dispatches Boot posthaste to cover civil war in Ishmaelia. His qualifications: being mistaken for one John Boot, legendary foreign correspondent.

But in time, I began to make sense of the numbers and to appreciate their importance. Demographics is not as incomprehensible, nor as boring, as it may at first seem. There's actually a logic and underlying simplicity to it, for those who stick with it. I gradually came to understand what my boss was talking about and to share his enthusiasm for demographics. I eventually realized that he had given me unusual freedom and a tremendous opportunity to do important, distinctive work, and thereby set myself apart from the many other reporters stuck on traditional beats.

The editor, Bill Giles, had just come to the *Detroit News* from Dow Jones, where he had been the founding editor of the *National Observer* and before that a reporter and editor at the *Wall Street Journal*. These are the very publications that pioneered demographic reporting back in the 1960s. Admittedly, demographics might not have the flash appeal of a congressional investigation, Middle East politics, the Super Bowl, or a presidential campaign. Yet demographics is every bit as important, perhaps more so, because it reveals not only what's happening now, but what may lie ahead.

Unlike most beats, where a reporter is writing today about what happened yesterday for tomorrow's paper, the demographic reporter is writing about the future. And there's nothing more important or intriguing in the 1990s—the decade opening onto the magical 21st century—than the future.

Here are just a few of the things forecasters say we can look forward to: working until our late 60s or beyond, having several totally different careers—not just jobs, but different careers, more and more people living to 100, bypassing Florida to retire in college towns or places like the Ozarks, and seeing a revival of Sixties-style rebelliousness by the same people at a later age—senior Baby Boomers determined to protect Social Security.

You don't need to be a mathematical wizard to become an expert demographic analyst or reporter. I say that from personal experience, having struggled through high school math. What it does take is a calculator with fresh batteries, a grounding in basic arithmetic, and understanding the difference between mean and median (see page 156 if you're not sure). Just as important are: curiosity, eagerness, and hard work.

If I, who got a C- in Algebra II and Trig I, can do it, you can do it. Give it time and I'm confident you'll realize as I did that, unlike William Boot, this was no mistake.

—*William Dunn, September 30, 1991*
Chevy Chase, Maryland

Preface

The U.S. is a fast-changing nation of more than 250 million individuals racing toward the future.

While the rate of growth is slowing, the population increased 22.2 million between 1980 and 1990—roughly as many people as live in all of Canada. In just the last decade, the country has become more racially and ethnically diverse and experienced another baby boom. It has seen a decline in divorces and the first signs of labor shortages.

New cities and jobs are emerging in the suburbs, yet some old and dying central cities show evidence of renewed life. And while the Sunbelt continues to boom, not everything that booms is in the Sunbelt and not everything in the Sunbelt booms.

Meanwhile, Asians have the highest household income of any Americans, while Hispanics are on the way to becoming America's largest minority, likely to surpass blacks by the year 2015, if not sooner.

These trends and countless others are altering the way we live, work, and play. They affect all of us—our institutions, all aspects of society, what collectively is the evolving American culture. They are powerful forces that cannot be ignored.

And it is demographics—the buzzword of Madison Avenue, but so much more than a catch-phrase—that spots and quantifies powerful social and economic forces, and even allows us to influence those trends.

Some wag once called sociology "the science of the obvious." If that is true, then demography, sociology's first cousin, is taking the obvious to its less-than-obvious conclusions.

Demography has also been called destiny. Demography—from the Greek 'demos' meaning people—is the statistical study of the population, ranging from people down the block to the estimated 5.5 billion people around the world.

Demographics and the Real World

It is demographics that literally determines political power in America through reapportionment and redistricting, and influences the allocation of $45 billion annually in federal funds. Demographics charts social problems, progress, and opportunities. The numbers are used by governments from the local zoning board to the White House to decide where to build schools and roads, and how to design an anti-poverty program or salvage Social Security.

The news media, as well as businesses of all types, are belatedly discovering the vital importance of demographics. Anyone concerned about the future or possible futures, and even ways to influence trends to arrive at the best possible future, must follow demographics. In the hands of business leaders, demographic data influence the cars we drive, the insurance we buy, and where the next McDonald's or shopping mall will be built. In a very real way, demographics influences where the jobs will and won't be.

There's no better time to start following demographics than now, with results from the 1990 census beginning to flow. For it is the Census Bureau's thankless but indispensable job through its head count every 10 years to gather the demographic data that create a statistical portrait of the U.S. and its people.

Despite controversy over the accuracy of the 1990 count, the census is the only game in town, or the nation. The results that will pour out for years to come form the baseline for much other social science research to be done within and outside the government, including at our elite universities and think tanks. Census results and the other research they will trigger represent a national treasure of data just waiting to be mined by those who know how.

Leading news organizations have assigned top reporters to provide ongoing coverage of the Census Bureau, other statistical agencies, and the demographics they produce. Among them: the *New York Times*, *Los Angeles Times*, the Associated Press, United Press International, *USA*

Today, Knight-Ridder, the Gannett News Service, *Time*, *Newsweek*, and *U.S. News & World Report*.

Interest is spreading beyond the elite media, evidenced by the fact that the managing editor of a chain of suburban dailies recently opined during a break in a golf game, "Demographics is the hot beat of the 1990s." If suburban editors are saying it at the country clubs, it must be true.

And there's further proof. In its November 17, 1990 issue, *Editor & Publisher* magazine ran a feature titled, "Census is Treasure Trove for Journalists." I myself have recently given talks on covering demographics to many groups, such as Investigative Reporters and Editors and the Society of American Business Editors and Writers, and have written a how-to piece on statistical reporting for *Writer's Digest* magazine.

Every day, an increasing number of newspapers, magazines, and broadcast stations run demographic stories. Often they're ripped right from the wire service printers. Unfortunately, such stories are typically superficial, lack color, and miss the local angle. Yet editors run them because readers and the broadcast audience want to know more. These are people stories, with the potential to inform Americans about themselves, their world, and what lies ahead.

Glimpsing the Future Through Demographics

While most demographers look ahead only a decade or two, one daring demographer at the Census Bureau made population projections to the year 2080. He explained it was safer that way, because when 2080 arrived, no one would be around to remember his projection on the chance he was wrong.

Demographic analysis and forecasting is risky. But American business and government discovered in the 1960s and 1970s that they could not afford to ignore demographic research. In an increasingly complex world, demographics can provide a glimpse into the future—a competitive edge.

Here's how it works. Current demographics provide a map to where we are now in terms of income, educational attainment, life expectancy, births, employment, and so on, broken down by race, ethnicity, age, region, and more. When current numbers are compared with historic data, clear trends emerge; we see the progress or backsliding that has occurred. If you know where you've been and where you are now, you have a good idea of where you're headed. Given that demographic trends are often like steam locomotives, with powerful momentum that carries them forward, demographic analysis provides a glimpse of the future, or possible futures.

It's not by chance that General Motors has a demographer on its staff, as do many other large companies, including the utilities. Firms of all sizes and in all industries are beginning to pick up on the importance of trend tracking. "Demographics has a big place in small business," Irwin Friedman of the Network of Small Businesses told me for an August 1991 story in *Nation's Business*. "Trend tracking can certainly give small business the edge," says Friedman, "because the turnaround time is more rapid for a small business than a large one. The adjustment to reality takes place very quickly. But, he adds, firms that ignore demographic trends are "flying blind. ... Unless they're lucky, they're gone in a year or two."

In recent years, some 3,500 freelance demographers have hung up their shingles to provide consulting services to businesses and anybody else who needs to know about the future. Two presidential administrations and a contentious and heatedly partisan Congress came together to spare the budget axe and authorize $2.6 billion for the 1990 census—the most costly, controversial, and computerized head count ever. From the Social Security Administration to the local board of education, government officials are paying close attention to the numbers, because indeed they must.

Average Americans too are catching on. Even if they don't know the name for it, they see the impact of demographics all around them and want to know more about changing neighborhoods; school enrollments that are growing after plunging; shorter work weeks but somehow less leisure time; two-income families with little extra money to show for it; stores closing downtown, with new shops and subdivisions springing up on the outskirts; traffic that's worse than ever; and planning for retirement amid fears that Social Security's in trouble. People want to know what's going on, and demographics can provide many of the answers.

Admittedly, the numbers by themselves can be deadly dull for the reporter or analyst, and lethal for the reader. It's not enough to scoop up some Social Security projections of beneficiaries or the newest numbers on births and report them undigested. Too often, the numbers mystify or bore the reader. The challenge is to analyze the numbers, dig below the surface, and get beyond the numbers to the people and lives that the numbers are quantifying. Where possible, show the repercussions of the numbers.

On a national level, the numbers can become overwhelming, when talking about millions of people and billions of dollars. But the story becomes very real and compelling indeed when it explores the generational conflicts between workers and retirees, how retirement is being redefined and pushed back, how baby boomers will retire later than their parents, and how baby busters and immigrants will shoulder the burden for boomer retirement.

It's my contention that most, if not all, stories are demographic stories or have strong demographic angles that are too often overlooked. And the stories are weaker for the lack of demographics.

There's a good recent example to be found in the U.S. and Coalition war with Iraq. Saddam Hussein had boasted, and the media took at face value, that he had an army of one million men. A quick check of the Census Bureau's *Statistical Abstract* and a few phone calls would have exposed this for the empty claim it was. Iraq has a 1990 population of 18.8 million, over half of whom are women. Of the remaining nine million males, almost one-half are boys under the age of 15; another 20 percent or so are men over the age of 40. When one excludes those put out of action by Iraq's war with Iran, that doesn't leave all that many able-bodied, willing young men still available to join the Iraqi army, much less the vaunted Republican Guard. This clearly was an important story of Iraqi vulnerability, one that was thoroughly overlooked by most reporters.

This book is written for journalists, business executives, researchers, and planners of all types, as well as the plain curious who want to find the demographic story and deliver it in an understandable, informative, and compelling way. While the statistics are essential to any demographic story, the numbers should be used sparingly to be effective. Demographics, after all, are essentially people stories.

Each chapter in Part I covers the trends in a particular subject area such as migration or income. 1990 census data are included as available at the time of writing. Sources are listed at the end of each chapter and a full list of references is available in the appendix, followed by a glossary of terms. Each chapter also contains a tip on doing demographic analysis, definitions of rates referred to in the text, and, most important, food for thought—a list of trends to track and questions to ask when you are exploring. In Part II, the chapters explore how to most effectively track trends and how not to track them. We'll discuss where to find gold mines of demographic data and how to dig into the riches there. Reporters will learn how to develop the solid stories buried in the numbers; researchers will discover ways to widely disseminate their work via the media. Read on and finally discover the most important demographic statistic of all.

This is not some dense theoretical textbook written by a remote Ph.D. journalism professor sitting in an ivy-covered tower. I've tried to write a straight-ahead primer, filled with practical information, leads, and sources. It's taken over 15 years to write, the time I've been covering the demographic beat.

Part I

....

The Trends

1 The Beginning and the End: Births and Deaths

Before you begin writing award-winning stories and producing the types of reports guaranteed to get you noticed and promoted, we need to get a few things straight about demographics.

Remember: demographics or demography is the statistical study of population. And as with life itself, it all starts at birth.

Consider these staggering numbers:

- Some 143 million babies were born worldwide in 1990.
- Fifty million people died that year, resulting in a net gain of 93 million new mouths to feed, bringing the world population to 5.3 billion. (In 1992, the total is up to 5.5 billion.)
- In the U.S., there were a surprising 4.2 million live births in 1990, the highest number since 1963. But the total number will begin declining again this decade.

Americans are having smaller families today than they did a generation ago, roughly two children per woman now, versus almost four in the mid-1950s. What accounts for the high number of births in recent years is what demographers call the "echo baby boom." The women now having babies are part of the massive post-World War II baby-boom generation. And while opting to have small families, there are so many of them that they're igniting a temporary boomlet.

American Generations

The end of World War II is credited with starting the original baby boom in the U.S., Canada, and Europe, as returning soldiers and their sweethearts became free to marry and start the families they had been postponing. In just a few years, births that had been unusually low during the Depression and war years jumped several hundred thousand in the U.S. A strong economic expansion and low unemployment helped keep births high in the U.S. for nearly two decades. The number of births topped 4 million in 1954 and stayed at that level for an unprecedented 11 years, through a prosperous era of economic expansion. The peak came in 1957, with 4.3 million births. The original baby boomers were born between 1946 and 1964. They number some 77 million and represent almost one-third of the U.S. population.

After 1964, births began a prolonged decline. Several causes have been cited: the introduction of the birth-control pill, legalization of abortion, changing social mores, feminism, and women's increasing educational attainment and career orientation. Because there are relatively fewer of them, people born between 1965 and 1976 are called the baby-bust generation. In 1992, the bust is aged 16 to 27 and has 41 million people.

This smaller generation may have less political and marketing clout than the original boomers have. But they may have one real advantage in that busters will have less competition among themselves for jobs and promotions. It started early in the 1980s, with labor shortages of entry-level workers in industry, at fast-food restaurants, and in retail establishments—that is, until the recession hit. In contrast, it's been slow going for baby boomers and will continue to be as they climb the ladder of success, because they're always bumping into one another.

In the late 1970s, births began to pick up again, as the boom started having its own echo baby boom, or boomlet. Births topped 4 million again in 1989 and 1990.

Helping fuel this latest jump in births is the fact that many women who postponed motherhood to launch their careers are now racing their biological clocks to start families. But births should begin dropping soon, as the baby boomers age out of the prime childbearing years. And even with the large numbers of boomers having children, the average remains at about two children per woman, and this echo-boom generation will ultimately be smaller than the original boom, which because of its vast size has been called the "pig in a python."

No matter where they are in life, the baby boomers ignite trends and influence all of society because of their sheer size. As Census Bureau analyst Gregory Spencer notes: "Society's attention is wherever the heck the baby boom is. Whatever concerns one-third of the population will be a major concern to our society."

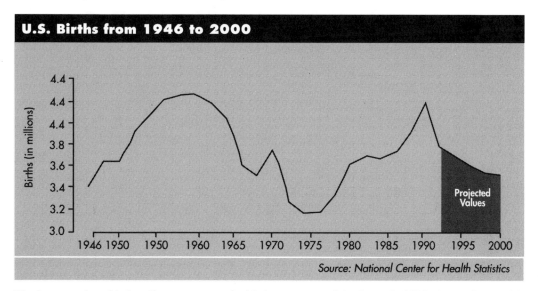

U.S. Births from 1946 to 2000

Births (in millions)

Source: National Center for Health Statistics

The boom-to-bust birth rollercoaster may be hitting a new peak in the early 1990s, but will probably fall off later in the decade (although less sharply than projections here indicate).

In the late 1960s, baby boomers crowded into classrooms, causing a building frenzy of new schools and a rush recruitment of new teachers to keep up with them. It happened all over again when boomers went off to college. They boosted sales for everything from 45 rpm records to blue jeans and Mustang convertibles. This is the original Pepsi generation and a big reason why America—as seen in advertising and the broader culture—has been so youth-oriented for the past 20 years.

But that's changing, because baby boomers are now aged 28 to 46, settling into middle age. Not so surprisingly, we're now seeing more middle-aged but active people in ads, pitching everything from hair dyes to fitness regimens and financial planning. And being the politically

3

active and vocal generation that boomers are, marketers are responding with politically correct ice cream and hamburgers that don't sacrifice the Bolivian rain forest.

Another birth trend to watch closely: births to single mothers. Births to unmarried women accounted for one-quarter of all births by the late 1980s, up from 18 percent in 1980. (This will be covered in more detail in Chapter 3.)

Demography: The Competitive Edge and The Big Story

While boomers are credited or blamed for starting most trends, it was actually the baby-bust generation and the fallout from plunging births that gave demography its big break, particularly in the business world. During the baby-boom years, the high levels of births boosted demand for everything from baby food to new houses. Little attention was given to long-range planning or product development. Business executives had all they could do to keep up with demand. Anything would sell, regardless of quality. People just assumed that sales—and births— would continue growing.

Then came the baby bust. Suddenly, companies that aimed their products and services at the infant and youth markets saw their target market shrink. Sales no longer automatically grew each year.

To grow now meant taking share away from the competition, expanding the product line, or diversifying into new fields. Countless firms that didn't react fast enough saw their sales decline. It was a rude awakening that forced a change in the way America did business.

A big part of that change was demographics, which corporate analysts began to track more closely as part of product development and marketing. "It can offer a competitive edge," says Vincent P. Barabba, a former Census Bureau director who went on to become executive director of marketing research and planning at General Motors Corporation.

Gerber Products, which always closely tracked birth trends, began expanding in the late 1960s beyond its baby-food line into insurance, children's apparel, even trucking and day-care centers. By the late

1980s, Gerber sold off its trucking and day-care divisions, but remains in insurance and children's apparel and has expanded its food line with products for the entire preschool set—infants to 4-year-olds.

In the cola wars, the giants battle with an ever-growing number of soft-drink products, catering to every taste, age, and waistline. Levi Strauss looked at the trends and, in the late 1980s, expanded its line to appeal to all ages, especially the aging baby boomers and their own children. While the company whose name is synonymous with blue jeans continued to produce the traditional denim pants that are so popular with the teen set, Levi Strauss in the early and mid-1980s introduced fuller cut jeans for men and women, maternity clothes, and a youthwear line. It also launched Dockers, a line of looser-fitting cotton pants in various colors.

"Dockers were clearly driven by demographic trends," acknowledges John Onoda, director of corporate communications. "They were targeted at this aging group. But we find it has universal appeal." There are Docker shirts and shoes, as well as the pants, selling to all ages. By 1991, Docker sales had topped $700 million; company-wide sales had risen strongly to around $5 billion.

In the hotly competitive radio broadcasting field, a steadily growing number of stations are now concentrating on playing oldies (music from the 1960s), while others are switching to the talk format—both strategies intended to bring in the aging baby boomers.

Demographics have also come to the attention of public officials and the public through the existence of the baby bust. The bust that followed the boom pointed up a dangerous flaw in the country's Social Security system. In 1940, Social Security had 42 workers contributing to its fund for each retiree drawing benefits. Today, that rate is down to 3.3 workers per beneficiary, and for baby boomers who retire around 2020, it will be down to 2.4 workers per retiree.

It was demographics that sounded the alarm and prodded Congress and the Carter and Reagan Administrations to action to shore up the system. Years of debate and analysis over the Social Security mess kept demographics on the front page, gave average Americans as well as politicians a crash course in Demographics 101, and put demographers on the nightly news.

Longer Life Means More Seniors and More Deaths

Births are only one important part of what's called vital statistics. Death is the flip side.

Americans are living longer than ever overall—a record high of 75.4 years at birth in 1990. Yet ironically, deaths are rising because the U.S. population is growing, and increased life expectancy puts more people in the vulnerable later years. While overall life expectancy at birth has increased dramatically, the remaining life expectancy for those aged 65 or older has risen slowly in recent decades. By 1988, men aged 65 could expect to live another 14.9 years on average; women could expect another 18.6 years.

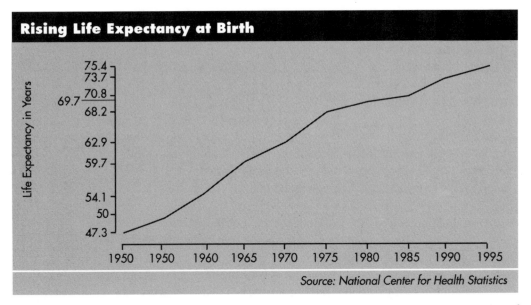

Average life expectancy in the U.S. has grown by more than 50 percent during the 20th century. Most of these gains have been made at the low end of the age spectrum with significant declines in infant mortality.

In 1990, there were 2.2 million deaths in the United States, slightly more than the year before. Deaths have been above 2 million annually since 1983. Despite the rise in deaths, however, death rates have fallen significantly in this century, due in large part to improvements in infant mortality brought about by advances in modern medicine in the first quarter of this century. The drop in infant mortality in turn led to declines in fertility.

For centuries, poor odds of survival caused parents to have many children in hopes that some would survive. This was especially important in agrarian societies, including the pre-industrial United States; children were needed to help with the farm work.

As infant mortality declined, so did a woman's primary reason for having a half-dozen or more births. Shrinking family size further accelerated as families moved from the farms to the cities, where big families were no longer a necessity and often proved a burden in crowded tenements.

The phenomenon of improving mortality rates preceding and contributing to decreasing birth rates is known as "demographic transition." The trend has occurred in most western nations. (Health trends will be discussed in more detail in Chapter 11.)

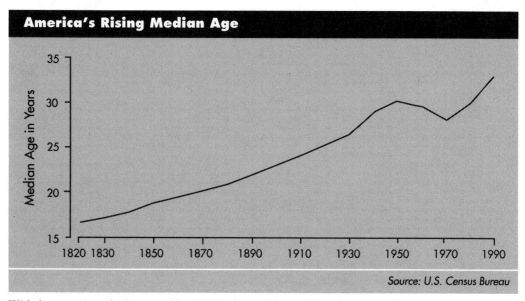

With the exception of a dip caused by the baby boom in its youth, median age in the U.S. has risen steadily since the nation's early years.

Increasing life expectancy, plus the aging of the population pushed along by the maturing baby boom, has sent median age soaring. It's gone from 28 years in 1970 to 33 years in 1990. Median age will continue rising, hitting 40 years by 2020, about the time that the bulk of baby boomers start retiring.

For a glimpse of the U.S. in the future, look now to Florida. One in five Floridians is now aged 60 or older, a share that the U.S. will reach in another 25 to 30 years.

The experience of black American males is the troubling exception to the fairly steady trend of increasing life expectancy for Americans. Life expectancy at birth for black males has been up and down and up again. It reached 65.6 years in 1984, then fell to 64.9 years in 1988. The decline is believed to be largely due to high mortality rates. For black men between the ages of 15 and 44, homicide is the leading cause of death.

Provisional data for 1989 and 1990 offer some encouragement, showing life expectancy for black males rising again, reaching a new high of 66.0 years by 1990, although that still lags years behind other groups.

Life expectancy for black females born in 1990 was 74.5 years, almost two years higher than that for white males, according to provisional data from the National Center for Health Statistics. For white females, it was 79.3 years. Historically, life expectancy for women has been longer than that of men because of men's more hazardous occupations and health habits. But one theory has it that the gap will narrow as more women get on the career fast-track and become subject to the same job stresses as men.

All told, for all groups, births far outnumber deaths. The difference between births and deaths is called natural increase. In 1990, the natural increase in the U.S. population was 2 million. Almost all countries have more births than deaths. But that could change if zero population growth advocates succeed in their efforts to achieve a stable world population in which births and deaths are roughly equal. The big challenge is to lower birth rates in developing countries, where six or more births per woman are not uncommon.

TREND-TRACKING TIP: The Differences Among Us

As for most demographic variables, differences emerge in birth and death rates when comparisons are made by age, race, region, income, and educational attainment. Age is usually broken down into cohorts, or five- or ten-year groupings. Demographics also vary by nation, state, even zip code. The smart demographic researcher should always be alert to these differences, because the differences hold clues to the whys.

Generally, the higher the income and educational attainment of a population, the more favorable are the vital statistics: longer life expectancy, lower death rates, and lower infant mortality. As income rises, so does access to regular and superior medical care. As educational attainment rises, so does the awareness of the benefits of regular checkups, good diet, and exercise.

Also, as income and educational attainment rise, birth rates fall, due to a combination of more access to and understanding of birth control and stronger commitment to careers. Blacks and Hispanics, who lag behind non-Hispanic whites in income and educational attainment, have higher birth and mortality rates but shorter life expectancies. Asian Americans go to school longer and have higher household income than other minorities and even non-Hispanic whites. Asians also have the lowest mortality rates and longest life expectancy in the U.S., as well as low birth rates.

It is interesting to combine demographic variables to delve into even more finely tuned differences. When one compares people from different racial and ethnic groups with similar demographic characteristics such as educational attainment, the gaps narrow but do not close. Some differences never disappear.

Future Growth/Stability/Decline Depends on the Balance of Births and Deaths

Despite continued high fertility in many developing countries, family size and the annual rate of growth have declined, offering hope that the so-called population bomb can eventually be defused before it explodes. At present fertility rates, women worldwide would wind up having 3.4 children by the end of their childbearing years. That's down from 4.9 children in the late 1960s.

There are a few Western countries where deaths have actually exceeded the number of births in recent years, and the population has begun shrinking. The populations in Hungary and what used to be West Germany have actually been dropping. They're shrinking because the total fertility rate (TFR) has been so very low for over a generation, below what's called replacement level. TFR is the number of children a woman would have if she finishes her childbearing years at the age-specific fertility rates for a particular year. Several other nations are close to shrinking, including Austria, Belgium, France, Italy, and Luxembourg. Replacement level is 2.1 children per woman, or the number needed for each man and woman to replace themselves. (The extra 0.1 is added to compensate for children who die before reaching reproductive age.) In several countries, the total fertility rate is as low as 1.7 children per woman.

While the rate in the U.S. is bobbing around replacement level, even this country's population conceivably could begin shrinking in the next century. The American experience roughly parallels what's happening in most other western countries. Many of these countries have even lower fertility rates than the U.S. One curious exception in recent years is Sweden, long a bellwether of social trends. After decades of fertility well below replacement level, Sweden's TFR has risen in recent years to about 2.1 children per woman, or replacement level. It remains to be seen whether Sweden's TFR will stay there or rise further and what this portends for other industrialized nations. Trend trackers are watching closely.

The United Nations and the Census Bureau have each done a series of population projections for the U.S., using various assumptions and coming up with a range of outcomes. Each has come up with a scenario, assuming low fertility and low-to-moderate immigration, that has the U.S. beginning a slow population decline sometime between the years 2030 and 2038, after the population peaks at 290 to 300 million.

Many analysts see a stable or even declining population as beneficial, contending it would ease the demand on already strained services and resources, and permit reallocation to those in need. But author and columnist Ben J. Wattenberg, in his provocative 1987 book *The Birth Dearth*, warns that a population decline in the U.S. would mean pervasive labor shortages, diminished creativity and economic and scientific progress, worsening pension problems, and rising tensions between generations.

He, like some in other slow-growth or declining countries, advocates pro-natalist, or pro-family, programs to encourage larger families, including tax breaks and child care. Such programs have had little effect in Europe, though. Immigration is the other variable—and one more easily regulated—that could keep the U.S. growing if it chooses to, by letting more people into the country.

While the U.S. may eventually stabilize or shrink, it will likely happen long after the census and United Nations expect it to. The census projection assumes annual net immigration of only 500,000; the United Nations assumes 435,000. In fact, annual legal immigration has been well over 500,000 annually since 1980 and has topped 600,000 since 1986. This figure does not include illegal aliens, who are estimated to be arriving at the rate of 100,000 to 300,000 a year. (Chapter 5 examines immigration trends in more detail.)

RATES: In addition to simple birth and death totals, rates are also frequently cited and are important for comparison purposes. There are several different kinds of rates:

- Birth rate, also known as a crude birth rate, gives the number of live births per 1,000 people in a particular year. To compute that number, take the total number of births, divide by the total population, and multiply by 1,000. In 1990, the U.S. birth rate was 16.7 births per 1,000 population.

- Fertility rate gives the number of live births in a year per 1,000 women aged 15 to 44 (considered the childbearing years). This is thought to be a more revealing measurement than birth rates. To compute the fertility rate, take the total number of births, divide that by the number of women in the childbearing years, and multiply by 1,000. In addition to overall fertility rates, rates can also be computed for different age groups. The 1990 fertility rate was 67.0 births per 1,000 women aged 15 to 44.

- Total fertility rate, also called TFR, is the number of children a woman would have by the end of her childbearing years if she continued having children at current age-specific fertility rates. U.S. TFR in 1957, at the height of the baby boom, was 3.7 children per woman. Currently, it's hovering around 2.0.

- Death rates are calculated basically the same way as birth rates. However, in addition to total rates and rates by age group, death rates are computed for the leading causes of death.

- Death rate, also known as the crude death rate, is the total deaths per 1,000 population. Take the total of deaths, divide by the total population, and multiply by 1,000. In 1990, the death rate was 8.6 deaths per 1,000 population.

- Cause-specific death rate is computed the same way as the death rate, except that one takes the number of deaths from a specific cause and divides that by the total population and multiplies by 1,000. The leading causes of death are heart attack, followed by cancer and stroke. Causes, however, differ dramatically by age and race. Asian Americans have the lowest mortality rates overall, while blacks and American Indians have the highest rates.

- Infant mortality rate is the total deaths of infants under age one divided by live births in a particular year, multiplied by 1,000. The 1990 U.S. infant mortality rate was 9.1 infant deaths per 1,000 live births, representing a 6 percent decrease over the previous year. Even so, more than 20 countries have lower infant mortality rates than the U.S.

Trends to Track; Questions to Ask

- **Baby Boomers.** Igniting trends every step of the way because of their size, baby boomers are now reluctantly entering middle age and settling down. What impact does this have on the economy, their own behavior, the towns they live in? Are they moving to the suburbs they previously abandoned, getting involved in local politics? What trends and fads are they starting now?

- **Baby Busters.** Who are they and how do they differ from their older brothers and sisters from the baby-boom generation just ahead of them? What are the advantages and disadvantages of belonging to the baby bust?

- **Echo Boom.** Why did it start? How big is it? How long will it last? How will people from this generation differ from those in the baby bust and the original baby boom? What's the impact of the echo baby boom on the economy and society? Will birth trends continue to ride a roller coaster, or will they eventually flatten out?

- **Birth Differences.** Explore differences in birth rates by age group, race, and region. Are women in their 20s, as well as older career women, contributing to the echo boom? While families remain small, has there been any increase in the total fertility rate? If so, why? Are gaps in fertility rates narrowing among racial groups? Why are birth rates highest in Utah and lowest in West Virginia? Jewish women in the U.S. have low fertility rates; what's happening with women in other religious groups? Catholics traditionally have had somewhat high rates; have they come down? How do U.S. rates compare with those of developed countries?

- **Abortions.** Abortions have averaged some 1.5 million annually in recent years. If abortions were restricted somehow, what impact might that have on the number of births and fertility rates? Would births rise significantly or not?

- **Birth Dearth.** Even with the echo baby boom, Americans are still hovering around replacement-level fertility. If it continues at low levels, would the U.S. begin shrinking in population? If so, when? What other factors would keep it from shrinking? What are the benefits/liabilities of growth/no growth on the economy and society?

- **Life Expectancy.** Life is not only easy, it's longest in Hawaii. How come? How do the other states compare? Why is it so high in some states and so low in others, like West Virginia and Mississippi? Are there differences by profession or religion, and if so, why? How high can life expectancy go? Does this mean more elderly with chronic conditions? What are the consequences—political, economic, and social—of living longer but being sicker?

- **Longer Life.** Women live, on average, seven years longer than men. Why? Is it genetic or behavior, or both? With women outlasting men, is there a significant shortage of men among seniors? What's the impact? In the black community, there is a growing shortage of men in their 20s and 30s because of high mortality rates for those ages. What are the implications?

- **Death Rates.** What are the trends in death rates? Where are the rates dropping, where are they increasing? What impact could AIDS have on overall death rates and life expectancy? If a cure were found for cancer, what impact would this have on mortality rates and life expectancy?

- **Infant Mortality.** Despite progress, more than 20 nations have lower infant mortality rates than the U.S. Why? What are they doing that we're not? Can we cut our rate further, and how?

SOURCES: The primary source for births and deaths and other vital statistics for the U.S. is the National Center for Health Statistics in Hyattsville, Maryland, which compiles these national data from state Departments of Health, which in turn collect birth and death certificate records from each county.

- The federal Centers for Disease Control in Atlanta keeps statistics on leading causes of death, including AIDS.

- The United Nations in New York City keeps tabs on births and deaths worldwide.

- Each year, the Population Reference Bureau in Washington, D.C. publishes a World Population Data Sheet, using United Nations and Census Bureau statistics.

2 On the Road Again: Migration

Every day, some 1,600 people move to Florida. Every day, another 700 move out.

Each year, about 18 percent of Americans change their address—more than 40 million people. Most go only a few miles, but some 8 million move to another state. Americans are among the most mobile people in the world, and people in their 20s have the highest rates of mobility.

Census Bureau analyst Kristin Hansen, writing in a bureau report on mobility, notes: "Long-distance moves are more frequently undertaken for economic reasons, including corporate transfers, military transfers, new jobs, or looking for work. Others move to attend school or for noneconomic reasons such as a desire for a change of climate, proximity to recreational areas, or family reasons." For those going only short distances, reasons include leaving the parental nest, switching apartments, or moving up to the dream house.

In explaining long-distance migration, demographers often say that people vote with their feet, moving in pursuit of opportunity. Or they're fleeing the lack of it, as with the many auto workers who fled the Midwest for the Southwest, especially Texas, during the Oil Patch boom of the early 1980s.

People may rave about the sunny skies and many outdoor amenities in the Sunbelt, including golfing year-round. But, "by and large, the jobs come first," says economist Nestor Terleckyj, who does employment and population forecasting at NPA Data Services. "Jobs are created, and people migrate to them. People move back and forth all the time. More people stick in the places where the labor demand is greatest and expanding. Fewer people stick around or come in when employment is depressed."

Rapid population growth then perpetuates itself. Terleckyj notes that a growing population "increases demand for all types of things. Housing is an obvious case. So is retail trade and all kinds of services. People go to dentists and doctors. They need public services. They get sick and go to hospitals. Kids go to schools. All this fuels more job growth. You end up with even more people in that place."

The Bureau of Labor Statistics calculates that the total number of jobs increased from 102 million in 1980 to 122.6 million in 1990. Well over three-quarters of the 20.6 million increase in jobs came in the South and the West; not surprisingly, that's where most of the population growth occurred last decade, too.

Newcomers vs. Leavers

Net inmigration from other states and overseas accounted for over two-thirds of the growth in Arizona, New Hampshire, Nevada, and Florida, and well over half of the growth in Alaska, California, Georgia, Texas, Virginia, and the state of Washington. The balance of growth came from an excess of births over deaths. Almost all of these states, not coincidentally, grew at two to three times the overall U.S. growth rate of 9.8 percent in the 1980s. It's a general rule of thumb that any state, county, or city that is growing significantly faster than the U.S. average (double or more) is experiencing a rapid influx of newcomers.

Of course, like Latin, demographics has an exception for every rule. An exception here is Utah, which grew at almost twice the U.S. rate yet had only modest inmigration. How come? Fueling that state's growth was a high birth rate, traceable to the historically large families that Mormons have. Utah is over three-quarters Mormon.

In any case where the demographics don't fit the pattern, dig below the surface. There's usually a logical explanation, as in the case of New Hampshire, which was booming amid the northeastern bust. The reason: a high-tech and services boom in the early and mid-1980s and the lack of a state income tax lured people from all over, especially neighboring "Taxachusetts."

The slower an area's population growth, the less growth comes from inmigration. In very slow-growing areas, like Michigan and elsewhere in the industrial Midwest and Farmbelt, there has actually been a net outmigration. More people moved out than moved in during the 1980s. Yet, most of these areas still managed to grow because those losses were counterbalanced by natural increase.

During the 1980s, only four states—Iowa, North Dakota, West Virginia, and Wyoming—experienced an overall loss of population. If not for natural increase, the list of decliners would have been much greater and would have included many of the farming, industrial, and Deep South states.

The exodus from the impoverished Deep South and Farmbelt is not new. The so-called "Okies" from Oklahoma and elsewhere fled the Dust Bowl in the 1930s and 1940s for the orange groves and factory opportunities—real and imagined—in California.

Many Southerners—black and white—headed straight north during that same period to high-paying factory jobs in Cleveland, Detroit, Chicago, and Milwaukee. So many transplants from the Appalachian "hollers" wound up in Ypsilanti, Michigan—drawn there by the auto jobs—that the town became jokingly known as "Ypsitucky."

Following the pattern of previous migrations, people on the move headed in fairly straight lines, often going to the towns where friends and relatives had already established themselves. In that way, they're not strangers when they arrive. Typically, people bring their music and culture with them.

The bands and the juke boxes at the taverns surrounding the auto plants around Ypsilanti and Taylor are just as likely to play songs by Tammy Wynette or the Oak Ridge Boys, as they are to play Bob Seger or Motown. In certain neighborhoods, the supermarkets make a point of stocking food items that appeal to Appalachian as well as local tastes. Amid the midwestern accents, it's not uncommon to hear southern drawls.

Despite the urban setting, many of the transplants and their children cling to the outdoor way of life by farming a few acres after their regular jobs. At harvest time, these hobby farmers proudly load their trunks with crops to bring to the factory to sell to co-workers. Hunting and fishing are also popular and a direct link to their roots.

Net Gain (Loss) in State Population 1990-91

State	Percent Change	1991 Population (in thousands)
Alabama	1.0	4,089
Alaska	2.9	570
Arizona	1.8	3,750
Arkansas	0.7	2,372
California	1.7	30,380
Colorado	2.0	3,377
Connecticut	0.1	3,291
Delaware	1.6	680
Florida	2.1	13,277
Georgia	1.8	6,623
Hawaii	1.9	1,135
Idaho	2.6	1,039
Illinois	0.8	11,543
Indiana	0.9	5,610
Iowa	0.5	2,795
Kansas	0.6	2,495
Kentucky	0.6	3,713
Louisiana	0.6	4,252
Maine	0.4	1,235
Maryland	1.3	4,860
Massachusetts	-0.3	5,996
Michigan	0.6	9,368
Minnesota	1.0	4,432
Mississippi	0.6	2,592
Missouri	0.6	5,158

Southern and Western states continue to grow faster, on average, than the Northeast and Midwest. (July 1, 1991 estimates of the resident population of states and percent change from April 1, 1990 to July 1, 1991.)

1990-91 Population Change, continued

State	Percent Change	1991 Population (in thousands)
Montana	0.9	808
Nebraska	0.7	1,593
Nevada	5.3	1,284
New Hampshire	-0.3	1,105
New Jersey	0.3	7,760
New Mexico	1.7	1,548
New York	0.3	18,058
North Carolina	1.3	6,737
North Dakota	-0.5	635
Ohio	0.7	10,939
Oklahoma	0.7	3,175
Oregon	2.2	2,922
Pennsylvania	0.5	11,961
Rhode Island	0.1	1,004
South Carolina	1.7	3,560
South Dakota	0.8	703
Tennessee	1.2	4,953
Texas	1.7	17,349
Utah	2.2	1,770
Vermont	0.6	567
Virginia	1.3	6,286
Washington	2.4	5,018
West Virginia	0.3	1,801
Wisconsin	1.0	4,955
Wyoming	1.0	460
District of Columbia	-1.1	598

Source: U.S. Census Bureau

The sense of identity and ties to the old home are further reinforced with frequent trips back there for vacation, typically once or twice a year. And many transplants eventually return to where they came from to retire.

Auto employment peaked in 1978; then the bottom fell out. The early 1980s recession spread from the automotive industry to related industries of steel, glass, and rubber. Jobs plummeted, and unemployment shot up throughout the industrial Midwest. A mass exodus began, with many heading to the booming Oil Patch to look for work.

As with earlier massive waves of immigrants from abroad, the influx of Michiganians and other Midwesterners to the Southwest triggered a backlash. Newcomers learned to get local license plates quickly, so they wouldn't be spotted as "black tag people," a derisive term that came from Michigan's black-and-white license plates. Bumper stickers appeared on Texas cars reading "Native Texan" and "Last One Out of Detroit, Turn Off the Lights."

The biggest recent losses in the Midwest and in places like New York and Pennsylvania came in the early 1980s, when their economies were in shambles. Since then, they've rebounded somewhat by overhauling and streamlining their basic industries, and diversifying and waiting for demand to come back, although they've been rocked a second time by the recession of the early 1990s. The Farmbelt has been helped by rising commodity prices.

But by 1986, the boom went bust in the Oil Patch and other mining areas, as world prices for energy fell. Soon oil exploration stopped; people were being laid off in states like Alaska, Louisiana, Oklahoma, even Texas, the very places people had flocked to only a few years before.

In some cases, the transplanted Midwesterners returned home, figuring they would rather be unemployed near family, and maybe they could get in on the industrial rebound. Native Texans either waited out their bust or headed for still-growing areas, like California, Florida, and Georgia.

TREND-TRACKING TIP: Tracking the Yearly Population Rollercoaster

When analyzing population trends over time, don't just look at the numbers at the beginning and end of a decade. It's very important to find out what happened between those points—year by year if possible—because population change is seldom a steady line up or down. It's more like a roller coaster, closely tied to the fortunes of the local as well as national economies.

Check intercensal and postcensal estimates (estimates for years between the censuses), which are produced by the Census Bureau, many state planning agencies, and others. These show year-to-year shifts that often paint a much different picture than just comparing the beginning and end of a decade, as we've seen in Texas.

Also, study the components of population change, remembering that growth is not merely a matter of births, nor totally a matter of inmigration. Population change is the bottom line on births, deaths, inmigration, and outmigration.

The switch in fortunes underscores how closely tied interstate migration is to opportunity, or the lack of it. A further complicating factor in looking at migration trends is that the growth or loss for a state may not hold for all regions within the state. For example, West Virginia, an impoverished state still dependent on mining and farming, suffered the biggest population decline in the 1980s, down 8 percent, or 156,167. Yet the three counties in its eastern Panhandle around Harpers Ferry grew by some 20,000 people last decade, after it was discovered to be a beautiful, affordable, and historic area within a two-hour commute by train or car to Washington, D.C. Similarly, while Oklahoma grew only 4 percent, its northern counties around Grand Lake of the Cherokees grew at triple that rate because of an influx of retirees, many of them native Okies returning from California.

This points up another complexity of migration and rapidly growing areas. While the net migration may be decidedly inbound, many boom areas still have a good number of people leaving for a variety of reasons.

California, the city of Los Angeles, and Los Angeles County all scored big numerical gains in the 1980s. Yet each had substantial outmigration—people being transferred, others escaping the congestion, crime, and exorbitant prices, some wanting elbow room and shorter commutes, and still others retiring back to Oklahoma or wherever.

Moves Often Reflect Life Stages and Resources

In many high-priced areas around the country, older couples sell their appreciated homes for substantial sums, then move to an inexpensive area like Oklahoma or Nevada, buy a palace for half the price, and bank the rest.

In Los Angeles, there was an actual net outmigration in the 1980s of so-called "Anglos," as non-Hispanic whites are called there. Even so, the city and county grew substantially from an influx of Latins and Asians pursuing jobs and low-end entrepreneurial opportunities. It's happening in other cities, too. The newcomers manage to trim housing costs in these expensive areas by sharing a house or apartment with extended family.

In Florida, where 1,600 newcomers arrive daily, 700 people leave every day, according to census data. Some of those leaving are workers giving up on "sunshine pay," the comparatively low wages Florida employers pay, knowing that they have a ready supply of newcomers. Others are retirees moving back home to be near their grown children after a spouse dies or health fails.

Still others are still-active retirees, the "go-goes" in marketing terms, who have grown tired of Florida's congestion, escalating prices, and summer heat. Many are skipping to northern Georgia, with its spectacular views, four seasons, and low prices. As we'll see later, a growing number of seemingly unlikely places are aggressively competing to attract retirees whose nest-eggs mean big business. Florida and Arizona definitely have competition.

While the majority of movers are in their young and middling adult years, some 5 percent of senior citizens move in a given year. In a lifetime, a person may make ten or more moves.

Rapidly growing states tend to have younger populations and more births, because young adults and families are the most mobile. Conversely, slow-growing or declining states have older populations, because the ones leaving tend to be young people seeking jobs elsewhere, leaving older, less mobile people behind.

But slow growth is not always a sign of a sluggish economy. During much of the 1980s, Connecticut, Massachusetts, New York, and New Jersey had fairly strong economies and below-average unemployment. But living costs in these states are very high, especially for housing, which discourages many young couples and those on modest incomes. Starter homes can easily top $200,000 in the New York suburbs. The average home in tony Greenwich, Connecticut, sold for around $780,000 in 1991.

Not surprisingly, it's not uncommon for children raised in the expensive New York metro area to have to move out of the region when they leave the parental nest. Some go all the way out to the Pocono Mountains in Pennsylvania to find affordable housing, only to suffer through two- and three-hour commutes to their jobs back in New York City.

Fairfield County, Connecticut, one of the wealthiest areas in the country where many Fortune 500 executives live, finds that local businesses and towns often have difficulty filling essential positions, because secretaries, clerks, and policemen cannot afford to live there. This bids up starting salaries, but even so, there are often unfilled vacancies.

Between March 1989 and March 1990, 47.3 million people moved in the U.S., or 17.9 percent of the population over the age of one. The highest rate of migration in the last 30 years came in 1960-61, when 20.6 percent of the population moved, closely followed by 19.6 percent in 1984-85.

Six in ten movers stay in the same county. Another 18 to 20 percent move to a different county within the same state; about the same proportion move to another state. The remaining few percent move in from another country.

Census Bureau mobility expert Kristin Hansen notes that "generally, local moves are housing adjustments—the purchase of a new home, a change of apartments, etc.—or are made in response to changes in family status or what is commonly termed a 'lifecycle change.' These lifecycle changes include marriage, divorce, birth of a child, and retirement."

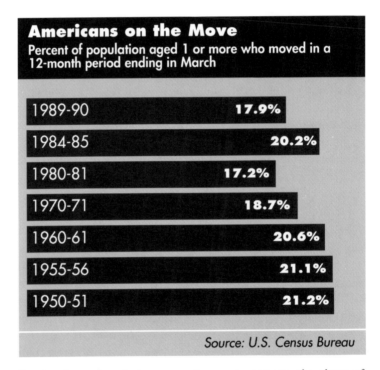

Americans on the Move
Percent of population aged 1 or more who moved in a 12-month period ending in March

Year	Percent
1989-90	17.9%
1984-85	20.2%
1980-81	17.2%
1970-71	18.7%
1960-61	20.6%
1955-56	21.1%
1950-51	21.2%

Source: U.S. Census Bureau

Despite the notion that no one stays put anymore, the share of Americans who move in a given year is now lower than in the past.

The economy directly affects both local and long-distance mobility. In times of national recession, people are less likely to buy a new house or rent a bigger apartment. They tend to stay put to ride out the downturn. Also, businesses retrench and are less likely to expand their staffs or transfer executives from one state to another.

But a spotty recession that is confined to certain regions can fuel a certain type of mobility. As we saw in the Rustbelt recession of the early 1980s, Midwesterners flooded into the then-booming Oil Patch in the South. The traffic was moving so heavily in the one direction that van rental firms like U-Haul and Ryder wound up with an oversupply of their equipment in the South and not enough back in the Midwest. So few were going the other way that the moving companies offered discounted rates for people heading north and tacked a surcharge on those moving from the Midwest to the South.

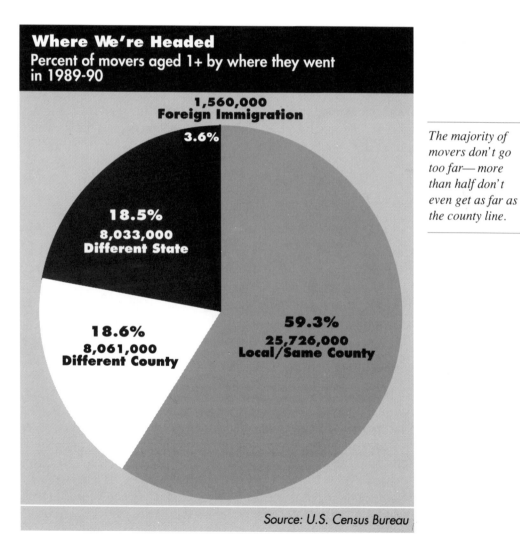

Where We're Headed
Percent of movers aged 1+ by where they went in 1989-90

1,560,000
Foreign Immigration
3.6%

18.5%
8,033,000
Different State

18.6%
8,061,000
Different County

59.3%
25,726,000
Local/Same County

Source: U.S. Census Bureau

The majority of movers don't go too far—more than half don't even get as far as the county line.

Families relocating because the husband or wife has transferred typically move all together. Often the move is paid for by the employer and handled by an interstate moving company. In cases where someone goes to a booming area to check out the opportunities without a firm job offer, that person typically goes alone to scout out the prospects. Only after finding work does he or she send for the family. And then, oftentimes, they are moving themselves. That was typically the case of the laid-off auto workers who went to Texas to start over.

Mobility tends to rise as the economy improves. People are ready to buy their dream house; companies are expanding and hiring and transferring people again.

Limits to Growth Posed by Dual-Earners and Water

Two demographic factors could slow mobility in coming years—the aging of the population, especially baby boomers, and the growing number of two-career couples.

Mobility is highest for people in their 20s. Baby boomers, who fueled the mobility boom along with all other trends, are aging out of the most mobile years. In 1992, they are aged 28 to 46 and settling down.

Also, corporations are finding it ever more difficult to transfer workers, who increasingly are considering the impact of a move on their spouses' careers as well as their own. More and more workers, particularly baby-boom men, are rejecting transfers even when they mean promotions because their spouses want to remain in their own jobs. Some couples, usually childless, have opted for commuter marriages, but they are the exceptions.

While projections expect the South and West to continue growing faster than the Northeast and Midwest, the gap will likely narrow, in part because of the aging of the population. Also, many of the fast-growth spots are becoming crowded, developing urban problems just like the North and becoming less desirable.

In some of these areas, water—or the lack of it—is another factor that could alter future migration patterns. California, Nevada, Arizona,

Colorado, and Florida in particular have severe water problems, while the Midwest has an abundance of water.

Nevada, the nation's fastest-growing state in the 1980s, grew 50 percent, due largely to growth in metropolitan Las Vegas. Las Vegas, which has seen vast residential development in what was desert only a few years ago, is expecting a continued influx of retirees and people working in the expanding gaming and tourism industry. But the growth is fast straining the region's water supply from the Colorado River. Even with stringent conservation, growth will stop by the year 2000, unless new water sources are found soon, warns the Las Vegas Water District. To keep the boom going, a controversial proposal calls for piping water in from rural northern Nevada to the southwestern deserts of Las Vegas. Northern counties are suspicious, because it would sharply curtail their own future growth prospects.

In Arizona, California, and elsewhere, a debate rages between farmers, who use over 90 percent of the region's water, and developers, who want to buy up and take farmland out of production to secure water rights and free up more water for development.

Worsening water shortages could slow population and employment growth in the Sunbelt. Conversely, the abundance of water in the struggling Rustbelt, which is surrounded by the Great Lakes, could provide a tremendous boost to the region in the 21st century and lure people and jobs back there.

No matter what the water situation in the U.S., the nation remains a land of milk and honey to many, and immigration from abroad shows no sign of letup. In fact, it will likely rise from 600,000 annually during the 1980s to some 700,000 a year in the 1990s, because many view immigration as vital to the nation's health.

Immigration Tells the Tale

As fertility rates remain low in this country and the overall growth rate declines, immigration since World War II has been rising and accounting for an ever-increasing share of national growth.

More than 600,000 people legally immigrated to the United States last year, and a few hundred thousand more came illegally. By the late 1980s, immigration accounted for about 30 percent of population growth, compared with 11 percent in 1960 and 17 percent in 1970.

In New York City, as in Los Angeles, it was immigrants who fueled the population growth of the 1980s. In many cities, immigrants are helping repopulate and reinvigorate tired neighborhoods and revive struggling commercial districts. Cubans did it in Elizabeth, New Jersey; Asians did it in San Jose, California; and Haitians, Jamaicans, and others from the Caribbean have done it in sections of Brooklyn.

Projections by the Census Bureau show that immigration's contribution to overall U.S. population growth could climb to 37 percent by 2010, and account for all growth by 2028. The U.S. population could actually begin shrinking by 2038 without fairly substantial levels of immigration. That prospect, along with labor shortages in some industries and problems with Social Security, are guaranteed to make immigration a hot front-burner political issue, likely to raise annual entry quotas but with ever-more emphasis on those with job skills in demand. (Immigration will be discussed in more detail in Chapter 5.)

RATES: Migration is usually calculated as the percent of an age cohort or the total population over the age of one that moved in a specific 12-month period. It does not include infants under 12 months because they would not have been alive for the entire year under study.

In addition to totals, immigration is also expressed as a rate, which is computed by taking the number of immigrants divided by the total population at the destination point, and multiplied by 1,000. In 1988, when there were 643,000 immigrants to the United States, the rate was 2.6 immigrants per 1,000 population.

Not all immigrants stay in America, nor do all native-born Americans. People who leave are emigrating. The emigration rate is the number of people leaving a country divided by the population of that country, and multiplied by 1,000. Emigration has been averaging about 40,000 per year, so the emigration rate is 0.16 per 1,000 U.S. residents.

Many of those emigrating are Mexicans—documented and undocumented residents of the U.S.—who return home. It's not uncommon for Mexicans and others to spend years in the U.S. building up nest eggs.

Then they go home to retire or buy a business. Then, too, thousands of native-born Americans are retiring abroad, particularly in Mexico and Central America, because living is so inexpensive there, and it's still relatively close to the U.S. for periodic visits back to see relatives.

Trends to Track; Questions to Ask

- **Local Mobility.** As the nation emerges from the recession of the early 1990s, what impact did the downturn have on mobility and migration nationally, to major regions, to your area? Who's moving where and why? Compare local moves with interstate moves.

- **Jobs.** Jobs grew by over 20 million in the 1980s. What fueled the growth? Where did it occur? What types of jobs? What impact did the job growth have on local economies, on migration patterns, and population trends?

- **Growth.** Population growth, in many minds, is assumed to be good. Is it? Why? Are there any downsides? What are the disadvantages of slow or no-growth states or areas; are there any advantages? What is the impact on demand for services, infrastructure, taxes?

- **Migration.** If people follow jobs, why did states like New Jersey, New York, and Connecticut, with strong economies during most of the 80s, have sluggish population growth? Is that situation preferable to rapid growth or not?

- **Mobility.** More than 40 million people move each year, roughly 18 percent of the population. Yet there are dramatically different rates by age group. Why? What are the most mobile age groups; the least? What are likely mobility trends in the 1990s and beyond? Will there be a slowdown in mobility, and why? Will this affect the economy; which industries?

- **Sunbelt.** Long synonymous with rapid population growth, the Sunbelt is a vast diverse region, where not everything is booming. Even the boom spots have downturns. Where? What is the impact? What's the likely future?

- **Water.** The life blood of any region, water could prove a major factor in determining future population trends in the United States. How? What is the water situation today in the different regions; is it affected by population and job growth? Could water help revive distressed areas; could lack of water hurt boom regions? How are different regions handling their water resources today? What are the local, state, and international politics of water?

- **Immigration**. Almost 30 percent of U.S. growth today comes from immigrants. What has the trend been in immigration over the decades; what lies ahead? What are the push/pull factors in immigration? What impact are immigrants having on the communities and regions they go to?

- **Emigration**. About one in four immigrants returns home for good or leaves for yet another country, according to the Immigration and Naturalization Service. Still other immigrants go back and forth between the U.S. and their native country. Are rates and trends changing? Why do people come so far, only to go home? What impact does emigration have on the U.S. and the countries emigrants return to? Are native-born Americans emigrating? If so, where and why?

SOURCES:

- The Census Bureau, Suitland, Maryland.
- Individual states, including California's Population Research Unit of the State Department of Finance, Sacramento, California; and Florida's Bureau of Economic and Business Research, Tallahassee, Florida.
- Internal Revenue Service, Washington, D.C., which does an annual migration study based on tax returns.
- U.S. Immigration and Naturalization Service.
- The Bureau of Labor Statistics, Washington, D.C.
- Allied Van Lines, Chicago, Illinois, and United Van Lines, Fenton, Missouri. Each do annual migration studies based on household shipments.
- Runzheimer International Ltd., Rochester, Wisconsin.
- NPA Data Services, Washington, D.C.
- Other sources of migration data are county and city planning departments, utility companies, and regional planning agencies, known as councils of governments, or COGs. One active one, serving the seven-county region of metropolitan Detroit, is the Southeastern Michigan Council of Governments (SEMCOG). Most metro areas have COGs that closely monitor population shifts.

3 The Ties That Bind: Households and Families

A household is not a family. And the family isn't what it used to be. The Andersons of "Father Knows Best"—a working father, homemaker mother, and three kids—are certainly not typical of American families today, although they once were. The family is evolving, coming in a wider variety of shapes, sizes, and arrangements than ever before. The family has been struggling of late but is surviving, while the household has been booming in recent decades.

The household is a basic, yet essential, building block in demography. It's nothing more, nothing less, than the person or persons who live in an occupied housing unit. Operating on the assumption that everybody has to be somewhere, the household is where the Census Bureau goes to find and count people every ten years in the decennial census and between censuses in the monthly Current Population Survey of 56,000 households.

While the household is a simple concept, things start getting complicated once the door is opened. Inside, one finds a proliferation of nontraditional households in the last generation. High levels of divorce, which create two households from one; young adults leaving the parental nest for their own digs, while others return to live with Mom and Pop; plus the coming of age of the trend-setting baby boomers all combined to trigger a rapid jump in the number and variety of households during the 1960s and 1970s.

Households increased 20.1 percent, or 10.6 million in the 1960s; they increased another 27.4 percent, or 17.4 million in the 1970s, and by 15.6 percent, or 12.6 million in the 1980s. Households numbered 94.3 million in 1991 and are more diverse than ever before. In terms of planning and marketing, the household is one of the main units of consumption; the other is the individual.

For marketers of goods and services, the assortment and growth in the number of households have helped to counterbalance a slowdown in overall population growth. Households have been growing roughly twice as fast as the population since 1960. So while the population slowdown has hurt sales of certain products, faster household gains have boosted sales for real estate, appliances, furniture, TV sets, home furnishings, soap, *TV Guide* magazine, and pillowcases.

As more and more people choose or are forced to live alone or in ever smaller households, there are fewer people within a household to share. The average household size has dropped from 3.3 people in 1960 to 2.63 by 1991. In that same period, the average family has gone from 3.67 people to 3.18.

As with many demographic trends, the rise in households has downsides as well as benefits. Rapid household growth has also increased demand for fire and police protection, sewers, streets, utilities, and the desperate search for tax dollars to pay for them, notes economist Jim Golden of the National Association of Counties. In an era of tight budgets and federal funding cutbacks, counties and cities, especially fast-growing ones, are scrambling to find the money to pay for expanding the so-called "infrastructure" and maintaining what they've already got. It's a hot topic at practically every annual meeting of organizations like the National Association of Counties, the United States Conference of Mayors, the National League of Cities, the Northeast Midwest Institute, and the Sun Belt Institute.

Even in areas of slow population growth, like the agricultural Midwest, households have been growing substantially. The household boom has turned millions of acres of farmland into lush fields of singles apartments, condominium developments, and malls.

It's important to bear in mind that household and family statistics do not include the homeless or those living in group quarters, such as college dormitories, military barracks, long-term health-care facilities, or prisons.

The numbers of people in group quarters are broken out separately. The 1990 census counted 6.7 million people in group quarters. Counting the homeless accurately is an almost impossible task. Estimates from various organizations—often politically loaded—have ranged from 250,000 to over 3 million. While not claiming to have found all the homeless, the 1990 census did conduct a Shelter and Street Night Count—S Night.

Enumerators counted 178,828 people at known emergency shelters for the homeless and another 49,793 at pre-identified street locations known to be gathering places for the homeless.

"S-Night was not intended to, and did not, produce a count of the 'homeless' population of the country," cautions Census Bureau spokesman John Connolly. "S-Night was designed to augment traditional census procedures to ensure the fullest possible count of America's population. Even if that (counting all homeless) had been our objective, the absence of a generally agreed-upon definition of homelessness would have made that task impossible."

Despite the bureau's disclaimer, many advocates for the homeless fear that the S-Night statistics are confusing and will be misused in future discussions on homelessness to downplay the extent of the problem. The debate still rages over the number who are homeless, with the unknowable truth probably somewhere between the extreme estimates.

The Basics: Households and Families

Let's get back to some elementary definitions before exploring trends further. Households—remember, those living in an occupied housing unit—are divided into two types: family households and nonfamily households.

Nonfamily households include various arrangements in which the occupants are not related by birth, marriage, or adoption. By 1991, nonfamily households numbered 28.0 million, or 30 percent of all households. That's up from 7.9 million and 15 percent in 1960.

Nonfamily households include various configurations of roommates, cohabiting couples, and people living alone. People living by themselves totaled 23.6 million in 1991, the most ever recorded. They represent 84 percent of all nonfamily households and 25 percent of all households, but only 10 percent of people living in households. People living alone have doubled since 1970 and quadrupled since the mid-1950s. They are the biggest factor in the jump in nonfamily households.

A 1979 study by the Population Reference Bureau of Washington, D.C., found that the live-alone boom has been caused by "increasing numbers of elderly, especially widows, who can afford the privacy of their own living quarters, and because of such factors as more marital dissolutions among childless couples and more independent living by young adults who are postponing marriage."

Unmarried couples totaled 2.9 million in 1991, also a record. That's up from 523,000 in 1970. The majority are in their 20s and have never been married, but a growing proportion are older and divorced. Demographer Kathryn London of the National Center for Health Statistics speculates that several trends could be fueling the cohabitation boom: college couples sharing expenses without long-range commitment, trial marriages, marriage postponement to launch careers, post-divorce readjustment, and widows and widowers sharing expenses and providing companionship. While results are not yet available, for the first time, the 1990 census will yield a breakout of same-sex couples—or gays—living together.

Despite the rapid growth of nonfamily households, family households remain the majority, although much more diverse than in the nuclear family heyday of the "Father Knows Best" 1950s. The family household, according to the Census Bureau's definition is a "group of two persons or more (one of whom is the householder) related by birth, marriage, or adoption and residing together; all such persons (including related subfamily members) are considered as members of one family."

TREND-TRACKING TIP: Households vs. Families vs. Others
Remember not to confuse the terms household and family. They are not interchangeable. Not all households are families. Families consist of two or more people who are related by blood, marriage, or adoption. Households consist of one or more persons occupying a housing unit and may consist of relatives or nonrelatives.

Nontraditional Lifestyles Mean More Nontraditional Families

Family households are subdivided into three basic categories: married couples, male-headed families with no wife present, and female-headed families with no husband present. Those three categories can be further subdivided into families with no children under age 18 present, those with children under age 18 present, and by the number of children under age 18 present. Among married couples with children are a record 2.2 million families in 1990 in which three generations live together: children living with one or both parents, together with their own parent or parents.

Family households do not always include married couples. A fast-growing share of family households consist of a single, divorced, or widowed parent with children, typically a female-headed family.

By 1991, 16.6 million children under age 18 were living with only one parent, up from 8.2 million in 1970. In contrast, 46.7 million children were living in two-parent homes in 1991, down from 58.9 million in 1970.

Family households with children have increased in number, reaching 32.4 million by 1991, up from 28.7 million in 1970. However, that increase is due to the rise in single-parent families. In the same 20 years, the number of female-headed families with children under age 18 grew 139 percent, to 6.8 million. Male-headed families with kids at home shot up 252 percent, to 1.2 million. In the same period, married-couple families with children at home declined four percent to 24.4 million.

Even so, married couples represent a majority—albeit declining—of all family households. As recently as 1960, married-couple families represented 87 percent of all families and 74 percent of all households; by 1991, married-couple families were 79 percent of families but only 55 percent of households. Among married-couple households are stepfamilies, frequently referred to as blended families.

The swiftest changes in family structure occurred during eras of unprecedented social and political upheaval and change in the U.S.: liberalized divorce laws, changing social mores, increasing educational attainment, women's liberation, the Pill, legalization of abortion, and a roller-coaster economy, all of which contributed to the household boom and realignment of the American family.

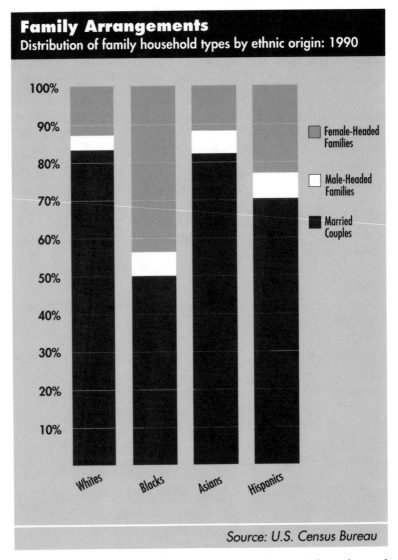

Black families are less likely than others to contain married couples, and more likely to be headed by women on their own.

Liberalization of divorce laws in the 1960s cleared the decks of a backlog of troubled marriages. The Pill, abortion, and rising educational attainment gave women increasing independence from men and marriage. The growing numbers of men and women getting college and advanced degrees and women pursuing careers pushed up the age at first marriage, because people tend to wait until they complete their schooling or launch their careers before they settle down. Median age at first marriage has risen from 20.8 years for women and 23.2 years for men in 1970 to 23.9 years for women and 26.1 years for men by 1990.

As life expectancy has increased, so has the lifecycle, with more stops along the way. In past eras, people frequently stayed in the parental home until marrying in their early 20s and setting up a new household that pretty much lasted until death. "Today's individual and family life courses involve many more important transitions as people form, dissolve, and re-form households and families," notes Arthur Norton, a family specialist at the Census Bureau.

Coming through an era of very high divorce levels, the drop in the proportion of married-couple families with children at home was inevitable. Another contributing factor was the easing, if not elimination, of the stigma of pregnancy outside of marriage. In previous generations, a boy who got a girl pregnant typically married her in a so-called shotgun wedding. Increasingly, women are postponing or foregoing such a marriage, opting for an abortion or out-of-wedlock birth. Abortions have almost tripled since the early 1970s, to about 1.5 million annually, while out-of-wedlock births account for one in four live births.

In 1991, 47 percent of married-couple families had children under age 18 at home. That's down from 57 percent in 1970. Two-parent families with kids still home were an even smaller proportion of all households, 26 percent in 1991, down from 40 percent in 1970.

The real drop, however, has been only in large families. The Census Bureau's report *Household and Family Characteristics: March 1990 and 1989* notes that "the drop in the number of two-parent families is attributable to the 4.2 million decline between 1970 and 1990 in the number of larger married-couple families with three or more children. During the same period, the number of smaller married-couple families with only one or two children actually increased by 3.2 million."

Interestingly, married couples without children at home have held fairly stable as a proportion of all households, at about 30 percent, although that could change, as we'll soon see. These couples include both those who never had children and those whose children have grown and left home.

By having fewer children, today's parents complete child-rearing years sooner than did parents a generation or two ago. Consequently, even though they start having kids later, today's parents are younger overall than parents a generation ago. This has implications for marketers. Having finished child-rearing at younger ages, today's parents can redirect their spending to themselves for vacations, entertainment, or whatever—a sort of second honeymoon.

Boomerang Kids and Demographic Differences

But there's a hitch: a growing number of young adults are postponing flying the coop or they are returning to the parental nest. By 1990, a record 13.4 million adults aged 18 to 24 were home with their parents. That's 53 percent of that age group, compared with 43 percent in 1960.

Writing in the May 1990 issue of *American Demographics* magazine, Martha Farnsworth Riche sees this as a new phase of life—pre-adults whom she says are acting like boomerangs. "Move out, move in. Start school, stop school. Get a job, quit a job. Get married, get divorced. Young adults go back and forth like boomerangs. It's not because they're spoiled or rebellious. It's because young adults face increasingly complex choices; they must investigate more options before they can settle into adult life. Boomeranging is a rational response to changes in our society and economy. It's here to stay."

Household and family formations and dissolutions come most frequently in a person's 20s and 30s. Those are the years of most dramatic transitions—graduating from school, leaving home, joining the military, starting a job, being transferred, marrying, starting a family, and divorcing. All directly influence household and family trends.

Among the different racial groups, all have experienced increases in the number of nontraditional family arrangements. But dramatic differences exist among the various groups, oftentimes related to other demographic factors. Households and families are larger for blacks and Hispanics than whites, a reflection of both higher fertility rates and lower income, which discourages separate household formation. Asians as a group have lower fertility rates than whites, yet larger households, because of extended families and friends sharing living quarters. The number of minority families is also growing faster than white families, due to a combination of higher fertility and immigration.

All groups have seen a rise in female-headed families. By 1991, 46 percent of black family households were maintained by a woman, compared with 13 percent of whites and 24 percent of Hispanics. The rate of increase, fastest in the 1970s, slowed significantly in the 1980s, most noticeably among blacks.

Whites are especially likely to be married. While 79 percent of all family households in 1991 were married couples, 83 percent of white families were couples, compared with 48 percent of blacks and 69 percent of Hispanics.

As is often the case, statistics can mislead even as they enlighten by telling only part of the story. Such is the case with a major contributing cause to the rapid jump in female-headed households: out-of-wedlock births.

Out-of-wedlock births rose from less than 10 percent of all births in 1960 to 24 percent by the late 1980s. For blacks, the share rose from 23 percent to 62 percent; for whites, from 2 percent to 16 percent. But the increases in proportions were so dramatic because the total number of births to married women declined as family size shrank. The actual increase in illegitimacy was greater for whites than for blacks. Between 1970 and 1987, the number of black babies born out of wedlock increased 86 percent, to 399,100; the increase for whites was 185 percent, to 498,600.

The numbers point up the importance of scrutinizing a trend from different angles to fully understand the complexities of what's going on. The fact remains that an alarmingly high proportion of births are to single mothers, which raises the risk of poverty, as we will see in a later chapter.

The Future of Households

In the coming years, household growth is likely to slow further, as it did in the 1980s. The baby-boom generation is aging out of its peak household formation years, followed by the smaller baby-bust generation. Also, as real-estate prices continue to escalate, people will be less inclined to branch out on their own. To the disappointment of some parents, who thought they were free at last after putting kids through college and waving goodbye as graduates finally flew the nest, some of those young adults are flapping their wings back home.

There is also a discernible trend of people both young and old pooling resources to share living quarters to cut expenses. Senior citizens, often widowed and living on fixed incomes, are teaming up in apartments, sometimes with people of the opposite sex. Such arrangements are often based more on economics than romance.

Immigrants who are trying to get a foothold in a new country and build a nest-egg frequently get a group of people together to pool resources. Such arrangements are common among Asians and Hispanics, today's two largest immigrant groups. They could contribute to a reversal of the downsizing of the American household and family.

To be sure, households will continue coming in a wide variety of configurations, maybe even some new ones we can't even imagine now. Yet a certain traditionalism is reasserting itself in some quarters. The family, battered and repeatedly challenged, has shown its durability. Indeed, California, which experienced rapid immigration and minority and overall population increases in the last decade, had family growth equal to that of nonfamilies, bucking the national trend, perhaps a portent of things to come.

Trends to Track; Questions to Ask

- **The Family.** Ozzie and Harriet are doing great in reruns. How is the American family doing, and where is it going? Is the nuclear family another victim of the anti-nuclear movement?

- **Household.** When is a household a family, and when is it not? Why are households growing faster than the U.S. population? What's the impact—positive and negative—of rapid household growth? What's the impact on housing and real estate as well as goods and services? Will household growth continue? What forces will change trends?

- **Living Together.** By 1991, 2.9 million unmarried couples were living together, up from 1.6 million in 1980 and 523,000 in 1970. The sexual revolution of the 1960s is long over; what's causing the continuing rise in living together? What's the economic and social impact? Where is the trend headed?

- **Female-Headed Families.** What are the trends, causes, repercussions? Are there differences by age, race, and ethnicity?

- **Education**. Educational attainment has risen steadily in the U.S. since the 1950s, with women making the strongest gains. What impact has educational attainment had on household and family formation?

- **Live-Alone Boom.** The biggest factor in the household boom is the quadrupling since the mid-1950s of people living by themselves. Who are they, and what's fueling the live-alone boom? Where is it headed?

- **Returning to the Nest.** Just when parents thought they had launched their children on a life of their own, the adult kids are coming back home in record numbers. Why? Do they pay rent? Are there curfews? How long are they staying? Do they keep their rooms neat?

- **Immigration**. About 30 percent of U.S. population growth is due to immigration, with most coming from Asian and Latin countries. How does immigration affect household and family trends? How do immigrant families compare with those native to the U.S.?

SOURCES:

- Census Bureau, Suitland, Maryland.
- U.S. Deptartment of Health and Human Services, Washington, D.C.
- U.S. House of Representatives' Select Committee on Children, Youth and Families, Washington, D.C.
- Population Reference Bureau, Washington, D.C.
- Family Research Council, Washington, D.C.
- National Association of Home Builders, Washington, D.C.
- Center on Housing Studies, Cambridge, Massachusetts.

4 I Do and I Don't: Marriage and Divorce

If record high divorce rates of recent decades continue, something approaching one-half of all marriages would eventually end in divorce—startling statistics that always generate headlines and worry about the collapse of American society. America's divorce rate has the dubious distinction of being the world's highest, although the lead is narrowing over other western nations.

Yet, clearly, half of all marriages have not yet ended in divorce—and may not, and probably won't. Think of your own families, colleagues, and neighbors. Unless you live in Nevada, far fewer than half have divorced so far, and fewer than half probably ever will.

Let's examine the 50 percent projection closer for a better understanding of divorce trends and also as a cautionary exercise to point out that demographic numbers often come with caveats, conditions, or assumptions. Too often the caveats are ignored or purposely discarded because they are complicated, cumbersome, clutter up an analysis, or dilute the point of the whole story. Still, the responsible demographics researcher should be mindful of the limitations of the data, and where appropriate, alert his or her audience.

In fact, 23 percent of the ever-married population in 1985 had experienced a divorce, according to unpublished data from the Census Bureau's Current Population Survey. The oft-quoted 50 percent projections are based on the continuation of trends of recent decades, which have not necessarily been typical. They may or may not continue.

It now appears that less than one-half of all marriages will end in divorce. The share is more likely to be between 30 and 40 percent, which is still high.

TREND-TRACKING TIP: Divorce American Style

One common mistake in trying to gauge the risk of divorce is to take the total number of marriages in a year and compare them with the number of divorces. This is an invalid comparison, like apples and oranges.

Those who get married in a particular year come primarily from a relatively narrow age cohort of people aged 20 to 30. Those getting divorced are from a different pool—those who are currently married, which includes people married this year, as well as couples married in years and decades past. At any given point in time, the pool of those who may divorce is larger than those who might marry, because the share of adults currently married outstrips those currently not married.

As with all trends, keep your eye on baby boomers. They're aging and settling down. The trends they ignited and kept at high levels will not necessarily remain at those levels. In these areas and others, the trends may moderate, because the boomers, in sheer size and other respects, were the exceptions to the rule.

After generations of strict divorce laws, the liberalization of those laws in the 1960s and early 1970s sent divorce rates skyrocketing as a backlog of bad marriages dissolved.

The 60s, which is a state of mind as much as a rebellious and trend-setting decade that extends well beyond 1969, also shattered tradition and taboos with regard to such matters as sex, marriage, and divorce, with help from baby boomers.

An unrestrained generation fond of experimentation and adventure, boomers eventually began marrying in large numbers in the 1970s and 1980s. And it wasn't long before many started divorcing, keeping rates high. Divorce, if it's going to happen, is most likely to happen in the first seven years.

Women pursuing careers brought more money into two-earner families, but also put new strains on marriages. It also gave these women, unlike their mothers, the financial wherewithal to leave a rocky marriage and go it alone, although it's not as easy when children are involved.

Divorces peaked in 1981, at 1,213,000, when the rate tied the 1979 record high of 5.3 divorces per 1,000 population. The 1981 total and rates are more than double what they were in the 1960s. During much of the 1980s, the annual number of divorces averaged 1.1 million, and the rate hovered around 4.9 to 5.0 per 1,000 population.

The risk of divorce is greatest for those who got married in their teens and lessens with age and education.

Another factor that has contributed to rising divorce—and will likely become an even greater, though secondary factor—is rising life expectancy at birth, which has gone from 69.7 years in 1960 (73.1 years for women, 66.6 years for men) to 75.4 years in 1990 (78.8 years for women, 72.0 years for men). The longer people live, the greater the risk that they might split up.

The National Center for Health Statistics projects that life expectancy at birth will rise to 80 years by 2010. Some forecasters contend it's possible to increase life expectancy to 90 or more years within the next 50 years. With people living longer and spending more time in active retirement, one theory suggests they will be less inclined than generations past to stay in unhappy marriages. "There will be more divorce because people will no longer regard a first marriage as their only marriage, in part because they'll be living longer and won't be satisfied with the same spouse for 40 or 50 years," write trends analysts Marvin Cetron and Thomas O'Toole in their book *Encounters with the Future*.

Other demographic and social trends are conspiring to push overall divorce rates downward. In fact, divorce rates dropped modestly in the late 1980s. Some analysts have taken a second look and now expect divorce rates to drop further in the 1990s and beyond. This would put them below record-high levels of recent decades, but still higher than the supposedly blissful Ozzie and Harriet era of the 1950s.

Divorce Rate Expected to Drop

Reasons for a likely downturn in divorce rates:

- **Aging**. Baby Boomers are in or approaching middle age and are more or less settled. They have homes, mortgages, and children. Their attitudes have changed. To borrow a political phrase from another context: "They've been mugged by reality." Many have now survived the vulnerable early years of marriage, during which divorce rates are highest. Boomers are turning inward and toward the home. "Baby boomers now have children to protect. They've become cautious.... They've always been self-centered, and now they have extended that to their children, families, and home," says Cheryl Russell, author of *100 Predictions for the Baby Boom*.

- **Baby Bust.** Behind the boomers is a smaller generation, the baby bust, which has been described as more conservative and tradition-bound. Many of these young people grew up with single parents and may react against their experience by staying put in their own marriages. Being fewer in number, there will be fewer young married couples eligible to divorce. This will help cause the absolute number of divorces as well as the divorce rate to decline.

- **AIDS.** Various sexual diseases and the rising alarm over date rape have all but ended the wide-open sexual revolution of past decades and its casual "anything goes" attitude. In contrast, steady dating and marriage are increasingly attractive options. Fear of AIDS and other sexually transmitted diseases and educational efforts may make people "consider monogamy more carefully. I think people are less inclined to be careless in their sex connections," suggests Ray Brown, professor of popular culture at Bowling Green State University.

- **Reappraisal**. Many experts, who a decade or two ago argued persuasively that troubled marriages were worse on parents and children than divorce, are having serious doubts about that. There's a growing consensus that divorce exacts a high financial and emotional price on all involved, and it should only be used as a last resort after counseling and other efforts have failed.

- **Economics**. Love aside, marriage is also, and always has been, an economic union, notes demographer Leon Bouvier. Two may not be able to live as cheaply as one, but a married couple can live cheaper than two singles or divorced people living separately.

There were 1,175,000 divorces in 1990. That's up slightly over 1989, but lower than the annual totals between 1985 and 1988. The divorce rate in 1989 and 1990 was 4.7 divorces per 1,000 population, the lowest rate since 1974.

The State of Marriage

In 1990, there were 2,448,000 marriages, a two percent increase over 1989, and the third highest total ever. Paul Glick, a former census analyst and now adjunct professor at Arizona State University, notes that the number has grown because of the vast numbers of people now in the marriageable ages.

Marriage and divorce rates were high in the 1970s and early 1980s because that's when the massive baby-boom generation was squarely in the peak years for marrying and divorcing. But the all-time high for marriage rates came, not surprisingly, in 1945, the year that World War II ended and returning GIs and their sweethearts could finally realize the wedding plans that the war had put on hold.

Marriage and divorce rates tend to fall in economically unstable times when unemployment and uncertainty discourage marriage and starting up a new household, as well as divorcing and starting over alone. In the Depression year of 1930, the marriage rate was only 9.2 marriages per 1,000 population, while the divorce rate was 1.6 divorces per 1,000 population.

Conversely, marriage and divorce rates tend to go up during economic expansions. The jobs, promotions, and prosperity that come with economic expansion encourage many couples that the time is right to marry. It also convinces others that they can succeed on their own.

Oddly, divorce itself also contributes to the number of marriages and keeps U.S. marriage rates among the highest in the world. For divorce is but the first step on the road to remarriage, and Americans keep trying, again and again.

Census Bureau analyst Arlene Saluter estimates that 70 percent of divorced people eventually remarry. That's down from around 80 percent in the mid-1970s. Even so, in 1990, nearly half of marriages involved at least one partner remarrying, according to demographer Barbara Foley Wilson of the National Center for Health Statistics. That's up from one-quarter in the early 1970s.

"Most people prefer the married state," contends Glick. In fact, the average American marries more than once, despite the fact that a growing share never marry at all. Historically, about 5 percent of the population never married. But this share has been rising in recent decades and may approach 10 percent. Even so, this is more than made up for by those who marry more than once.

While the total number of marriages is high, the 1990 rate was quite low, at 9.8 marriages per 1,000 population. That compares with the recent peak of 10.9 marriages per 1,000 population reached in 1972. Rates have bobbed up and down since then. The 1990 rate was 1 percent higher than the two previous years, when it was 9.7.

Several factors have depressed marriage rates in recent decades. One certainly is the declining number of what were commonly called "shotgun weddings," in which a man married a woman after getting her pregnant. Typically, both spouses were teenagers. A sense of moral duty and the stigma of an illegitimate child prompted many expecting couples to marry. Today, in an age when celebrities routinely have and often want children outside of marriage, the stigma of illegitimacy has greatly lessened, with one alarming result: one-quarter of all births in the U.S. are now out of wedlock, compared with only 11 percent in 1970 and 5 percent in 1960. More than half of all black children are born to unmarried mothers.

Also keeping marriage rates down is the rising age at first marriage, which many analysts view positively. Median age at first marriage has risen from 20.3 years for women and 22.8 years for men in 1960 to 23.9 years for women and 26.1 years for men by 1990.

Pursuing education, launching careers, and/or sowing wild oats are often cited as the reasons for the rising age at first marriage. Some people reason that by delaying marriage, couples are likely to have a bigger nestegg, and be better established and more mature, thus improving the odds for a successful marriage. By 1988, six of ten women and nearly eight of ten men aged 20 to 24 had not yet married, according to the Census Bureau. That compares with 36 percent of women and 55 percent of men in 1970.

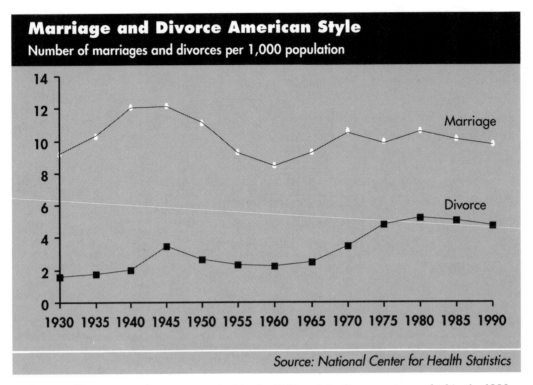

Marriage and Divorce American Style
Number of marriages and divorces per 1,000 population

Marriage

Divorce

1930 1935 1940 1945 1950 1955 1960 1965 1970 1975 1980 1985 1990

Source: National Center for Health Statistics

In the past 60 years, marriage rates peaked in the 1940s, while divorce rates peaked in the 1980s.

To Boost Income, Get Married

One unsolicited demographic endorsement for marriage is the fact that people who are married tend to live longer than those who are single or divorced. That could reflect the higher income in married-couple households, which in turn affords better medical care. There is also research that suggests married people, especially men, are more satisfied and content with life, which can have a positive effect on physical health.

Married-couple households have higher incomes than other households, partly because they have the potential for two incomes. Married men also have higher incomes than unmarried men. A 1990 University of Michigan study found that married men in the U.S. and 11 other countries consistently earned more money than single men. Even when age, race, education, and work experience were similar, the gap persisted. The income of married men in the U.S. was 30.6 percent higher than that of unmarried men.

The study's author, Robert F. Schoeni, offers three possible explanations: married men, feeling obligations to their families, work harder and are paid more for it; productive and financially successful men are viewed as attractive mates and thus more likely to be married; employers are more inclined to hire and promote married men, believing they are more stable, rooted, and less likely to change jobs.

Both marriage and divorce rates differ markedly by age, education, income, and race. Marriage rates for a first marriage are highest for people in their mid-to-late 20s. The next highest first-marriage rate is for people in their early 20s. A steadily rising share of marriages now involve people in their 30s—over 20 percent of all first marriages and about 40 percent of all remarriages.

Despite determination to get it right the second and subsequent times around, the risk of divorce is somewhat greater for people involved in a remarriage than for people in their first marriage, according to research by the Census Bureau and National Center for Health Statistics. For all marriages that end in divorce, the median duration of the marriage is about seven years. The median age of people divorcing is 35 years for men, 32 years for women.

Marriage and divorce rates are highest—by far—in Nevada, where people go for quickie divorces and quickie remarriages. Nevada's divorce rate is roughly 3 times the U.S. rate, while its marriage rate is 11 times the national rate.

Schooling and Marriage—Men and Women

While education offers no guarantees, the higher the level of education a man has, the less likely his chance of divorce. The correlation is not as strong for women. In their *Population Bulletin* on marriage and divorce trends, Paul Glick and Arthur Norton write: "Marital stability is greatest for men who have graduated from college or who have gone on to graduate school. Women differ in that those who have gone on to graduate school (17 or more years of completed schooling) record below-average marital stability."

They continue: "For men, the relationship between socioeconomic status (whether measured by education or income) and marital stability is consistently positive. For women, however, an exception occurs among the highly educated. The reasons vary from woman to woman, but probably include such factors as the many more options for career development these women have, which often conflict with harmonious marriage, and, sometimes, personality traits that reduce their prospects for both entering and remaining in marriage."

The 1988 National Survey of Family Growth (NSFG) found that white women were more likely than black women to have married in all age groups between 15 and 44. There was little difference between Hispanic and non-Hispanic women. Marriage rates are lower for black women in large part because of what some have identified as a shortage of eligible young black men. A combination of high rates of unemployment, incarceration, and mortality among young black men results in too few economically stable men available for the number of single women seeking marriage partners.

Research by University of Chicago sociologist William Julius Wilson finds that by the early 1980s, there were only 60 employed nonwhite men aged 25 to 34 for every 100 nonwhite women in that age group. The comparable ratio for whites was 85 percent. "Black women, especially young black women, are facing a shrinking pool of 'marriageable' (i.e. economically stable) men," writes Wilson in his book *The Truly Disadvantaged*.

The NSFG survey, which did not include Asians, found that black women's marriages were more likely to have dissolved than white women's marriages. The risks for Hispanic women were only somewhat higher than for non-Hispanic women. Research by William P. O'Hare and Judy C. Felt, shows that Asians marry later than other groups, are less likely to divorce, and more likely to have adult children still at home. All this plus high levels of education and employment combine to give Asians the highest income level of any household group in the U.S., including whites.

Once rare and frowned upon, numerous studies reveal a growing number of marriages across racial, ethnic, and religious lines. The report by O'Hare and Felt notes that about 17 percent of Asian Americans have non-Asian spouses, roughly the same rate of intermarriage as for Hispanics. The Census Bureau estimates that by 1990 there were some 211,000 black/white married couples.

RATES: The marriage rate is computed by taking the total number of marriages in a specific period of time, typically a year, and dividing it by the total population, multiplied by 1,000. In 1990, there were 2,448,000 marriages, for a rate of 9.8 marriages per 1,000 population.

Since close to one-half of all marriages now involve at least one partner remarrying, the remarriage rate has become important. It's calculated differently than the marriage rate. To arrive at the remarriage rate, take the number of remarriages, divide by the number of divorced or widowed people, and multiply by 1,000.

Marriage and remarriage rates are frequently calculated by age, race, and sex. In any case, take the number of marriages or remarriages involving a particular age group, race or sex, divide that number by the total number in that age cohort, racial group, or sex, and multiply by 1,000. These cohort breakdowns are valuable because they reveal significant differences among various groups.

Computing age distributions is also revealing. Simply take the total number of marriages, remarriages, or divorces involving a certain age group, and divide by the total number of marriages, remarriages, or divorces.

Divorce rates are computed in the same manner as marriage rates. Take the total number of divorces in a given year, divide by the total population, and multiply by 1,000. In 1990, there were 1,175,000 divorces, for a divorce rate of 4.7 divorces per 1,000 population.

Trends to Track: Questions to Ask

- **Marriage Rates.** The number of marriages has risen in recent years, yet marriage rates are rather low. What accounts for this anomaly? Is marriage in or out of style in the 1990s? What are the trends, implications, impact on society and the economy, and prospects for staying married in the 1990s and beyond?

- **Economic Union.** True love aside, marriage has also been described as an economic partnership. While a married couple might not be able to live as cheaply as one person, they can live more economically than two single people. What are the economic ramifications of marriage on couples and children? What impact does marriage have on life expectancy, household income, and a husband's or wife's career advancement?

- **Postponement.** Americans are getting married later than ever before. Median age at first marriage in 1990 was 26.1 years for men, 23.9 years for women. What are the benefits and disadvantages of getting married later? Does it improve the chances for a successful marriage? Are more people foregoing marriage altogether or simply delaying it? Will there be a rush to marry as people approach middle age? What are the social and economic ramifications of postponement?

- **Shotgun Wedding.** A relic of the 1950s, shotgun weddings have declined rapidly. Why? What are the ramifications of the drop?

- **Divorce.** Whither divorce? Projections suggest that half of all marriages will end in divorce if current rates continue. Will they? What ignited the divorce boom? What forces could continue fueling it; what trends could cause it to fall? Who's most susceptible to divorce; least susceptible? What are the financial consequences of divorce?

- **Remarriage.** Close to half of all marriages today involve at least one partner getting remarried—a record high. What's triggering the remarriage boom, and what are the chances for success? Explore who is remarrying, the consequences of remarriage, and the growing number of blended families.

- **Interracial marriage.** Once discouraged, a growing number of couples are marrying partners outside their racial or ethnic group. What are the trends among different groups, the reaction of those involved and their families, the consequences, and future direction of intermarriage?

- **Asian marriage.** Asians marry later and divorce less; their households are often bigger with more grown children and three generations at home. How do marriage and divorce trends compare and contrast among racial and ethnic groups?

- **Good Times/Bad Times.** Marriage and divorce trends are both affected by the economy. How and why? What have the trends been? What is likely to happen in a recovery following a recession, and a downturn after an expansion?

SOURCES:

- Census Bureau, Suitland, Maryland.
- National Center for Health Statistics, Hyattsville, Maryland.
- American Association for Marriage and Family Therapy, Washington, D.C.
- University of Michigan's Population Study Center, Ann Arbor, Michigan.
- Population Reference Bureau, Washington, D.C.
- Stepfamily Foundation, New York, New York.
- The Urban Institute, Washington, D.C.
- The Joint Center for Political Studies, Washington, D.C.

5 Beyond the Melting Pot: Race, Ethnicity, Immigration, and Religion

America, long a WASP bastion where minorities were just that, is becoming more ethnically, racially, and religiously diverse. New York City Mayor David Dinkins' description of his city as a "mosaic" may become an appropriate metaphor for the nation, replacing the image of the melting pot.

In Prince George's County, Maryland, one of the most racially and ethnically diverse in the U.S., a local newspaper editor described it as a "suburban lower East side." In 1980, whites accounted for 59 percent of residents in Prince George's, which borders Washington, D.C. Blacks now are 51 percent of the county's population, the first suburban county where blacks are the majority due to black suburbanization.

Minorities are already the majority in dozens of major cities, including New York and Chicago. Blacks constitute a majority in Atlanta, Baltimore, Detroit, Wilmington, Newark, and Washington, D.C. Hispanics are a majority in Miami, San Antonio, and El Paso; and more than one-third of the population in Tucson, Arizona, and the city of Los Angeles. In the public schools of Los Angeles, more than half of the student body is Hispanic.

In addition to the central-city strongholds, minorities are also showing strong numerical gains throughout the nation, including remote states where few minorities have been before. Alaska's Asian population increased 145 percent in the 1980s, to almost 20,000, while Hispanics grew by 87 percent, to 17,803. Minnesota's Asian population jumped 193 percent, to 77,886, or almost 2 percent of the total state population. Asians represent fully 7 percent of the residents of St. Paul. Even remote Vermont, the whitest state of all, at 98.6 percent, saw its Asian population grow by 137 percent last decade and its black population by 71 percent.

In Maryland, one in four residents is black; one in four Californians and Texans are Hispanic. Hispanics account for over one-third of the population of New Mexico; Asians are 10 percent of California's population. Based on current projections, non-Hispanic whites would no longer represent the majority in Texas and California as early as 2010. Like never before, minorities are on the move—to America and within the country.

Minority Population's Rapid Rise

Combined, minorities currently represent 24 percent of the U.S. population and are growing rapidly. By 2030, minorities could make up almost one-third of the population, according to a 1989 report by the Population Reference Bureau.

Asians, helped by massive immigration, saw their numbers more than double in just ten years, the fastest-growing group in America. Between 1980 and 1990, Asians grew 108 percent, to 7.3 million. Blacks, the largest minority, increased 13 percent, to 30 million. This is faster than the national average, due mostly to higher fertility rates. Hispanics scored the biggest numerical gains among minorities, up 7.7 million, or 53 percent, to 22.3 million. Their growth was a combination of higher fertility and immigration.

To the surprise of many, the number of American Indians increased 38 percent in the 1980s, to 2 million. This growth rate is well beyond what one could expect from the surplus of births over deaths, and native Americans do not, by definition, immigrate to the U.S. Analysts suggest that the reported increase in the native population could be the result of better promotional efforts to alert Indians to the political and financial importance of being counted, improved census methods and accuracy, as well as growing Indian pride and willingness to identify oneself as Indian.

The racial breakdown of the 1990 U.S. resident population of 248.7 million works out this way: 80.3 percent white, 12.1 percent black, 2.9 percent Asian or Pacific Islander, 0.8 percent American Indian/Eskimo/ Aleut, and 3.9 percent other races.

Hispanics, an ethnic not a racial grouping, accounted for 9.0 percent of the total population, or 22.3 million people. (The Hispanic figure excludes residents of the Commonwealth of Puerto Rico, which would add another 3.5 million people.)

Just who is what race and who is Hispanic are matters of self-identification—whatever the individual considers him or herself, including the offspring of interracial or interethnic couples.

As seen in the case of American Indians, self-identification can result in some shifts in population size, as people who are a mix of races or heritages change their identification from one census to the next.

TREND-TRACKING TIP: Race vs. Ethnicity

One frequently misunderstood factor in discussions of the minority population is the designation Hispanic origin, which refers to people descended from a Spanish-speaking nationality or Latin culture. As mentioned before, this is a category of ethnicity, or heritage, not race. Thus, people who identify themselves as Hispanics can also be of any race: white, black, or other.

In all census reports, Hispanics are broken out separately from the racial categories. However, Hispanics would also be included—but submerged—in the racial categories.

Analysis of 1990 census results indicates that just over half of the 22.3 million Hispanics identified their race as white, but many others put themselves in the "other" category, while 770,000 identified their race as black, and far fewer as Asian or Indian.

So, to estimate the total minority population, one must add up the racial categories, including "other." To that, add another 11.6 million, who are the Hispanics who identify their race as white. This yields a 1990 figure of 60.6 million minorities, or 24 percent of the total U.S. population.

A common mistake is to add the totals for the various racial minorities, plus the separate Hispanic total. This significantly overstates the minority population, because Hispanics wind up being double-counted in that erroneous formula.

Despite the rapid growth of minorities, their numbers are actually understated, because of what's called the "undercount"—people missed in every census. In something called the Post-Enumeration Survey, the Census Bureau double-checks its own work and estimates that it missed as many as 5.3 million people in the 1990 census. As in previous censuses, a disproportionate number of those missed were minorities. The undercount results from a combination of faulty address lists, census-taker error, as well as citizen error, indifference, or resistance. Some critics say the actual undercount was much higher than that.

In contrast to America's minority populations, the so-called white, or majority, population has been growing slower than average in recent decades. While the U.S. population grew 9.8 percent in the 1980s, whites increased only 6 percent. Some reasons for this slower growth include lower fertility rates than other groups and a diminishing supply of European immigrants.

Immigration's Shifting Tides

Most of America's rich diversity derives from its constant influx of immigrants from all over the world. These waves have shifted from time to time, altering the mix of new arrivals. Between 1931 and 1960, 58 percent of immigrants to the U.S. came from Europe; another 21 percent came from Canada. At that time, only 5 percent came from Asia and 15 percent from Mexico and other Latin countries, according to the U.S. Immigration and Naturalization Service.

Reform of the immigration laws in the 1960s, which eliminated past discriminatory policies that heavily favored Europeans, opened America's doors wider to others. There have been several revisions

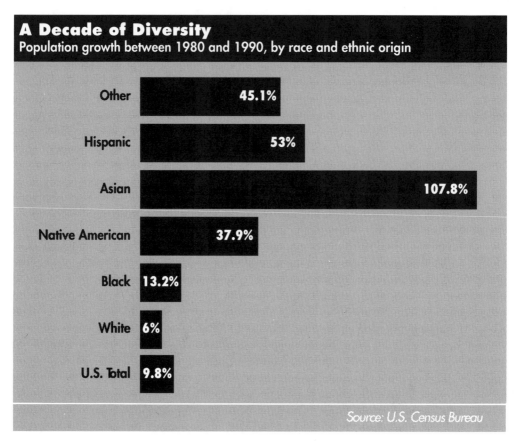

A Decade of Diversity
Population growth between 1980 and 1990, by race and ethnic origin

Other	45.1%
Hispanic	53%
Asian	107.8%
Native American	37.9%
Black	13.2%
White	6%
U.S. Total	9.8%

Source: U.S. Census Bureau

Asian Americans more than doubled in number during the 1980s, although they remain the nation's smallest minority after Native Americans.

since, including the 1986 Immigration Reform Act, aimed at normalizing the status of many undocumented aliens already here. By the 1980s, 42 percent of America's immigrants came from Asia, 42 percent from Mexico and other Latin and Caribbean countries, 11 percent from Europe, 2 percent from Canada, and 3 percent from Oceania, Africa, and elsewhere.

There are also what demographers call 'push/pull' factors influencing immigration. People who leave relatives and their homeland are often pursuing opportunity and freedom not available at home, and/or fleeing political upheaval, persecution, or poverty.

Western Europe, which is experiencing slow population growth, has been politically and economically stable in recent decades, compared

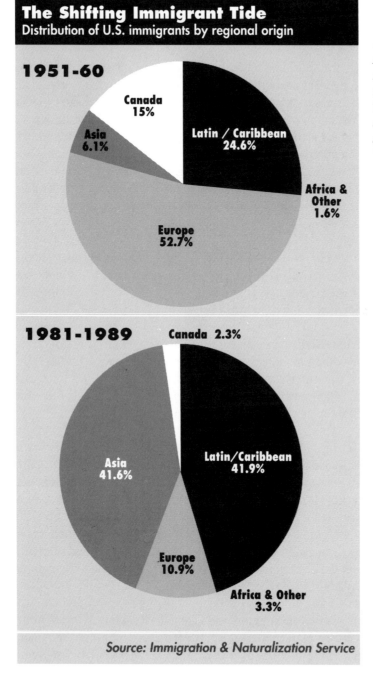

The Shifting Immigrant Tide
Distribution of U.S. immigrants by regional origin

1951-60

Canada 15%

Asia 6.1%

Latin / Caribbean 24.6%

Africa & Other 1.6%

Europe 52.7%

1981-1989

Canada 2.3%

Asia 41.6%

Latin/Caribbean 41.9%

Europe 10.9%

Africa & Other 3.3%

Source: Immigration & Naturalization Service

As recently as the 1950s, the majority of immigrants to the U.S. were from Europe. Today, more than four-fifths come from Latin America and Asia.

59

with faster-growing Asia, Central America, and Mexico, where the push factors are much greater. However, immigration from Eastern Europe might rise in the wake of the economic turmoil there, now that movement is no longer restricted as it was under Communism.

Mexicans are the single biggest group of immigrants today, followed by Filipinos. But the numbers coming from Mexico are likely understated, because of the many undocumented immigrants who cross the border without visas. The Census Bureau estimates that during the 1980s, between 100,000 and 300,000 undocumented aliens arrived in the U.S. annually—the majority were Mexican. Mexico, which shares a 1,500-mile border with the U.S., is growing by 2 million people a year, which the country cannot absorb into its economy. Like it or not, the United States has become the release valve for Mexico's rapid population growth.

The majority of refugees in the last decade came from Southeast Asia, including the so-called "boat people" from Vietnam, Laos, and Cambodia, who dramatically risked their lives on the open seas as they fled their homelands in overloaded boats.

More recent Asian refugees have tended to come from more rural areas, escaping with little more than the clothes on their backs. Earlier Asian refugees, particularly those who arrived in the months and years after the U.S. withdrawal from the Vietnam Conflict, were more often educated merchants and professionals and their families.

Of course, during the 1980s, significant numbers of refugees also came from the Soviet Union, Central America, and, in the early 1980s, Cuba. While all immigrants come seeking opportunity and a better life, there are a few key differences between immigrants of generations ago and those arriving today. Sociologists have called the earlier group "Ellis Island immigrants." Many were poor, unskilled, and uneducated, crossing the ocean in steerage class to arrive at Ellis Island with little more than the clothes they wore. Once here, there was little contact, except by mail, with relatives back home.

Many of today's immigrants, nicknamed "Kennedy Airport immigrants," arrive by jet within a matter of hours from their homeland. Certainly, some are impoverished and uneducated. But a greater proportion than ever before are educated professionals or merchants.

That's especially true of Koreans and Filipinos who have come in recent decades. Because of inexpensive jet travel, today's newcomers maintain closer ties to home, flying back every few years for a visit.

Diversity Within Diversity

In assigning people to various broad racial and ethnic categories, the statistics, as well as the marketers and politicians who use them, often fail to capture and appreciate the variety within groups. Cuban Americans are dramatically different from Puerto Ricans, who are different from Mexicans, Filipinos, and Central Americans, who are all different from each other.

A census report notes that average 1989 household income for Hispanics was $27,992, compared with $36,520 for all U.S. households. Within the Hispanic community, income was $35,091 for Cubans, $31,220 for Central and South Americans, $26,542 for Mexicans, and $25,269 for Puerto Ricans.

Even within subgroups, there are important distinctions. *The Hispanic Almanac*, published in 1990 by the Hispanic Policy Development Project, notes: "It is widely believed that most U.S. Cubans are professionals, managers, and entrepreneurs, and it is true that about one-third of the earlier refugees could be so described. From 1965 to 1972, however, more than one-quarter of a million Cubans were brought into the United States, and only one-sixth of these and more recent arrivals can be called members of the middle class."

Fifty-eight percent of the Hispanics in the U.S. have roots in Mexico, 12.6 percent in Puerto Rico, 6.7 percent in Cuba, 13.6 percent in Central and South America, and 9.0 percent elsewhere in the Caribbean or Latin America.

While their politics and cultures differ, Hispanics are bound together by a common language and religion. This cannot be said of Asians, the country's fastest-growing minority.

"The old stereotypes, even the informed ones, no longer apply, and that increasing variety is the hallmark of the contemporary Asian American experience," write Harry H. L. Kitano and Roger Daniels in their book *Asian Americans: Emerging Minorities.*

"The newer Asian and Pacific Islander immigrants are much less cultur-ally homogeneous than their predecessors," note Kitano and Daniels. "Whereas the overwhelming majority of pre-World War II Asian immi-grants were of peasant stock (with a smattering of intellectuals and political dissidents), today the range is from premodernized groups, such as the Hmong, to medical professionals from the Philippines and PhDs from India."

Japanese, the most numerous Asian group in the U.S. in 1970, now ranks third. Filipinos, who are second, are expected to be the biggest group by the year 2000. Chinese are currently the largest Asian group in the U.S. While still concentrated on the West Coast, over half of the Asian-American population now lives elsewhere in the country.

And while Asian Americans' household income and educational attain-ment are higher, on average, than that of whites, they also have a higher-than-average share of the people in poverty, a reflection of their varied backgrounds and circumstances.

Within the black community, too, there is a surprising range, often obscured by the statistics on poverty and single-parent households. Without denying the fact that 32 percent of blacks are impoverished, one must also acknowledge the growth of a black middle class, as the number of black college graduates topped 2 million in 1990, compared with only 300,000 in 1960.

The increasing number of minorities is already having a direct impact on many aspects of American society, including public schools where the minority enrollment is often greater than in society at large, the work force and global economy, the political arena, and, ultimately, the popular culture and American identity. Clearly, rapid minority growth has fueled the debates over bilingual education, the so-called "inclusive" curriculum in public schools and at universities, and affirmative action.

America's fast-growing minority communities become sources of new writers and artists, new music, new concepts, new products, and idioms that enter the mainstream, from social commentator Shelby Steele to screenwriter Spike Lee; from Surgeon General Antonia C. Novello to the Miami Sound Machine, from novelist Amy Tan to Silicon Valley's computers and chips. Some observers believe that the sheer number of minorities and immigrants and their collective clout will help shift U.S.

attention in foreign policy and international trade more toward the regions to which they are culturally linked.

It's already happening in business, with southern California becoming corporate Asia's gateway to America and a jumping-off point for American firms wanting to crack the Asian market or establish joint ventures. By 1989, California ports accounted for $121 billion—or 39 percent—of America's total trade with Pacific Rim countries. America's trade with Pacific Rim countries rose 170 percent between 1980 and 1989, and California has the lion's share of that.

In a similar way, the Hispanic presence has "transformed Miami into the premier financial and commercial center of Latin America," reports *The Hispanic Almanac*. Twenty-five of the 40 foreign banks in the Miami area are Latin, with assets of $2.4 billion.

While there are obvious places of concentration, the minority influence goes well beyond the first ports of entry. Cubans have helped revitalize the city of Elizabeth, New Jersey, as black immigrants from the Caribbean have re-energized neighborhoods of Brooklyn. The sixth-largest Hispanic concentration in the U.S. is in metropolitan Chicago, which boasts a daily Spanish-language newspaper, *El Mañana*, and seven other nondailies, six radio stations, and two TV stations, all aimed at Hispanics.

Asians have established vibrant enclaves in such unlikely places as Minneapolis/St. Paul; Fairfield County, Connecticut; Arlington, Virginia; even in the heart of the Deep South. Some immigrants, such as those running mom-and-pop shops, bypass or leave the major ethnic communities, because business niches there have already been filled. While giving up the friendship of their countrymen, they venture farther afield, where there is less direct competition. In so doing, they establish new beachheads for others to follow.

Growing Minority Clout and Competition

Look for minorities to play an increasingly active—but unpredictable— role in the political arena. Given their numbers and concentrations in key states and districts, minorities have the potential to build powerful coalitions, especially on issues that bind them: education, crime, poverty, municipal services, and a fair shake from the majority and political parties. But the federal funding pie is only so big. There is the potential for competition among groups, including whites, for pieces of the pie. Additionally, the diversity of minority communities means that they view some key issues differently. For example, immigration may be a more pressing issue to Asians and Hispanics than to blacks; blacks and Hispanics are strong proponents of affirmative-action programs; while some Asians, who have seen quotas used against them in college admissions, are wary.

Despite the homogenizing effect of group averages, remember the general rule that educational attainment and income tend to rise the longer a family or group of people has been in the United States. The children of immigrants tend to have more schooling than their parents did and more fluency in English, which usually results in higher income and social status and fewer barriers to success.

But in a 1991 Population Reference Bureau report on Asian Americans, demographers William O'Hare and Judy Felt caution: "In some cases, Asian Americans seem to be hampered by their success. It appears that some universities have set quotas limiting the number of Asian-American students they will admit. This could become a divisive issue for minority groups. While some minority groups favor quotas or racial preferences as a way of making sure they have access to educational institutions, Asian Americans may find themselves resisting these measures because it limits their access to some colleges and universities."

Since many immigrants are entrepreneurs involved in small family businesses, they may not be enthralled with liberal prescriptions of higher taxes and tighter business regulation. Long viewed as loyal liberal Democrats, today's changing minority and immigrant mix may prove more independent and demanding. While surveys reveal that the vast majority of blacks are Democrats, 35 percent view themselves as conservative or very conservative, according to 1991 *Washington Post* surveys. There has also been an emergence from the black community of thought-provoking, fiercely independent leaders and intellectuals like General Colin Powell, the Hoover Institution's Thomas Sowell, University of Chicago sociologist William Julius Wilson, not to mention Supreme Court Justice Clarence Thomas. Prominent blacks among the ranks of the Republican Party include Connecticut Representative Gary A. Franks, the Reverend Keith Butler of the Detroit City Council, Health Secretary Dr. Louis Sullivan, and TV producer and talk-show host Tony Brown.

Washington Post reporter E. J. Dionne Jr. wrote that President Bush's nomination of Justice Thomas in the summer of 1991 "underscored the diversity of viewpoints that exist in America's black community, giving new visibility to the nation's black conservatives and highlighting a century-old debate among black intellectuals over the best path to political power and economic success." While contending that conservative Republicans like Thomas are only a "small sliver" of black opinion, Dionne found that the Thomas nomination was a "chance to make clear that there are alternative views among African Americans."

The political clout of Hispanics is undercut somewhat by the fact that many are not yet citizens, while others are too young to vote. But that suggests a powerhouse in the making. The majority of Hispanics identify with the Democratic party, note Rafael Valdivieso and Cary Davis in their 1988 Population Reference Bureau study, *U.S. Hispanics: Challenging Issues for the 1990s.* "However, like other Americans, they increasingly support candidates on the basis of issues and personality rather than party affiliation," report Valdivieso and Davis. "Their political views can often be traced to their national origin and history. Cubans, for example, many of whom came to the U.S. fleeing a Communist regime, tend to be more conservative than other Hispanics."

The bottom line is that both major political parties and all candidates will have to work hard—and deliver—to get and retain the support of America's minorities. Republicans could narrow the wide gap with Democrats, because much minority growth is found in a handful of Sunbelt states that happen to be Republican strongholds. Under reapportionment, there will be new congressional seats created in these states, based on the results of the 1990 census.

Just as political parties must be ever more responsive, so too must marketers of goods and services. Their clientele are changing. And to keep them as customers, business operators must meet their needs and tastes. (This will be taken up in more detail in Chapter 9).

Other factors that contribute to the shifts in America's racial and ethnic makeup are better counting methods as well as changing views of ourselves. The Census Bureau and pollsters like George Gallup let people decide for themselves what and/or who they are. It's a matter of self-identification, which can be affected by changing social attitudes and personal pride in one's roots.

As America has become more accepting and supportive of diversity and best-selling books like *Roots* have encouraged pride in one's identity, there have been more and more people in recent decades standing up to acknowledge their ethnic or racial heritage. This has contributed to the numerical increase in various minority groups, who in decades past might have identified themselves in a census as white or "other."

In recent decades, the Census Bureau has encouraged participation in the decennial census within minority communities and this has boosted the numbers further. Even though the undercount was higher in 1990 than in 1980, it likely would have been higher still without such promotional efforts.

Stayers and Leavers

Three major forces will cause the minority proportion of the American population to rise steadily in coming decades: minorities, particularly blacks and Hispanics, are younger than non-Hispanic whites, more of them are in their childbearing years, and they have higher fertility rates. Furthermore, because of the nation's overall low level of fertility, possible labor shortages in certain sectors will increase demand for more immigration.

One thing to keep in mind about immigration is the often overlooked flip-side: emigration. The Census Bureau calculates that although 827,000 people came into the U.S. in 1988, the net influx of immigrants that year was 667,000 after subtracting the estimated 160,000 people who left the U.S. These figures do not include undocumented immigrants.

The Immigration and Naturalization Service, which regulates immigration, does not keep tabs on emigration, because no permission or application is required to leave the country. When people leave, it's unknown whether they're going on a brief vacation or business trip, leaving the country for an extended period, or leaving for good. However, the Census Bureau does estimate emigration, based on surveys, as a way of gauging the overall components of U.S. population change (births minus deaths, plus immigration minus emigration, equals annual growth).

Emigration, which mostly involves immigrants eventually returning to the land of their birth, has been made easier by inexpensive jet travel, as compared with the arduous steamship travel of Ellis Island immigrants. Some immigrants come to America and work hard for a given number of years to build up a substantial nest egg to then take home. This pattern has been seen among many immigrants from Mexico.

The expatriates also include a small but growing number of native-born Americans who retire abroad as a way to make their nest eggs and pensions go farther. Colonies of retired Americans can be found along the Pacific Coast of Mexico and throughout Central America, including one mountaintop in Costa Rica nicknamed "Gringo Gulch." These newcomers are welcomed for the money they bring and spend.

Religion in America

In addition to the changing racial and ethnic mix of the U.S., there is also a subtle shifting in the nation's religious makeup. The Census Bureau does not gather statistics on religious affiliation because of the strictures of separation of church and state. However, other data sources reveal slow shifts in the religious makeup of America. Again, as for race and ethnic self-identification, the persistent problem for surveyors—and denominational leaders themselves—is one of definition. Do we count the people born into a faith, only those who practice it regularly, or those who identify but don't attend regularly? And what about children of mixed marriages?

Fueled largely by Latin immigrants and their bigger families, the share of the U.S. population that is Catholic has reached 24 percent, according to the Official Catholic Directory, published by P. J. Kennedy & Sons. That will probably rise, helped also by the steady immigration of Filipinos, projected to become the single largest Asian group by the year 2000.

The growing Latin population in the U.S. may also present opportunities for various evangelical Protestant denominations, which have been successful in proselytizing in Central and Latin America. Substantial levels of Asian immigration could also boost U.S. membership in various eastern religions, which have always been small here, as well as mainline Christian denominations.

The recent influx of Jewish refugees from the Soviet Union caused a small numerical increase in America's Jewish population, which remains at risk of declining due to below-replacement-level fertility and intermarriage of American-born Jews. The Jewish population was 6 million in 1990, or 2.4 percent of the total U.S. population, reports the *American Jewish Yearbook 1991*.

 RATES: The Immigration and Naturalization Service (INS) tabulates immigration as the gross total of people moving to this country in a given year. The INS numbers do not reflect emigration.

While not often used, an immigration rate is computed by dividing the number of immigrants in a year by the total U.S. population. It may also be calculated for a longer period of time, such as a decade.

The Census Bureau calculates net immigration, taking its own estimate of annual immigration, minus an annual emigration estimate of 160,000. The result, net immigration, is a key component of population change, along with natural increase (the excess of births over deaths).

 ## Trends to Track; Questions to Ask

- **Asians**. The fastest-growing group in America, Asians increased 108 percent in the 1980s, to 7.3 million. They are the most highly educated of any racial group and also have the highest household income; yet their poverty rate is higher than that of whites. Explore the diversity, anomalies, and problems within the Asian community. Why are they growing so fast and in what parts of the country? Are Asians assimilating; how do they differ by generation and among different Asian groups? What impact are Asians having on their communities, the country, the economy, politics, culture? Will their rapid growth continue?

- **Hispanics**. As early as 2015, Hispanics may surpass blacks to become America's largest minority group. What's fueling the rapid growth of Hispanics; will the growth rate continue? What are the political ramifications of their growth and becoming the biggest minority? Will this encourage or discourage coalition building with other minorities; will it affect how government resources are allocated? What are the differences among the various Hispanic groups; are they united; will Hispanic growth benefit Republicans or Democrats?

- **Blacks**. Despite 32 percent of blacks living in poverty, the black community is diverse and includes a growing middle class and dramatic increases in college graduates. One-fourth of blacks now live in suburbia, although they are concentrated in older, inner-ring suburbs. Explore the uneven progress of blacks. What are the prospects in the coming decades? Will there be any loss of clout and prestige when they are no longer the nation's biggest minority?

- **Diversity**. Currently, 24 percent of the U.S. population is minority. This share is projected to reach almost 33 percent by the year 2030. What benefits, challenges, and opportunities will this shift pose? How will this growing diversity affect and change American society, its institutions, practices, people, and, ultimately, the American identity?

- **Intermarriage**. There are well over 1 million interracial married couples, including 211,000 black/white marriages. While this contributes to the growing diversity of the U.S., it also complicates the counting of various racial and ethnic groups. How? What is the racial identity of interracial couples and, especially, their children? How much does growing pride and willingness to be counted with one's group account for population growth among Hispanics, blacks, and native Americans? Does this skew the data? Additionally, the census misses millions of people in its decennial headcounts, a disproportionate number of whom are minorities. How accurate are the census numbers? Can they be trusted?

- **Emigration**. What are the push/pull factors in immigration and emigration? How significant is emigration; who's going and why? How much emigration is actually return migration to country of origin? What are the economic considerations; what impact does it have on the U.S. and the countries to which emigrants move?

SOURCES:
- U.S. Immigration and Naturalization Service, Washington, D.C.
- The Census Bureau, Suitland, Maryland.
- The Hispanic Policy Development Project, Washington, D.C.
- Population Reference Bureau, Washington, D.C.
- Center for Migration Studies, Staten Island, New York.
- The Asia Society, New York, New York.
- East-West Policy Institute, Honolulu, Hawaii.
- Center for the Continuing Study of the California Economy, Palo Alto, California.
- National Association of Latino Elected and Appointed Officials, Washington, D.C.

- Southwest Voter Research Institute, San Antonio, Texas.
- National Urban League, New York, New York.
- Joint Center for Political Studies, Washington, D.C.
- Urban Institute, Washington, D.C.
- Election Data Services, Washington, D.C.
- United States Catholic Conference, Washington, D.C.
- American Jewish Committee, New York, New York.

6 Making the Grade: Educational Attainment

Average SAT scores have plunged 90 points in recent decades, yet "grade inflation" has sent classroom marks upward, swelling the ranks on the honor roll.

Debate rages over what students are and are not learning, ignited by the hard-hitting 1983 presidential commission report, *A Nation at Risk.*

University of Chicago professor Allan Bloom writes a dense scholarly book on the failures of higher education, and it becomes a 1987 bestseller.

President Bush has declared himself the "education president," vowing to straighten out education, with lofty goals for the year 2000. And still, American students spend more than twice as much time watching television as doing homework, and less time in the classroom than students in most developed nations.

Fueling much of the debate and reappraisal about education in the U.S. are statistics on various groups' educational attainment—a key factor that directly influences other demographic variables, including income and employment. Enrollment data show a student population of rapidly changing size and ever greater diversity, posing added challenges to educators.

The education report card is mixed indeed, and complicated. There has been genuine progress over many decades in raising graduation rates, cutting dropout rates, and narrowing the gaps between whites and minorities. The baby boomers, aged 28 to 46 in 1992 and now entering the years of peak work force productivity, have been called "the best-educated generation ever."

But progress has slowed or stalled since the boomers left school. Women continue to gain in numbers and achievement in college, but others, notably Hispanics, are losing ground. Studies also reveal alarming gaps in student knowledge and proficiency at a time when the U.S. economy is becoming ever more high-tech and service-oriented in an increasingly competitive global marketplace.

The marks:
Good—The annual dropout rate for grades 10 through 12 declined from 5.3 percent in 1963 to 4.1 percent in 1990. The rate fell most for blacks, from 9.2 percent in 1975 to 5.1 percent by 1990. Rates that year were highest for Hispanics, at 8.1 percent; for whites, 3.4 percent. The rates are all-time lows.

Fair—The high school completion rate for persons aged 25 to 29 increased by 15 percentage points between 1965 and 1977 to 85 percent. That's a record high, although it has not improved since then.

Mixed—High school completion rates for blacks aged 25 to 29 jumped from 50 percent to 83 percent between 1965 and 1986 and have hovered around that level since then. Hispanics, after gaining several points in the 1970s, stalled at around 60 percent.

Poor—An international study found that U.S. high school seniors ranked last among six developed nations in mathematical skills and second to last in science comprehension. Another study of geography knowledge found that 13 percent of high school seniors could not identify Canada on a map; 15 percent couldn't locate the Soviet Union.

Poor—Between 1963 and 1981, combined SAT scores fell 90 points to a verbal/math total of 890. Between 1981 and 1989, they rose to the unimpressive low 900s, then dipped again slightly.

Fair—For this, the U.S. invests $4,719 per public school pupil per year, quadruple the expenditure in 1950 in constant dollars. The total K-12 education expenditure is $184.5 billion, or 3.6 percent of the GNP.

Good—The proportion of Americans with four or more years of college has risen steadily, from 11 percent of adults in 1970 to 21 percent in 1989.

Good—By 1989, 22 percent of white adults over age 24 were college graduates; 12 percent of blacks; 10 percent of Hispanics; and 40 percent of Asians. The proportions are higher still for adults aged 25 to 34.

Poor—Students are taking longer to complete college, and the share of men enrolling directly out of high school has declined somewhat.

Good—Since the late 1970s, over half of all college students have been women, and an increasing share of graduate degrees are going to women. By 1988, women earned one-quarter of dental degrees, one-third of medical degrees, and 40 percent of law degrees.

Fair—Almost half of blacks graduating from high school in 1977 went to college that fall. That fell to 38 percent in 1983, rebounding to 46 percent by 1990. The rate was only 5 percentage points below that of whites in the mid-1970s; 15 points lower in 1990. Hispanics who graduate from high school have generally been somewhat more likely than blacks to enroll in college. However, Hispanics are less likely than blacks or whites to complete high school.

Mixed—Foreign students make up an increasing share of graduate-school enrollment, particularly in the sciences. The share of engineering doctorates going to foreign students rose from 33 percent in 1980 to 47 percent by 1988. One-third of the doctoral students in computer sciences and 44 percent in mathematics were foreign by the late 1980s.

"Much of the new talent these programs create will not stay in the U.S.," warns a study by the Department of Education titled *The Condition of Education, 1990*. The statistics quoted thus far also come from the Department of Education's National Center for Education Statistics.

Better Grades, Better Grads Needed in 21st Century

The Hudson Institute's "Workforce 2000" study and many other studies caution that jobs of the future will require more training and higher levels of skill than in the past. The Department of Education projects that 30 percent of new jobs in the 1990s will require a college degree, compared with 22 percent the decade before. If Americans don't pursue educational opportunities and colleges can't produce adequate numbers of qualified workers, this will put added pressure on the government to adjust immigration policy to admit more highly skilled immigrants to fill the worker gap.

Family welfare, as well as America's global competitiveness, are at risk. Studies clearly show that income and job opportunities rise with education, and illegitimacy and family size decline. The rule of thumb is: the more you learn, the more you'll earn later in life.

This is true for all racial and ethnic groups. While disproportionate numbers of blacks and Hispanics are among the poorly educated and poor, the income gap between minorities and whites narrows significantly as education increases. For example, the average earnings of blacks overall are only two-thirds that of whites. But college-educated blacks earn 74 percent as much as comparably educated whites. And as Ben Wattenberg notes in his 1990 book, *The First Universal Nation*, "There are more than 2 million black college graduates, 1600 percent more than in 1950."

TREND-TRACKING TIP: The A's to F's of Grading

There are many ways to assess educational attainment, and the smart demographic analyst looks at them all to determine what's going on. The problem in looking at only one measure is that it will provide an incomplete picture of education in the U.S. and a flawed understanding of what's going on.

Example: Asian Americans, without question, have the highest level of educational attainment. Forty percent of Asian Americans aged 25 and older have at least four years of college—more than double the national average.

But there's a flip side: 20 percent of Asian Americans have less than a high school diploma, a rate higher than for non-Hispanic whites. Also within the diverse Asian community, there are wide differences in attainment among different ethnic groups.

Even within groups, look for differences by age. This reveals the much higher levels of attainment among young blacks who benefited from affirmative action, as compared with older blacks who were educated in the age of segregation. The same age pattern holds for women.

Tending to depress the overall achievement levels of Hispanics is the massive influx of immigrants, many of whom are poorly educated people who do not speak English. However, educa-

---

tional attainment rises significantly with second- and third-generation Hispanics.

Because of immigration, U.S. schools educate a much more diverse student body than any other country, including many students not fully fluent in English. For example, in the public schools of San Jose, California, 7,000 out of 29,000 students have limited proficiency in English. Some 55 languages are spoken by San Jose students.

Also because of the U.S. concept of universal education and mandatory attendance until age 16, elementary and secondary schools have a broader spectrum of students, including the disadvantaged, poorly motivated, and nonachievers, who would likely have quit school sooner in other countries.

At the college level, America's open admissions, part-time options, and community colleges make postsecondary education available to practically everyone; this is certainly not the case in most other countries, where universities are reserved for the elite. In this sense, Americans *are* the world's best-educated people. Even though American universities sometimes appear to be armed camps of competing 'isms,' the best of them remain among the very finest universities in the world, evidenced by the influx each fall of foreign students sent by their governments to study in the U.S.

The Boom in Babies Creates a Boom in Students

The first wave of post-war baby boomers began swamping American schools in the fall of 1951. Schools launched massive building projects that continued for years and relied on portable classrooms and double sessions to expand capacity in the short term. Hundreds of thousands of teachers were added in just a few years to cope with the enrollment bulge; many newly minted teachers were former G.I.s back from World War II. The author, himself a first-year baby boomer born in 1946, distinctly recalls a grade-school class of 57, with one teacher and no assistants.

The high school completion rate for blacks is now nearly as high as for whites, but dropping out remains common among Hispanics.

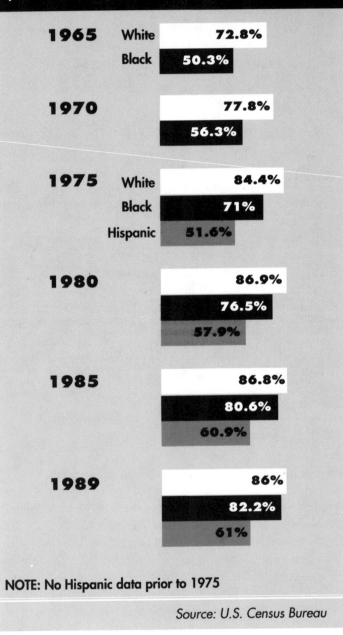

Rising Educational Attainment
Percent of 25-to-29-year-olds completing at least 12 years of school, by selected ethnic groups

1965
White — **72.8%**
Black — **50.3%**

1970
77.8%
56.3%

1975
White — **84.4%**
Black — **71%**
Hispanic — **51.6%**

1980
86.9%
76.5%
57.9%

1985
86.8%
80.6%
60.9%

1989
86%
82.2%
61%

NOTE: No Hispanic data prior to 1975

Source: U.S. Census Bureau

College Graduates

Percent of population aged 25 and older with 4 or more years of college, by ethnic origin

1970

White	11.3%
Black	4.4%
Hispanic	4.5%

1980

	17.1%
	8.4%
	7.6%

1989

	21.8%
	11.8%
	9.9%

Source: U.S. Census Bureau

Whites continue to graduate from college at rates nearly twice as high as those for blacks and Hispanics.

Many of the boomers' fathers were veterans of World War II who used the G.I. Bill to go to college, often the first in their families to ever go to college. Previously, college in America was viewed as only for the elite and not essential to success in life. For generations before that, it had not been uncommon to leave school before getting a high school diploma to take whatever jobs were available to help out with family expenses.

But millions of World War II veterans, with college degrees in hand, pursued white-collar careers during the prolonged post-war boom of the 1950s and 1960s. Their own improving prospects gave them the wherewithal and determination to give their own children the best opportunities. This included college for daughters as well as sons. Suddenly, college was middle class, for the masses, the ticket to success.

Thirteen years after the baby boom hit kindergartens, the wave swamped college campuses, where dorms and classrooms were quickly built as enrollments skyrocketed. Again, the author's own experience brings to mind a shortage of dorm space, prompting the administration to squeeze three students into rooms designed for two. Colleges, like high schools before them, beat the academic bushes to find enough people to teach the jammed classrooms. In addition to the sheer size of the baby boom, the Vietnam Conflict and the draft caused enrollment to swell during the 1960s, as many young men went to college rather than enter military service.

Boom to Bust to Boomlet

Portable classrooms and "triples" were commonplace at schools and colleges throughout the 1960s and 1970s. But ultimately, K-12 enrollment began declining, as the baby boom was followed by the baby bust. Grade schools and high schools that opened in the 1950s and 1960s were closed or turned into senior centers in the 1970s. K-12 enrollment peaked in 1970 at 51.3 million, then fell to 45.1 million by 1985.

Enrollment at the elementary and secondary level directly parallels population trends. This isn't necessarily the case at the college level. While the baby bust has shrunk the pool of traditional students, total college enrollment has actually managed to grow modestly in recent years, to 14.1 million students in the 1991-92 school year, by opening its doors to more women, older, and part-time students, and lowering standards to accept a greater proportion of high school graduates.

In 1990, 60 percent of those who graduated high school in June enrolled in college that fall, compared with 49 percent in 1980, according to the U.S. Department of Education. Forty-one percent of college students are now aged 25 or older, versus 28 percent in the early 1970s. Meanwhile, the number of foreign students enrolled, many sent by their governments, doubled between 1976 and 1988, to 356,000, or 3 percent of total enrollment. (Foreign students are heavily concentrated in engineering and the sciences at the graduate level.)

Even so, many private colleges have suffered enrollment declines, as competition for students heats up with a growing share of students opting for less expensive state schools.

College enrollment should begin an upswing by the mid-1990s because of the echo baby boom, which is already working its way through grade schools and junior highs. K-12 enrollment has increased by 1 million since 1985, to 46.1 million in 1990. Thoroughly confused administrators, who a decade ago were converting or selling off school buildings, are now opening up some of them again to handle the echo boom. Many baby-boom mothers also hold down jobs, which has fueled a sharp increase in enrollment at pre-primary schools. In 1970, 1 million children were enrolled in pre-kindergarten programs, representing 14 percent of all 3- and 4-year-olds. By 1987, 2.3 million children—32 percent of those aged 3 and 4—were in preschool.

Classroom Mixes

At all levels of education, enrollment is growing ever more diverse. Immigration and differences in birth rates have combined to dramatically increase the minority share of enrollment.

In 1976, 24 percent of K-12 enrollment was minority. A decade later, the minority proportion was up to 30 percent. Some projections show it rising to 46 percent by the year 2020.

"As minority students enter the schools in increasing numbers, they are bringing new languages, cultures, and conceptions of education to the classroom," notes *The Condition of Education, 1990.* "Generally, a higher percentage of minorities have incomes below the poverty level than nonminority individuals. Since minority status and poverty are positively correlated, this increase could portend an increasing demand on schools for a number of educational and social services which traditionally either have not been provided or provided on only a limited basis."

While operating with chronically limited budgets, Catholic schools may provide public-school educators with some answers about how to successfully meet the needs of a diverse student body and turn out capable graduates. Research by University of Chicago sociologist James Coleman has shown that Catholic-school students, who include many minorities, consistently outperform public-school students on achievement tests in math, science, and reading. Reasons cited by analysts for the higher parochial achievement include tougher discipline and course requirements, more homework, greater parental involvement, and the ability to expel unruly students.

Despite the success of their graduates, Catholic schools have seen their K-12 enrollments decline dramatically, from 5.3 million in the early 1960s to less than half that today. Contributing to the decline was the fact that 4,300 Catholic schools were shut down in the last three decades, primarily in the cities, as families moved to the suburbs and more parishes could no longer afford to operate the historically underfunded schools. There are currently 7,300 parochial grade schools and 1,300 high schools in the U.S., down from 10,500 and 2,400 in 1960.

Of the 5.3 million children enrolled in America's private schools, roughly half attend Catholic schools. In 1970, 80 percent of all private school students were enrolled in parochial schools. At the K-12 level, about 12 percent of students attend a private school, up modestly in recent decades.

The National Center for Education Statistics forecasts a significant K-12 enrollment increase in the 1990s. Between 1990 and 2000, K-8 will increase 11 percent, while high school enrollment should jump 20 percent. Causing that upswing, as previously noted, is the echo baby boom.

Of the more than 14 million students now attending college, 78 percent are enrolled in public institutions. That's up from 67 percent in 1965. The rising share opting for public college is no doubt prompted by skyrocketing fees at private colleges. A year at an Ivy League school can easily cost more than $20,000, while public schools can cost one-half to one-third of that.

Over 40 percent of all college students now attend part-time, up from one-third in 1970. Students are getting older, as a growing portion are employed people attending for job-related training or to improve their skills. In 1972, 28 percent of college students were over the age of 25. By the 1990s, the proportion had risen to over 40 percent. Over one-third of all students now attend two-year colleges.

Goals for the Class of 2000

In his 1990 State of the Union Address, President Bush set out six goals for the year 2000:

- All children in American will start school ready to learn.
- We will increase the share of students graduating from high school to at least 90 percent (from its current level of 85 percent).
- Students will leave grades 4, 8, and 12 having demonstrated competency in challenging subject matter, including English, mathematics, science, history, and geography.
- America's students will rank first in the world in science and math achievement.
- Every adult will be literate and possess the knowledge and skills necessary to compete in a global economy.
- Every school in America will be free of drugs and violence and offer a disciplined environment conducive to learning.

We have a long way to go.

Complicating efforts to get there, at a time when K-12 enrollment is rising again and growing more diverse, is a looming teacher shortage. The millions hired to educate the baby boom during the 1950s and 1960s are hitting retirement age. Others are quitting to go into more lucrative fields. "The projected annual demand for new hiring of all teachers is expected to rise from 233,000 in 1990 to a high of 243,000 in the year 2000," according to *The Condition of Education 1990*." Demand should be greatest at the elementary school level."

By the late 1980s, the annual dropout rate for teachers was 5.6 percent in public schools and 12.7 percent in private schools. Only a decade ago, college and universities, which produced a record number of PhDs, were unable to hire most of them as tenured faculty, giving rise to so-called nomadic scholars who roamed the campuses going from one untenured teaching post to another. Eventually, many tired of the elusive search for job security and left teaching for industry. But even colleges will soon need a new generation of professors to fill the growing number of vacancies now opening up as the teachers who taught the baby boom start retiring.

Corporate America will provide some teachers of the 1990s. No longer sitting on the sidelines except to write checks for donations, businesses and even labor unions are getting increasingly involved in education from grade school through graduate school. They're helping devise courses and providing top talent from their own ranks to teach on sabbaticals or as part-timers.

The move is a matter of survival as much as civic-mindedness. Businesses want better-prepared graduates than they have been getting as new employees in recent decades, and in an ever-changing high-tech world, they are requiring regular retraining for experienced staff to keep their companies competitive in the global marketplace. The challenge becomes especially acute in states and districts experiencing rapid population growth due to an influx of newcomers, such as California, Arizona, Nevada, and Florida.

The public-school system in Clark County, Nevada, which serves metropolitan Las Vegas and is one of the fastest-growing counties in the nation, added 1,300 new teachers in fall 1990 and opened 13 new schools. It expects to add another 1,000 teachers and 18 schools by 1992.

RATES: Educational attainment is typically expressed in terms of median completed years of schooling (the point at which half of people have more and half have less) and simple percentages of the population or particular group that reach or fail to reach a certain level.

The dropout rate is the percentage of students who failed to finish the school year. Divide the number who dropped out during the school year by the number who started in the fall.

High school graduation rates are determined by taking the number of students who graduate in a given year divided by the original size of the class when it entered high school. This is an imprecise measurement, because half of all dropouts eventually return to school or get an equivalency diploma. This type of rate is best described as an on-time graduation rate, showing the percentage who complete their education in the traditional span of years.

A growing number of students are taking longer to finish school, particularly at the college level. Therefore, a more revealing measurement than graduation rate is one that determines the maximum years of school completed. This calculates, for example, the proportion of the population, or a particular group, that has completed a maximum of eight years of school; one to three years of high school; four years of high school; one to three years of college; four years of college; more than four years of college. To show improvements over generations, completion rates are often computed for various age groups. While completion rates are sometimes given for the entire population, completion rates are much more likely to be given for the population aged 25 and older, or for cohorts starting at age 25. To include people under age 25 skews the results, because many people in their early twenties are still in school and have not reached their highest grade level.

Trends to Track; Questions to Ask

*   **Quality Education.** Debates rage over the quality of education in America, yet some statistics suggest Americans now are the best-educated ever, the most educated nation in the world. What are the facts and the trends; what are the anomalies in the statistics? Progress has been made, but some ground lost. Where? How? What challenges lie ahead; how can education be improved?

*   **Minorities.** Are there gaps in educational attainment between whites and minorities? Are they closing, or widening? Are there differences among minority groups? Within minority groups?

*   **Parochial Schools.** Research by University of Chicago sociologist James Coleman shows that parochial-school students, including minorities, consistently outperform public-school students on achievement tests. What are the differences, and how can this be, given the much lower funding of parochial schools? Are there lessons here for public schools?

*   **Enrollment.** The baby boomers launched school enrollments on a wild roller-coaster ride that affected funding, capital construction, staffing, and curriculum. How and why? What are the aftershocks? What have K-12 and college enrollment trends been since boomers graduated; what does the future hold?

*   **Colleges.** After decades of rapid enrollment gains, colleges saw enrollment growth slow dramatically in the 1980s. But renewed growth is expected later this decade. Are schools prepared for the newest surge? How? Is this merely a reflection of the echo baby boom or are more

forces at work? Has college marketing changed and proved a factor in renewed growth? What changes are evident in the composition of enrollment?

- **Women.** Men had long been the clear majority of college enrollment, their share rising during the Vietnam era. By 1978, women moved into the majority and remain the majority of college students. What are the trends, causes, and impact? What's happening at the graduate level?

- **Corporations.** Companies are not merely training employees on the job, they're also going right to the schools to become involved in curriculum design, counseling, and teaching. Xerox, 3M, R.J. Reynolds, and countless others are involved in public-school education. What prompted the trend; what's the point; how does it work; what are the results?

- **High-Tech Education.** Thirty percent of new jobs created during the 1990s will require a college degree, up from 22 percent in the 1980s. What impact is this having on schools and curricula? Can and how will American education keep American industry competitive in the global economy of the 21st century?

- **Teacher Shortage.** Will there be one, and why? Is American education prepared to find over 200,000 new teachers annually during the 1990s, at a time when teaching is held in low esteem and salaries are low? Who's going into teaching; who else can be attracted to the profession, and how? Will standards be relaxed, changed?

SOURCES:

- U.S. Department of Education's National Center for Education Statistics, Washington, D.C.
- Census Bureau, Suitland, Maryland.
- National Education Association, Washington, D.C.
- National Catholic Education Association, Washington, D.C.
- American Council of Education, Washington, D.C.
- Council for the Advancement and Support of Education, Washington, D.C.
- Association of Governing Boards of Universities and Colleges, Washington, D.C.
- College Entrance Examination Board, Princeton, New Jersey.
- The American College Testing Program, Iowa City, Iowa.
- Hudson Institute, Indianapolis, Indiana.

7 Help Wanted; Exp. Prf'd: The Work Force

As America's population grows ever more diverse racially and ethnically, so does the labor force, only more so. The share of minorities, immigrants, older workers, and women will rise steadily in the coming decades. Conversely, the proportion of white men and young workers will decline.

"Entrants will more likely be women, blacks, Hispanics, and Asians," reports the Bureau of Labor Statistics (BLS) in its latest series of projections, published in the November 1991 *Monthly Labor Review.* Contributing to that will be net immigration, both legal and illegal, which the BLS projects at 800,000 annually in the 1990s. "Leavers from the labor force, on the other hand, are more likely to be male, and almost one-half of the leavers are projected to be white non-Hispanics. The composition of entrants and leavers explains the changes expected in the composition of the labor force between 1990 and 2005."

Workforce 2005

Between 1990 and 2005, the labor force is projected to increase 21 percent, or 25.9 million, to 151 million people. This compares with a growth rate of 33 percent between 1975 and 1990. (The labor force includes both employed people and those unemployed but actively looking for work.)

The BLS forecasts that between 1990 and 2005, the number of Hispanics in the labor force will increase 75 percent, Asians 74 percent, blacks 32 percent, women 26 percent, whites 17 percent, and men 16 percent.

The number of young workers aged 16 to 24, which declined 6 percent in the previous 15 years, will grow 13 percent. Older workers, those aged 55 to 64, will increase 43 percent.

By 2005, the U.S. labor force will look like this (1975 comparisons in parenthesis):

- 83 percent white (down from 88 percent).
- 12 percent black (up from 10 percent).
- 5 percent Asian (up from 2 percent).
- 16 percent aged 16 to 24 (down from 24 percent).
- 53 percent men (down from 60 percent).
- 47 percent women (up from 40 percent).

Despite the declining share of workers aged 16 to 24, the actual number of these young workers will begin increasing again. This comes after a decline of 1.4 million, or 6 percent, of entry-level workers between 1975 and 1990, due to the entry of the baby-bust generation into the work force. But right behind them is a larger group—the echo baby boom, born starting in 1977—which will begin entering the job market later in the 1990s.

The BLS explains: "The very pronounced decline in the youth labor force is behind us. While declines in the number of youth in the labor force will continue for a few more years, until about 1996, this group will begin to increase gradually, and by 2005, is projected to be 2.8 million larger than in 1990. Consequently, the worry about lack of entry-level workers, which was of concern in the late 1980s and early 1990s, should ease considerably, if not disappear entirely, as we progress through this decade."

While almost half of the labor force will be female by 2005, almost two-thirds of all women will be working. The former is known as share of the labor force, while the latter figure is the participation rate. Projections show that the participation rate in 2005 for women aged 25 to 54 may reach 82 percent.

However, one-fourth of all employed women work only part-time. That plus interruptions in careers due to child-rearing and other commitments, have contributed to women's lagging earnings. Even when such factors are eliminated, women's earnings still trail those of men with comparable experience and education, although the gap has narrowed in recent decades.

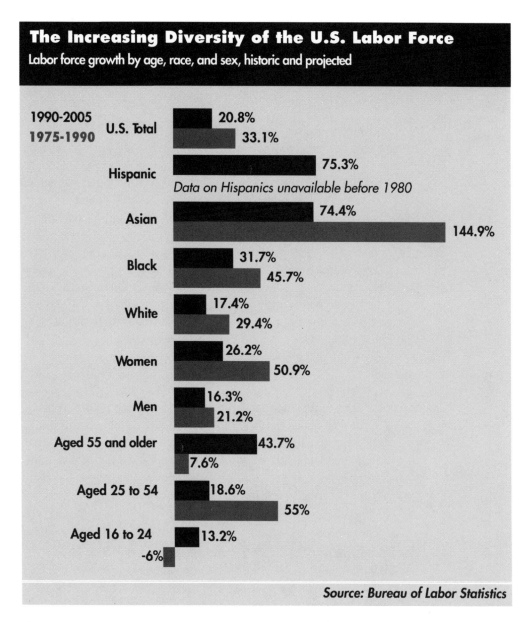

The Increasing Diversity of the U.S. Labor Force

Labor force growth by age, race, and sex, historic and projected

	1990-2005	1975-1990
U.S. Total	20.8%	33.1%
Hispanic	75.3%	*Data on Hispanics unavailable before 1980*
Asian	74.4%	144.9%
Black	31.7%	45.7%
White	17.4%	29.4%
Women	26.2%	50.9%
Men	16.3%	21.2%
Aged 55 and older	43.7%	7.6%
Aged 25 to 54	18.6%	55%
Aged 16 to 24	13.2%	-6%

Source: Bureau of Labor Statistics

The number of Asian-American and Hispanic workers will grow fastest in the 1990-2005 period, while the number of workers under the age of 25 may gain ground after losses between 1975 and 1990.

87

Single women are more likely to work than married women. Among married women with children under age 18, labor force participation rises steadily as the children get older. Just over half of married women with children under age one had jobs, compared with 64 percent of moms with 5-year-olds and 74 percent of those with teenagers.

While women's progress in employment is indisputable and many have broken through barriers and risen to the top, the majority of women remain in so-called traditional positions—nursing, secretarial, retail sales, teaching. By 1990, 40 percent of all executives and managers were women; yet three-quarters of K-12 teachers were women, as were 98 percent of secretaries, 87 percent of librarians, and 82 percent of cashiers.

Many growth fields are tied to demographic trends: day care, home-delivery services, education, health care, insurance, financial services. Some are tied to correcting society's problems: recycling, waste management, drug and delinquent counseling, urban renewal, family mediation, environmental reclamation, etc. Still other jobs are barely glimpsed today, growing out of our ever-changing technology and wealth of knowledge.

Edward Cornish, president and founder of the World Future Society, writes in the 1988 book *Careers Tomorrow*, "All of these proliferating career choices make it more difficult than ever for people to decide what they want to do. And choices promise to be even more numerous in the future. People must be prepared to change not just their jobs but their careers four, six, maybe ten times during the course of their lives."

TREND-TRACKING TIP: Who's Working and Who Isn't

Don't confuse the terms labor force and employment. The civilian labor force comprises all noninstitutionalized people aged 16 or older who are classified as either employed or unemployed. Employment, however, is the total number of jobs, which are divided into sectors, divisions, and industries. A distinction must also be made between employment and employed workers. In 1990, there were 122.6 million jobs; but only 118 million jobholders. Why? Several million people were holding down more than one job.

Since World War II, unemployment has gone up and down with the tides of the national economy. The low of 2.9 percent came in 1953; the high of 9.7 percent in 1982.

The jobless rate is based on the number of people out of work but looking for employment, plus those on layoff but available for work or waiting to report to a new job within 30 days, divided by the civilian nonagricultural labor force, which includes the total of these groups and all those currently working.

Specific and detailed as that definition sounds, it tends to understate the unemployment picture, because it does not include so-called "discouraged workers," the long-term unemployed who are no longer actively seeking work.

In the third-quarter of 1991, there were 8.5 million people in the labor force who were unemployed, for an official jobless rate of 6.8 percent. However, if one includes the estimated 1.1 million discouraged workers at that point, the unemployed rate rises to 10.1 percent.

Employment 2005

Employment—jobs—are projected to increase by almost 25 million between 1990 and 2005, according to the BLS's moderate forecast series. Jobs will rise from 122.6 million to 147.2 million, an increase of 20 percent, or 1.2 percent annually, which is half the growth rate in the previous 15 years.

To keep better track of how the total economy and its various parts are doing, the Labor Department divides employment into various categories. The first broad classification is: nonfarm wage and salary, agriculture, private households, nonagricultural self-employed, and unpaid family workers.

The nonfarm wage and salary category, accounting for 90 percent of all jobs, is divided into two sectors: goods-producing and service-producing.

The goods-producing sector, which is projected to grow very slowly, is composed of three divisions: mining, construction, and manufacturing. The latter is split into durable manufacturing and nondurable manufacturing.

The various divisions are further broken down into industries. For example, durable manufacturing includes automotive, electronics, computers, and industrial machinery. Nondurable manufacturing includes food, tobacco products, printing and publishing, and chemicals. On the service-producing side, the retail trade division includes industries such as department stores, restaurants, taverns, service stations, convenience stores, and automotive dealers. The BLS produces employment projections for over 300 industries.

The projections show the continuation of the shift from a manufacturing economy to a service-based one. Mining jobs, half of which are in petroleum/oil industries, are expected to decline in the coming years, due to further introduction of labor-saving devices and a growing use of foreign oil. While growth in foreign demand for U.S. coal will boost coal output, jobs will not keep pace, due to increased mechanization in mines.

Construction employment will grow 1.1 percent annually, somewhat slower than employment overall. "The slowing of population growth and household formation will dampen demand for new housing units, and eliminating the excess stock of office and commercial space may take much of the 1990-2005 period," cautions the BLS report "Outlook 1990-2005" in the November 1991 *Monthly Labor Review.* "However, increased spending for construction and repair of roads, bridges, and other infrastructure components is assumed, as well as increased spending on educational facilities to accommodate the children of the baby boomers as they come of school age."

While real manufacturing output is forecast to grow 2.3 percent annually, wage and salary employment is projected to decline 0.2 percent annually, to a 2005 level of 18.5 million jobs. Output will grow due to improved productivity and mechanization. Manufacturing as a share of the economy's total real output will hold at about the 1990 level of 34 percent.

The service-producing sector will contribute 23 million of 25 million new jobs projected. The sector consists of six divisions: transportation/communications/utilities, wholesale trade, retail trade, finance/insurance/real estate, services, and government. Each of those divisions is made up of dozens of industries.

Within the service-producing sector, the service division will generate the most jobs, 11.5 million, according to the BLS. Trucking and air transit jobs are expected to grow due to increased domestic and overseas freight shipments. Airlines will also benefit from more business and vacation travel. New technologies and heightened competition are expected to further cut communications jobs.

Wholesale trade employment, boosted by projected increases in exports, is expected to grow at about the national rate. Retail trade is projected to have the second-fastest employment growth, after the service sector. "The fastest projected job growth in this industry is in apparel and accessory stores and eating and drinking establishments, as higher levels of personal income and continued increases in the labor force participation of women stimulate purchases of clothing and restaurant meals," explains "Outlook 1990-2005."

"Within the services division are 16 of the 20 fastest-growing industries and 12 of the 20 industries adding the most jobs. Most of these industries are in business, health, social, legal, and engineering and management services."

"The projected 2.3 percent-a-year employment growth for the services division is almost twice as fast as the projected average increase in total nonfarm wage and salary jobs, but does not match the division's performance during 1975-90, when its employment grew 4.8 percent annually. This performance is not possible to repeat, given the projected slowdown in population and labor force expansion."

Health services and business services combined are projected to account for 6.1 million of the new jobs, about one-fourth of the employment increase.

The ten fastest-growing industries are projected to be, in descending order: residential care, computer and data processing services, health services, management and public relations, water and sanitation, libraries/ vocational and other schools, offices of health practitioners, passenger transportation arrangements, social services, and legal services. Jobs in those industries will grow at two to four times the national rate of 1.2 percent.

In addition to tracking industries, the BLS also produces employment estimates and projections for occupations.

Get a Job

Occupations are divided into nine major occupation groups: executive/administration/managerial, professional speciality, technicians and related support, marketing and sales, administrative support including clerical, service occupations, agricultural/forestry/fishing and related occupations, precision production/craft/repair, and operators/fabricators/laborers.

Within those nine groups, there are almost 800 specific occupations. The professional group includes physicians, attorneys, dentists, registered nurses, engineers, scientists, teachers, librarians, computer analysts, and statisticians.

Computer programmers, opticians, dental hygienists, and licensed practical nurses fall in the technicians and related support group, along with paralegals, aircraft pilots, and lab technicians. Secretaries, clerks, postal workers, bank tellers, and receptionists are in the administrative support group.

The precision production/craft/repair group includes skilled trades-people such as automotive workers, carpenters, electricians, mechanics, and blue-collar supervisors.

The fastest-growing occupations in descending order are: home health aides, paralegals, systems analysts, physical therapists, medical assistants, operations research analysts, human services workers, radiologic technologists, medical secretaries, and physical therapy assistants. Over half of the 30 occupations facing large projected declines are in manufacturing.

The major occupational groupings of executive/administrative/managerial workers, professionals, and technicians/related support, which now represent over one-fourth of total employment, are projected to account for 41 percent of the job growth by 2005.

The projections clearly put added pressure on the nation and particularly its straining educational system to prepare entry-level workers and retrain experienced workers for a changing economy. "Those jobs growing the fastest currently are filled by workers with higher levels of education. This clearly does not mean that everyone must have a 4-year college degree to find a job. But it does point out that an increasingly important opportunity difference is emerging along the lines of education preparation," writes Ronald E. Kutscher, BLS associate commissioner, in "Outlook 1990-2005."

The decline in manufacturing means a decline in high-paying jobs for those with little schooling. And the restructuring of manufacturing and global competition increasingly demand new skills and advanced training for many blue-collar workers. "This does not mean jobs are not expected to be available for high school dropouts, because the list of occupations projected to have extensive job growth show many for which they could qualify.… It does mean, however, the risk of unemployment for high school dropouts is higher," writes Kutscher.

The risk is highest for Hispanics and blacks, who lag in educational attainment. They are also expected to become an increasing share of the labor force. "Therefore, the challenge is to emphasize the need for more education for Hispanics and blacks so that these groups can compete in the likely labor market of the next 15 years," Kutscher concludes. At the same time, schools must improve the achievement levels of all students, particularly in the sciences and math, to be ready to work productively in an increasingly high-tech world.

If American schools and universities cannot produce all the technicians and professionals needed, business will look outside the country to fill strategic vacancies. There will likely be yet another adjustment in America's immigration policy to tie it even more closely to the economy and to give top priority to those with job skills in demand.

More Schooling for a High-Tech Workplace

The Department of Education estimates that 30 percent of the new jobs created during the 1990s will require a college degree, up from 22 percent a decade ago. Even those not requiring degrees will require increasing schooling and training, including better English-language skills than in recent years, at a time when employers are complaining that America's schools are producing too many unqualified graduates. Employers and others are increasingly demanding that schools and universities become more flexible in their instruction, tailoring courses to the shifting needs of industries and employers.

With the growing diversity of the work force, debate over affirmative-action programs will surely grow. In the short-term, tension among competing individuals and groups may also rise, as workers and bosses try to understand and adjust to one another. Employers themselves may find they have go back to school—to learn a foreign language or two, to better communicate with their immigrant workers, and to understand the disparate cultures of their employees.

A 1990 survey of 645 companies by the Hudson Institute and Towers Perrin found a mixed response to the demographic and economic shifts under way and some uncertainty about what to do. The study found that just under three-quarters of respondents reported some degree of management focus on minority hiring and promotion; 68 percent are mindful of the special needs of female workers.

Sixty-five percent admitted concern about labor shortages; over half of these firms have responded with management strategies and decisions. Forty-two percent of firms concerned about labor shortages recruit nontraditional workers (handicapped, elderly). Forty-two percent cited concern about gaps between worker skills and job demands.

"More telling, perhaps, 46 percent were either unable or unwilling to answer the question on management concern about skills mismatches. This high percentage of nonrespondents … may be indicative of just how unknown this particular territory remains for many companies. Their unfamiliarity with the issue appears great enough to discourage many from making any sort of determination about current or looming skills gaps," warns the *Workforce 2000* study by the Hudson Institute and Towers Perrin. Three-quarters of the companies surveyed offer workers tuition reimbursement; only 8 percent provide remedial training. But another 9 percent are piloting remedial education programs, and 14 percent are planning to adopt one.

"In the 1990s, American business will become ever more deeply involved in our schools," forecast futurist Marvin Cetron and education consultant Margaret Gayle in their book *Educational Renaissance*. "Large corporations and small ones all over the country will send their executives to work as mentors with students at risk of dropping out. They will sponsor classes designed to teach the skills students will need for success in later life. They will pay to send teachers to training seminars. They will even pay their own employees to drop out of the corporate life and become teachers themselves."

There were already 140,000 so-called educational partnerships between industry and schools as of 1988, up from 42,000 four years earlier, according to the National Center for Education Statistics. The partnerships, which take different forms and degrees of involvement, currently involve 40 percent of the nation's elementary and secondary schools and more than 9 million students. Cetron and Gayle expect such partnerships to reach virtually all schools by the year 2000. Not only does this improve the quality of education, it's an effective way for businesses to spot, nurture, and eventually recruit talented students.

Boomers and Busters on the Job

Because of rapid technological advances and changes in the economy, workers will increasingly be returning to the classroom over the course of their careers to update or expand their skills. This trend will in part counterbalance the temporary college enrollment slump due to the baby bust.

Members of the comparatively small baby-bust generation, born between 1965 and 1976 may find their own career prospects quite bright after the economy shakes free of the recession. Because there are few of them, busters will have less competition as they move up in their careers. This shortage could bid up their wages.

The situation is much different for the older, massive baby-boom generation, born between 1946 and 1964. Numbering 77 million and representing one-third of the population, there are so many of them that they've gotten in each others' way on the climb up the ladder of success. They have not advanced as quickly as their parents did. The competition has been heightened by the large number of women who entered the labor force during the 1970s and 1980s.

The sheer number of boomers, compounded by the smaller generation following them, is expected to strain the Social Security system in the 21st century. Congress has responded by hiking FICA withholding taxes and gradually pushing back the age for collecting full benefits from 65 to 67. Those born before 1938 will continue to receive full benefits at age 65. The age to receive full benefits then rises two months per year for those born between 1938 to 1943, to 66 years. It remains at 66 years for those born between 1943 and 1954. The age for full Social Security benefits then rises again two months per year for those born between 1955 and 1960, until it reaches age 67, and remains at age 67 for those born in 1960 and later.

Even so, some analysts predict that many baby boomers, who know how to enjoy themselves, will opt for early retirement or semi-retirement. Corporate downsizing and realignment are already encouraging or forcing younger retirement.

Peter Dickinson, publisher of *The Retirement Letter*, notes, "We're getting a lot of these baby boomers. Our base of readers is becoming younger, because these people are wondering what the future will hold for them. They have the feeling—and they are probably right—they won't be able to depend that much on Social Security, or even the longevity of a job." While they begin building their nest eggs, Dickinson expects many boomers and others to retire before traditional retirement age or cut back to part-time work.

Another increasingly popular option is what has been called 'downshifting,' quitting the rat-race at mid-point to slow down and enjoy oneself, often launching a new career, growing out of a hobby or personal interest. For many, that means working at home at one's own pace. By the mid-1980s, 2.2 million persons worked entirely from home. Two-thirds are women. The numbers of home-based workers are expected to continue rising, especially as computers find their way into more homes and as more working wives with kids to raise face up to the unexpected expenses of going to the office.

While some employers currently wrestle with labor shortages brought on by the baby bust, there is some relief in sight. Right behind the baby bust is the larger echo baby boom, the generation born in the late 1970s and throughout the 1980s. The oldest echo baby boomers turn 16 in 1993 and are expected to help ease any shortage of young entry-level workers.

College administrators, who have been struggling to prop up enrollment in recent years by taking in older students and more part-timers, are hungrily awaiting the arrival on campus of the echo boomers for their sheer numbers, if not their academic acumen.

Robots for Coworkers in the Office of Tomorrow

By 1989, a decade after the introduction of the personal computer, 15 percent of households already owned one. Computers, as well as robotics and increasing mechanization, all combine to cut the work week. Futurist Marvin Cetron and co-author Owen Davies in their 1989 book *American Renaissance* predict that "by 2000, Americans will spend just 32 hours each week at work, a full day less than their parents did." By the year 2000, they also expect that up to 20 percent of American workers will work at home.

While a second paycheck significantly boosts a family's gross income, expenses also jump. A 1988 study by Battelle Memorial Institute for *Cosmopolitan* magazine found: "The income of families where both husband and wife are working was 35 percent higher than the income of families without a working wife. Income taxes reduce this advantage to 17 percent. If the additional expenses incurred by the wife in going to work (transportation, lunches, clothing, dry cleaning, etc.) are subtracted, the net benefit is only 5 percent."

For those who choose to or must work at the business site, more and more employers in the 1990s will offer flex-time, part-time scheduling, job-sharing, even some sort of child-care benefit, because they must keep good workers satisfied. One-fourth of all employed women work part-time. The proportion rises for mothers with young children; the younger the children, the higher the share who work part-time.

A 1987 Bureau of Labor Statistics survey of 1.2 million businesses with at least 10 employees found that only 2 percent had employer-sponsored day care, 3 percent assisted with child-care expenses, 5 percent provided child-care information or referral, and 5 percent had counseling services. However, the same survey found 61 percent of the firms did have varied work-schedule policies to assist in child care: flextime policy, 43 percent; voluntary part-time, 35 percent; job sharing, 16 percent; work at home, 8 percent; flexible leave, 43 percent.

RATES: Unlike many other demographic variables, the rates for gauging changes in the labor force are simple and straightforward: labor force participation and unemployment rates are simple percentages; none of that per 1,000 population business. But remember that unemployment rates are the number of unemployed people who are actively seeking jobs divided by the entire labor force, which consists of workers and those seeking work.

 ### Trends to Track; Questions to Ask

- **Labor Shortages.** The U.S. grew by 22.1 million people during the 1980s, or 9.8 percent. Additionally, the country is experiencing a temporary echo baby boom. Yet there have been labor shortages in some sections. Where are the labor shortages; among which age groups? Will they continue? What are the current repercussions and future prospects? Will the trends affect U.S. productivity, competitiveness, cost of living? What strategies are there to alleviate labor shortages and skill mismatch?

- **Women Workers.** Projections show that 47 percent of the work force will be women in 2005, up from 40 percent in 1976. What proportion of women will be working? What's fueling the upward trend; is it moderating? What impact has women entering the work force had on the economy, the workplace, the home, and the careers of men? What are the special needs of women workers, especially working mothers; how are companies responding? How has the growth in working mothers/wives created opportunities for entrepreneurs in the service sector? What proportion of women work part-time; will it grow? What is the net financial benefit—and expenses—to a family of a mother/wife going into the work force?

- **Minorities.** One in four workers in 2005 will be a minority, up from 16 percent in 1976. Many of the new workers will be immigrants. What accounts for the rapid increase; how else is the work force changing, and why? Does the growing share of minority workers present special opportunities and challenges? How are the educational system and employers responding?

- **Educational Partnership.** Over 140,000 corporations, dissatisfied with the quality of today's young job applicants, have gotten involved with schools in an effort to improve the quality and preparedness of graduates. What forms do these educational partnerships take; are they needed; are they working; what's the payoff? How are educators and students responding?

- **Baby Boomers.** Boomers, representing one-third of the population, are now approaching mid-career, normally a period of peak earning power and productivity. Yet their advancement has been slow and their wages depressed. Why? How have they affected the economy, pension programs, Social Security? What lies ahead? Can America afford baby boomers in retirement?

- **Baby Bust.** Right behind the boomers is the much smaller baby-bust generation, which was responsible for shortages of entry-level workers prior to the current recession. What impact does this have on the salaries, employment, and advancement prospects of busters? How are they faring? Will they do better than their older boomer brothers and sisters? Are there any liabilities to being the generation after the boomers? Will baby busters bear an undue burden for keeping Social Security afloat?

- **Early Retirement.** Americans are now retiring younger than ever. But because of the massive size of the baby-boom generation and strain it is expected to put on Social Security, the age for collecting full benefits is being pushed back to age 67 for boomers. Will that help; will Social Security stay afloat? Despite concerns, many baby boomers are expected to retire—or semi-retire—well before the age of 67. Why? How? What impact will that have on the economy, on Social Security, on boomers and subsequent generations, and insurance/financial industries?

SOURCES:

- Bureau of Labor Statistics, Washington, D.C.
- Census Bureau, Suitland, Maryland.
- National Center for Education Statistics, Washington, D.C.
- Forecasting International, Arlington, Virginia.
- The Conference Board, New York, New York.
- NPA Data Services, Washington, D.C.
- The Hudson Institute, Indianapolis, Indiana.
- Towers Perrin, New York, New York.
- Battelle Memorial Institute, Columbus, Ohio.
- WEFA Group, Bala Cynwyd, Pennsylvania.

- Woods & Poole Economics, Washington, D. C.
- U.S. Chamber of Commerce, Washington, D.C.
- World Future Society, Bethesda, Maryland.

8 Making Sense of the Dollars: Income and Poverty

In the most powerful and arguably richest nation in the world, with the biggest middle class anywhere, about 13 percent of all Americans are poor. More than 33 million people are impoverished, including almost one-third of all blacks.

But what is poor? Is or isn't America the richest nation in the world? It all depends.

Income and poverty demonstrate the complexity of seemingly simple concepts and the need to get them straight and use them properly. Income and poverty are important demographic measurements frequently used in combination with other variables such as education, fertility, marital status, employment, and mobility to establish relationships in behavior and isolate cause and effect in social problems such as illegitimacy and crime in an effort to design policies and programs to alleviate the problems.

Each year, the federal government allocates some $45 billion in grants programs, which use census data and statistics from other government agencies to determine who gets how much. Income and poverty figures are among the census statistics frequently used to help calculate program grants. The data, which derive from the decennial census and the Current Population Survey, are also vital to policy debates in Congress and the legislation th t is written there. You can't write corrective legislation to combat poverty or other problems if you first don't know the size and scope of the problem.

While many millions more Americans feel impoverished than actually are (including free-spending baby boomers after making a payment on the Volvo), the official poverty rate is based on an index set by the Social Security Administration and updated annually based on the consumer price index. In 1990, the official poverty rate for the U.S. was 13.5 percent.

Not surprisingly, the government's efforts to gauge poverty have come under attack from all sides. "The Census Bureau is dramatically over-stating the number of persons in poverty and understating the living standards of low-income Americans," insists Robert Rector, a policy analyst at the Heritage Foundation. "The average 'poor' American lives in a larger house or apartment than does the average Western European. America's poor have twice as much living space per capita as the average Japanese and four times as much living space as the average citizen in what was the Soviet Union." Over one-third of poor house-holds own their own homes; 62 percent own their own car, says Rector.

Liberals are quick to dismiss the analysis of the conservative Heritage Foundation. The Center on Budget and Policy Priorities traces rising poverty rates to the recession, wages not keeping pace with inflation, and inadequate government help for the poor. In terms of real household income, the middle class, as well as those officially in poverty, have lost ground, contends the center.

Deciding Who's Poor and Who Isn't, and Who Decides

The consumer price index, which considers the normal living expenses of Americans, sets a poverty threshold. Anyone whose income is below that threshold is considered to be living in poverty. In 1990, the threshold was $6,652 for a household of one person, $13,359 for a family of four, and $26,849 for a family of nine or more. This is gross money income, which includes salary/wages, bank interest, dividends, rental income, pension, Social Security, alimony and all regular sources of income before taxes, union dues, and FICA withdrawal. The poverty thresholds for various-sized households are curiously the same across the country—the same in the pricey New York metropolitan area as in the deep-discount heartland of Joplin, Missouri, where more than half of families live on less than the 1990 median household income of $29,943, which is what yuppies may spend on cars and country-club memberships alone.

Official poverty rates do not calculate the benefit of such noncash programs as food stamps, Medicaid, public housing, and school lunches. But in unofficial experimental calculations by the Census Bureau that included such items, the 1990 poverty rate dropped by 2.2 percentage points to 11.3 percent. Heritage critics say that noncash benefits are undervalued in the experimental calculations, and that including all such benefits would cut the poverty rate to under 10 percent.

The Families USA Foundation counters that Census Bureau calculations seriously underestimate the actual level of poverty, because the formula for setting the annual thresholds, first designed in 1964 and last revised in the early 1980s, has not kept up with skyrocketing medical and housing costs and the changing needs of today's families, including child care. Using its own standard of basic needs, the Families USA Foundation estimates that some 45 million people, or 18 percent of the population, were poor in 1990—far above official estimates.

What's puzzling is that the official poverty rate fell from 34 percent in 1940 to 15 percent by 1960, a period that saw little direct effort by the government to alleviate poverty. "Yet when the welfare state expanded in the 1970s, progress toward eliminating poverty came to a halt. What is more, poverty increased among young families and inner-city residents," writes Harvard professor of government Paul Peterson in a 1991 Brookings Institution report, *The Urban Underclass.*

Despite the expenditure of billions of dollars in anti-poverty programs, the poverty rate has hovered in the low- to mid-teens in recent decades, bobbing up and down along with the economy.

The reality of poverty often defies stereotypes and requires close scrutiny to be properly understood. Consider:

- While blacks and Hispanics are three times more likely than average to be impoverished and represent a disproportionate number of the poor, whites actually account for two-thirds of the nation's 33 million poor.

- Asians, who have the highest level of educational attainment in the U.S. (see Chapter 6), still have higher rates of poverty than whites, 12 percent compared with 11 percent in 1990. The poverty rate for blacks is 32 percent; for Hispanics, 28 percent. At the same time, Asians have the highest household income of any group, including whites.

- Many millions of minorities, however, are not impoverished, particularly married couples. Eighty-seven percent of black married couples are not poor; the same is true for 92 percent of Asian couples and 83 percent of Hispanic couples. The comparable figure for white married couples is 95 percent.

- Forty percent of poor persons aged 15 and older in 1990 worked in 1989; although only 9 percent worked full-time year-round.

- Senior citizens, often viewed as the most economically vulnerable part of the population and squeaking by on dwindling savings, actually have lower-than-average poverty rates. In fact, they are the one group to see significant declines in their rates, dropping from 30 percent in 1967 to 12 percent by 1990, thanks to Social Security and pensions. Vice versa, poverty rates for children have been rising, in part due to the increasing number of single-parent families.

The Feminization of Poverty

Still, some perceptions of poverty are sadly accurate. A disproportionate number of the poor are women and children in female-headed households, inner-city residents, and unemployed or underemployed minority men.

Of the 33.6 million people who were poor in 1990, 40 percent were children under age 18. Over half of all poor families were headed by a woman with no husband present (53 percent); the proportion was 75 percent in poor black families.

Most analysts see discrimination as a factor in poverty; how big a factor it is today is open to debate. But there are clearly other factors also at work, perhaps even more important. The economy's shift to high-tech and services and the movement of manufacturing jobs to suburbia have destabilized many central cities and increased unemployment there, particularly for blacks, contends University of Chicago sociologist William Julius Wilson. Writing in the 1991 Brookings report *The Urban Underclass*, Wilson observes: "The rise in joblessness has in turn helped trigger an increase in the concentrations of poor people, a growing number of poor single-parent families, and an increase in welfare dependency." Dim prospects, plus high rates of mortality and incarceration of minority males, have created a shortage of marriageable young men in the central cities, which only adds to the poverty and single-parent problems, contends Wilson.

The Census Bureau's 1991 "Family Disruption and Economic Hardship" study, based on 1984-86 survey data, found that family income fell 37 percent in families with children where the father left during the survey period. Children who lived throughout the three-year survey period with only their mothers were the worst off. At present rates of illegitimacy, divorce, separation, and widowhood, Census Bureau analyst Arthur Norton has estimated that as many as half of all American children will spend at least one year in a single-parent household before reaching age 18.

In her book *100 Predictions for the Baby Boom*, Cheryl Russell writes: "The best insurance for affluence is a marriage certificate. And the importance of marriage is growing." The reasons are: a married couple has the possibility of two earners in the household, even if just the husband works; men earn and work more than women; women's jobs are often part-time and low-paying, with added expenses like day care; and many absent fathers do not fulfill financial obligations to their children or former spouses. Across all racial and ethnic lines, poverty is lowest for married-couple families and highest for single-parent families.

Other trends in poverty include:

• The higher the educational attainment, the lower the risk of poverty for all groups.

• The South remains the poorest region, a reflection of its agricultural base and large black population. But poverty there has declined significantly as the region has diversified. It's gaining on the other three regions.

• Nonmetropolitan areas had the highest poverty rates for generations. But rates there have moderated in recent decades. Now central cities have the highest poverty rates. Suburbia has the lowest poverty rates.

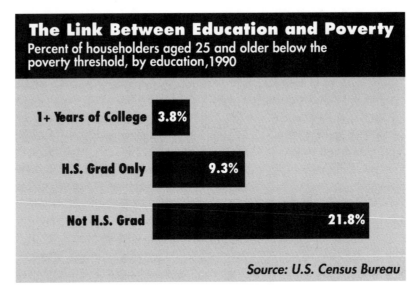

High school dropouts are most likely to have incomes below the poverty line, but even a college education does not guarantee economic security.

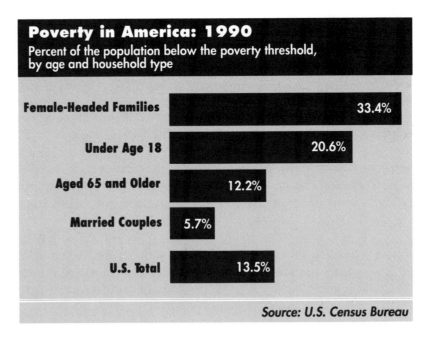

Women who head families on their own have the highest poverty rates, and their growth means that children in general have a higher poverty rate.

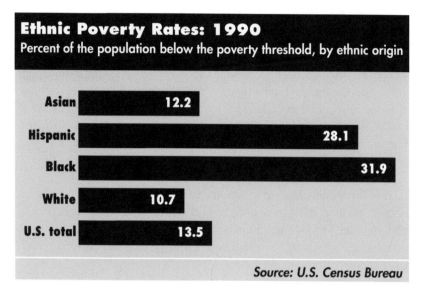

Ethnic Poverty Rates: 1990
Percent of the population below the poverty threshold, by ethnic origin

Asian	12.2
Hispanic	28.1
Black	31.9
White	10.7
U.S. total	13.5

Source: U.S. Census Bureau

Poverty rates for blacks and Hispanics are more than twice as high as those for whites and Asians.

Income: Count Carefully

As complex as it is, assessing poverty is a simple matter compared with the various ways to gauge and compare income. In demographics, if not at the bank, there are many ways to measure income. There's money income, earnings, effective buying power, per capita income, wealth, etc. Each of these measures can be further broken down by household, family, race, region, and so on.

Income figures pop up in the media all the time. Income is an effective bit of detail, a revealing indicator of a person's success or lack thereof, an engaging fact that encourages the reader or listener to compare himself or herself with the person being reported on.

But the reporter, marketing analyst, business executive, or anyone else using income figures must be very careful with them. The statistics can be easily misunderstood simply because there are so many types of income. Always double-check income figures. When including them in a story or analysis, make clear what type of income is being used and what the source is.

The most common income used is money income: gross income from salary/wages, interest, dividends, Social Security, alimony, and other sources all before taxes. It does not include savings, investments, capital gains, life-insurance payments, or home equity. Those goodies are included in something called net worth or wealth, which is the total of assets after taxes. Effective buying power, which marketing firms use frequently, is the spendable money left over after federal, state, and local taxes are paid. It doesn't include capital gains or home equity.

Each of the above can then be computed as mean, median, or per capita income. Mean is what most people think of when they say average. It is the figure derived by adding up income for all units and dividing by the total number of units. The median is a mid-point—the point at which half are above and half are below.

Both means and medians have their advantages and disadvantages. They also yield different results with the same set of numbers. The mean, in particular, which is easy to compute and commonly used by most people, can be distorted by an unusually high or low number. Mathematician Mario F. Triola in his book *Elementary Statistics* notes: "Unlike the mean, the median exhibits the advantage of not being affected by some exceptional extreme values. However, a disadvantage is that the median is not sensitive to the value of every score."

Household and family income are two different, but often confused, measures. Household income is the money income of an occupied housing unit and the people living there. A household can consist of one or more persons; they may or may not be related. In contrast, a family household consists of two or more persons related by blood, marriage, or adoption. Money income and earnings in family households are typically higher than income in households, generally because family households tend to be larger and are more likely to have two wage earners.

Per capita means per person. Per capita income is computed by taking the total income for a group and dividing it by the number of people in that group. The group could be a family, a racial group, a state, or the nation. In 1990, per capita income was $14,387, while median family income was $35,353, and median household income was $29,943. All of these are money income figures.

Asians Earn Less But Have More

Asians have the highest household income of any group, because they tend to have more people and workers in the household.

In 1990, Asians had the highest median household income in the U.S., $38,450, compared with a national median of $29,943, and $31,231 for whites. Yet Asians' median per capita income is below that of whites. Why? Asians, the best-educated among us, tend to have large households, often extended families living together with several people working, which boosts total income.

Despite the overall high educational levels of Asians, many struggle with language barriers in the workplace. Some speak of a glass ceiling that prevents rising to the very top, while others are newly arrived refugees who have not yet assimilated. These factors combine to pull down the per capita income figures of Asians somewhat, although they remain well above those of other minority groups.

Within the broad Asian category, however, there are major income differences among various groups, a reflection of different levels of education, assimilation, and background. Chinese and Japanese Americans who have been here for several generations have incomes much higher than those of recently arrived refugees from Southeast Asia.

TREND-TRACKING TIP: Money for Real, not Monopoly
When making income comparisons from one year to another, be sure of what you are comparing. The dollar amounts can be expressed in current dollars or constant dollars. There's a big difference.

Let's compare per capita income change between 1979 and 1989. Per capita income rose from $7,168 to $14,056 in current dollars, which gives the value of the dollar in the years in question. Constant dollars eliminates the distorting effect of inflation by recomputing income in earlier years to reflect subsequent levels of inflation. In 1989 constant dollars, per capita income went from $12,243 in 1979 to $14,056 in 1989, a "real" increase of 15 percent.

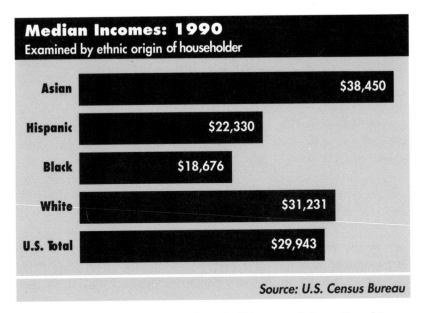

Asian-Americans have the highest household incomes, followed by whites.

Black and Hispanic households, families, and individuals continue to trail far behind whites. In 1960, the median money income for black families was 55 percent of white families (no comparable figures were then available for Hispanics). In 1972, black family income was 59 percent that of whites; Hispanics, 71 percent. In 1990, black family income was 58 percent of whites; Hispanics, 63 percent.

A changing economy, the shift of jobs to the suburbs, rising out-of-wedlock births, lack of aggressive enforcement of equal opportunity statutes, and resistance to affirmative action are among the reasons often cited for the loss of ground in recent years by minorities. However, the gap between blacks and whites is much closer between college-educated and/or married minorities and whites, reflecting the financial advantages that schooling and marriage bring.

In 1990, black married-couple families had 84 percent of the median income of white married-couple families, up from 76 percent in 1975. Hispanic married couples, however, had 69 percent of the income of white couples in 1990, down from 76 percent in 1975, which may reflect massive immigration during the 1980s of people who have not fully assimilated and are working at low-paying jobs. In 1989, black householders with four or more years of college earned 78 percent as much as white college-educated householders; Hispanics earned 85 percent as much.

The gap between women's and men's earnings (salaries/wages) has narrowed steadily, as a growing number of women enter the labor force and advance in their careers. In 1967, women working full-time year-round earned 58 percent of what men were making. By 1989, the difference had narrowed to 68 percent. In 1990, it was up to a record high 71 percent, although this was due in part to three consecutive years of declining earnings for men.

Household Income: 1990
Median income for selected household groups

College Grad Households	$50,549
H.S. Grad Households	$28,744
Renters	$20,722
Homeowners	$36,298
Two-Earner Households	$41,656
One-Earner Households	$24,575
Women Living Alone	$12,548
Men Living Alone	$19,964
Female-Headed Families	$18,069
Married Couples	$39,996
All Households	$29,943

Source: U.S. Census Bureau

Households headed by a college graduate are the most affluent, followed by two-earner households and married couples (which are often the same households).

Another slow but steady trend has been the widening gulf between the haves and the have nots, but also between the haves and the middle class. In the Census Bureau's "1989 Income and Poverty" report, Gordon W. Green, Jr. notes: "The share of aggregate income received by the highest quintile of households was 46.8 percent, no higher than in 1988, though significantly higher than the comparable figures for 1979 and 1969 (44.2 and 43.0 percent, respectively). This change was accompanied by somewhat lower shares of aggregate income going to the lowest and the middle three quintiles."

Green continues: "The reasons for this trend are not as clear. Certainly, part of the growing inequality of the income distribution can be attributed to the changing composition of families and households. One of the compositional changes is the growth in the elderly population....Another compositional change is the growing number of persons living in nonfamily situations....A trend that is associated with the increasing inequality of the family income distribution is the growing percentage of families with a female householder, no husband present....[Other factors include] the aging of the baby-boom generation, the growth in the labor force participation of women, and the changing occupational structure." Once again, the baby boomers rear their 77 million heads and prove a major factor in yet another trend.

Another Census Bureau study has found that the percentage of households that fall into the middle-income category rose from 69 percent in 1964 to 71 percent by 1969. It then fell to 63 percent by 1989.

Living Well, A Matter of Timing

Boomers, to their regret, will not live as well as their parents have. It's a matter of timing and numbers.

The parents of baby boomers, coming of age during the Depression and World War II, were molded by those events, becoming thrifty and conservative. A comparatively small generation, they returned from World War II to take advantage of the G.I. Bill and buy homes in the new suburbs with Veterans Administration mortgages. They launched their careers and advanced during the economic expansion of the 1950s and 1960s, as their homes escalated in value.

Now they're retiring, reaping the full benefits of Social Security, sitting atop hefty savings accounts, and selling their 1950s tract houses for ten times the purchase price.

In contrast, their children, the baby boomers, are bumping into each other every step of the way. Unlike their parents, they have been slow to start saving, preferring to spend their money on high-tech electronics and fast cars. Because of their numbers, their advancement will be slower and their pensions uncertain.

Boomers have already weathered at least two recessions, upheaval in the U.S. corporate world, and the emergence of a fiercely competitive global economy. The bottom line is that despite the early years of partying, boomers will not live as well as their parents nor have as much in the bank.

One indicator of this is homeownership, which showed signs of falling in the last decade. In 1940, only 44 percent of American households owned the home they lived in. That jumped to 55 percent by 1950, rose steadily to 63 percent by 1970, and peaked at 64.4 percent in 1980. By 1988, the proportion had slipped to 63.6 percent. Even more alarming, in the spring of 1988, 57 percent of all families could not afford to buy the median-priced home in the region where they lived because of escalating prices and high interest rates, according to a 1991 Census Bureau report by Peter J. Fronczek and Howard A. Savage. Over one-third of current owners and 91 percent of current renters could not afford the median-priced house. Especially hard hit are the youngest boomers, in their late 20s and early 30s and just settling down.

Among the four regions, the West had the highest percentage of people who could not afford to buy the median-priced house (63 percent), followed by the Northeast (59 percent), the South (56 percent), and the Midwest (51 percent). The value of the median-priced house also differed significantly by region, with the Northeast and West having higher prices than the Midwest and South.

This in turn is a factor in explaining income differences. People in expensive regions tend to have higher incomes, because the higher living costs force employers to pay higher salaries and wages. The Northeast consistently finishes tops in various measures of income, due to the concentration of high-paying professional jobs there. In the last few years, residents of Connecticut and New Jersey have enjoyed the highest per capita, household, and family incomes. The West usually comes next, followed by the Midwest. The South is at the bottom, but the gap is closing.

Income is clearly sensitive to the fortunes of the economy. Poverty rises and income tends to decline during recessionary periods. Alaska, with a high cost of living that boosts salaries, had the highest per capita income for a few years during the early 1980s, when the oil industry was booming. But since the downturn in prices and the rise of unemployment there, Alaska has dropped several slots.

Income generally rises with educational attainment. More schooling means better jobs that pay more money. That's especially true in the technical and scientific fields, where there is often a shortage of adequately trained workers.

Income also increases with age because age brings experience, seniority on the job, and promotions. The years of peak earning power typically are in one's mid- to late-50s, and then begin dropping off.

However, they may come earlier for some in the 1990s because of the developing trend of career downshifting. It's clear that a growing number of people, particularly baby boomers, are getting off the high-paying fast track earlier to pursue more enjoyable, but often lower-paying, work.

Despite tremendous strides in education and the workplace, women continue to earn less than men at all levels, although the gap has narrowed. Clearly, barriers have fallen, yet some remain for women, who still must contend with the old-boy network and pockets of discrimination. In many cases, career interruptions due to pregnancy, child-rearing, and household responsibilities also hold back their earning potential.

 RATES: To compute the poverty rate, first determine the Census Bureau's current poverty threshold. People in households with income below that threshold are living in poverty. Divide the number living in poverty by the total population. To compute the rate for a specific group, say whites, take the number of poor whites and divide by the total white population. This can be done for all demographic groups, including household types and educational attainment, to compare levels of poverty.

Another revealing measure is to take the number of poor from a specific group, say single-parent households, and divide that by the total number of all poor to determine what share of the poor the particular group represents.

Except for income distribution, income is not expressed as a rate. Rather, income is typically reported as a mean or median, or per person. See the first pages of this chapter for an explanation of median, mean, and per capita. Income distribution is a complicated calculation, requiring data for every household or person. Leave it to the Census Bureau, which does it every year. The bureau takes all 93.4 million households and separates them into five groups by income level, called quintiles. It then adds up the total income in each group to determine how much each quintile controls of aggregate household income. In 1989, the top fifth had 46.8 percent of the aggregate income; the bottom fifth 3.8 percent. The gap between the top and bottom has been widening and is called income disparity.

Trends to Track; Questions to Ask:

- **Wealth.** America has long been viewed as the richest country in the world. Is it? What are the complex facts and trends in income and poverty in the richest nation? What's contributing to the trends?

- **War on Poverty.** Who won? Since the administration of President Lyndon Johnson, billions have been spent to combat poverty in America. Yet progress has been slow, while real progress was made in the 1950s when there was very little anti-poverty effort. What's causing this anomaly? Explore the views of sociologist William Julius Wilson and others for the causes and possible solutions to poverty.

- **Poverty Threshold.** Just who and what is poor? How is it determined? And are the government's measurements of poverty accurate?

- **Northeast.** The East Coast has the highest level of income, but it also has a high cost of living. Are they related? What other factors make North-easterners the richest among us? How do the other regions stack up?

- **Asians.** The nation's fastest-growing racial group, Asians, has the highest overall household income. Yet their per capita income is lower than whites, while Asians' poverty rate is higher. Why are their income and poverty rates so high? Are there differences within the Asian community? Is discrimination a factor; what else is at work?

- **Homeownership.** The American Dream of homeownership is a reality for 64 percent of American households. But the dream is becoming elusive for many. What have trends in homeownership been; what does the future hold; how are people responding to make their dream reality?

- **Baby Boomers.** What are the income prospects of baby boomers as they reach middle age, and how do they compare and contrast with those of their parents? Who will have the bigger nest egg and more comfortable retirement? Are demographics a factor? What other influences are there?

- **Marriage.** A marriage license is a certificate for affluence, according to one analyst. Why? What are the trends in income and poverty for different household types, including married couples?

SOURCES:
- The Census Bureau, Suitland, Maryland.
- The United States General Accounting Office, Washington, D.C.
- U.S. Department of Labor, Washington, D.C.
- Joint Economic Committee of the U.S. Congress, Washington, D.C.
- Brookings Institution, Washington, D.C.
- Rand Corporation, Santa Monica, California.
- The Heritage Foundation, Washington, D.C.
- Center on Budget and Policy Priorities, Washington, D.C.
- Children's Defense Fund, Washington, D.C.
- Americans for Generational Equity, Washington, D.C.
- The Urban Institute, Washington, D.C.
- University of Michigan's Institute for Public Policy Studies, Ann Arbor, Michigan.
- University of Wisconsin's Institute for Research on Poverty, Madison, Wisconsin.

9 Attention All Shoppers: Consumer Trends

In the 1930s, salesmen for Gerber baby food would begin their sales pitch at the local grocery stores by telling the merchants how many babies there were in the area and how many mothers would be needing the product. Following standard Gerber practice, the salesmen had calculated the number of babies in the neighborhood by counting the number of homes that had diapers drying on the clothesline.

Since the 1950s though, when births were skyrocketing due to the post-war baby boom, Gerber headquarters in Fremont, Michigan, has sent its sales representatives monthly birth totals from the National Center for Health Statistics.

By the late 1960s, seeing births starting to nosedive because of the baby bust, Gerber Products began to diversify, going into trucking, apparel, insurance, and day-care centers, while continuing its baby-food line. In the 1980s, births were rising again, as baby boomers belatedly started having children.

Once again, Gerber has repositioned itself, selling off its trucking and day-care centers, and broadening its marketing focus beyond babies to produce food items for the entire preschool set. Building on the brand loyalty that mothers develop, Gerber aims to feed their children through age 4.

"We see births for the next decade being fairly level, a slight decline, but not dramatic, roughly through the year 2000. Then we'll see what happens from there," says Gerber's spokesman Steve Poole.

Gerber was one of the first companies to realize that demographic trends drive consumer trends, trigger the expansion and contraction of various product markets, and should influence the advertising pitches used to sell the products. As the U.S. population has grown ever more racially and ethnically diverse and middle-aged, the models making the pitches are now clearly older, but young at heart, with more black and brown faces alongside the white ones.

The fact that baby boomers number 77 million and represent one-third of the population makes them especially influential in setting agendas and igniting trends, including consumer trends. They started out fueling sales booms for baby carriages and hoola hoops. Eventually, they grew into blue jeans, 45 rpm records, and Mustang convertibles. Now they're in their 30s and 40s. The median age of boomers in 1992 is 37. But their musical tastes haven't changed much since their teen years, which is why so many radio stations now play classic oldies from the 1960s and 1970s.

Nostalgia is also a boom industry, in the form of books, movies, and retro-rock albums, as these folks look back fondly, even as they prepare for the future. They still sip the soft drink of their youth, although it's often now the diet version. At the same time, they're increasingly preoccupied with careers, families, and homes.

Home: Where the Boomer's Heart Is

Cheryl Russell, in her book *100 Predictions for The Baby Boom*, writes: "The home will symbolize the social stability of the next few decades. It will be the center of American life, equipped with VCRs, home computers, compact-disc stereo systems, cable television, large-screen and pocket-sized televisions, security systems, answering machines, microwaves, exercise equipment, and a host of new technologies not yet on the drawing boards. Middle-aged consumers, short on leisure time and busy raising children, will spend more time at home. The businesses that catered to the young adults (such as singles bars, laundromats, and ski resorts) will have to change their strategies."

It's starting.

Club Med, which succeeded in the 1960s and 1970s catering in large part to single boomers, launched a $15 million advertising campaign in

1991 to help reposition itself to "a broad spectrum that includes couples and families," explains Club Med president Michael Kubin. Club Med, in its western hemisphere division, now has six resorts designed for families, complete with day-care workers. There are another five resorts aimed at couples without kids and only three expressly geared to singles. By 1991, the median age (half above, half below) of Club Med guests had reached 37. That's smack in the middle of the baby boom.

The home as a new focus, compounded by the escalating cost of buying a house, has prompted a new trend among boomers and others—to expand and remodel their current home rather than trade up. Seeing an opportunity, an architect left the vice presidency of a 50-person firm in suburban Washington, D.C., to launch a contracting business in which he works alongside do-it-yourself homeowners on remodeling projects. He serves as both the expert and the extra pair of hands. This service cuts costs to the customers because they don't hire everything out; it also lets the architect work on more jobs because he is not fully responsible for any one project.

Another big priority for boomers these days is their children. Boomers are having smaller families than the ones they themselves grew up in. Yet in many cases, they have more money to lavish on fewer children— and they are. Boomers spend a sizable chunk of their budgets on their children on such items as clothing, toys, sports gear, lessons, and computers to ensure their future success.

Another way to ensure the well-being of the next generation is to save. In this area, the boomers aren't doing so well. Slow to begin saving, boomers are belatedly getting around to it as they think ahead to their children's education and their own retirement. They don't have much in the bank yet, but many will be coming into a lot of money. Ken Dychtwald, president of the Emeryville, California, consulting firm Age Wave, Inc., notes that the thrifty parents of the baby boomers have amassed $3 to $4 trillion in wealth and assets. "Many are going to be passing on. And you'll see $3 to $4 trillion in cars, insurance, stocks, and homes come cascading down on to the boomers," he says in an August 1991 *Nation's Business* article.

But the boomers' actual inheritance could wind up being substantially less than that. While Congress debates the controversial issue of national health care, medical bills and nursing-home costs continue their rapid rise and eat away at nest eggs of many senior citizens.

Seeing opportunities there, insurance companies, brokerage houses, banks, and financial planners are racing to come up with new annuities, mutual funds, and other projects, eager to help boomers and their parents retain and protect their money, and effectively deal with the burden of elder-care.

Not All Boomers Are Yuppies

Even considering this expected windfall, however, one mistake that marketers often make is to assume that all boomers are yuppies. They're not. As *American Demographics* magazine asserted in its September 1985 issue: "The yuppies—and who doesn't know by now that the acronym stands for young urban professionals—have been crowding the media spotlight, and they don't deserve the attention they're getting. Only 4.2 million baby boomers (a minuscule 5 percent) are yuppies." It classified yuppies as living in major central cities or their suburbs, working in a professional or managerial occupation, with a household income of at least $40,000 in 1985, which by 1990 would be the equivalent of around $50,000, often touted as the threshold to affluence.

The reality is that U.S. median household income in 1990 was only $29,943, half of what yuppies might spend on a "little cabin in the woods." In the overcrowded competition for the dollars and brand loyalty of upscale consumers, many marketers are ignoring the very real opportunities in catering to the masses. This has left a wide-open and less competitive field to smart marketers like Wal-Mart, Dollar General, and Shoppers Warehouse, which have focused on meeting the needs of the downscale. This vast audience doesn't have the per capita disposable income to squander on high-priced luxury items, but their collective wealth is in the billions, and they do spend substantial sums wisely on essential items, while saving up for the occasional luxury.

Downscale marketers succeed by keeping expenses and prices low and turning profits on volume. Their operating costs are lower, because they avoid high-rent malls and forego frills in their stores. Buying in volume, they can sell brand names for less, along with store brands, seconds, and close-outs.

As the population ages and the number of retirees on fixed incomes grows, such discount shopping should become more appealing. The growing number of immigrants may also cause discounting to spread, because many immigrants come from cultures where dickering over price is routine and you never pay the asking price. As the number of immigrants and minorities at all income levels grows, so too will the demand for a wider array of goods and services at all price levels, tailored to consumers' diverse needs and tastes.

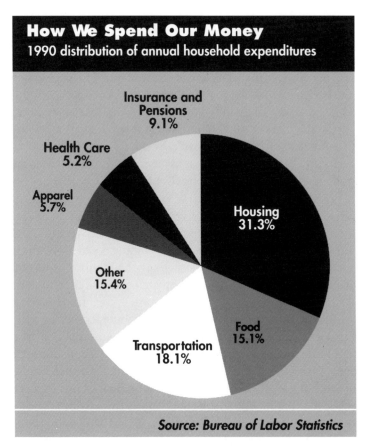

Nearly one-third of every dollar goes to housing expenses. The other basics—food and clothing—take up another 21 cents per dollar.

To attract and keep this more diverse clientele, merchants will have to consider advertising in foreign languages and even hiring workers who speak foreign languages. Executives and managers will have to learn about the cultures and ways of the newcomers. In addition to staples and common brand names and items, smart supermarkets will stock more specialty vegetables and meats to please the tastes and cultures of a diversifying base of shoppers. Bookstores, record shops and clothing stores will carry items of broad appeal, but also more finely targeted publications, music, and fashions.

That's not to say that marketers should run amok with segmentation. A little goes a long way. While demographics and other variables can point to different consumer preferences and needs, there are some products, attitudes, and issues that cut across demographic lines. Everybody needs the basics, such as soap and light bulbs. Also, American adults to varying degrees are showing more concern about such matters as nutrition, health, fitness, and pollution than in decades past, regardless of age, education, or income level. Residents of Pittsburgh, long identified with belching smokestacks and blue-collar issues, are as concerned about air quality as trendsetting Californians and have probably done more about it.

As pollsters and political candidates are belatedly discovering, attitudes and tastes these days are increasingly complex and defy the neat categories of past eras. Despite the pat simplistic analysis of nightly newscasters, the old coalitions have long ago been shattered.

The so-called "ethnic vote" is no longer a sure thing for Democrats. The family is not the exclusive issue of Republicans; get-tough on crime is not a code word for anything, but a simple plea to get tough on criminals, voiced by blacks as well as whites; all women are not feminists, certainly not in the NOW-mold; and not all feminists are Democrats. Meanwhile, baby boomers, despite the rhetoric from over 20 years ago, have been "mugged by reality" and are now all over the political landscape. In fact, they always were, something the mass media never adequately conveyed.

The Selling of Convenience

What is also becoming increasingly apparent is that people at all income and educational levels are, with experience, becoming smarter and more demanding consumers. Business must offer a good product at a favorable price. Even rich people comparison shop and appreciate a bargain, which has given rise to a seeming oxymoron—upscale outlet stores.

At the same time, retailers of all types are seeing increasing competition from a new source: direct marketers and their catalogs, which offer staggering variety, often at attractive prices. Using commercial mailing lists, which categorize consumers by demographics and by past purchases based on credit-card records, businesses who send catalogs can reach beyond their immediate area to sell nationally. By calling a toll-free 800 telephone number to order a product, charging it on their credit card, and having it delivered to their home, consumers are buying convenience as well as the product advertised.

Convenience will be increasingly important to consumers in the 1990s and beyond. With the growing numbers of working women, including wives and single mothers of all ages, we've already seen a proliferation of convenience services that let busy people pay others to handle onerous chores, thereby saving themselves precious time to do the things they really want. There are now franchise operations of nannies and house cleaners. Entrepreneurs have sprung up to do your shopping, mind your children, pick up and deliver your laundry, plan your parties, even handle your correspondence.

Milkmen, who were nearly driven to extinction by competition from supermarkets and convenience stores a few decades ago, have staged a strong comeback in southern California, Chicago, suburban Detroit, central New Jersey, and countless other places. The chief milkman for Chicago's Lincoln Park Dairy Service, is its founder Mark Kominkiewicz, an accountant by training who quit a secure job as a financial analyst to have some fun, be his own boss, and make some real money. He launched his business in 1990, after detecting a need for the delivery service. He says many of his customers are "DINKS—dual income, no kids." Others are parents who are juggling careers and children, and whose shopping time is scarce.

> **TREND-TRACKING TIP: Psychographics—Demographics With a PhD in Psychology**
> Demographics can tell you a lot about people trends and the world in which we live, but they can't tell you who's most likely to prefer pistachio ice cream, Russian novels, or neo-conservative politics. For these or other preferencs and attitudes, the curious should turn to psychographics and geographic information systems (GIS). Psychographic systems use attitude and lifestyle analysis to discern patterns of behavior. GIS takes all of the above, including demographic and purchase data, and plots them on maps to show concentrations of consumer markets.

Baby Busters: The New Market

While marketers often zero in on the baby-boom generation because of its vast size, they should not ignore the smaller but still attractive generations right behind them, the baby bust and echo boom, and those preceding them: their parents.

Following the baby boom as it does, the baby bust is forever having to settle for trends that the boomers have ignited. Many busters long ago grew tired of that and are eager to distinguish themselves from boomers. A 1990 *Fortune* magazine cover story on this "smaller overshadowed generation" finds they possess "a quirky individualism." *Fortune*, which coined the term "yuppies" in 1980 to describe upscale boomers, now directs its name-calling at the busters. "Let's call them yiffies, for young, individualistic, freedom-minded, and few."

After interviewing 30 college-educated baby busters, *Fortune* concluded: "Their attitude: other interests—leisure, family, lifestyle, the pursuit of experience—are as important as work." While busters are largely apolitical, the environment is "the one issue that inspires even the most apathetic among the busters, the issue they view as their own."

First *Fortune*, then a PBS special and a spread in *Newsday*. And now *Generation X*. After years of being ignored, finally the busters are starting to get the attention they've long craved.

A 1991 best-selling novel by Canadian Douglas Coupland, *Generation X,* effectively explores the insecurities and uncertainties of the complex yet simple, seriocomic world of the "twentysomething" crowd. It does for them what the movie *The Big Chill* did for boomers.

Yet, with any fiction and factual reporting, there is the risk of stereotyping. Just as all boomers are not yuppies, all busters are certainly not the same. As a clothing-store proprietor in a college town told me for an article in *American Demographics* magazine: "You're always thinking, what do they want? It's like the rest of the population. It's so segmented as far as their political beliefs, socio-economic status, or where they're from. It's hard to pin down. When I think about my customer, I think of about 10 different people."

There may be fewer baby busters, but this younger group could well have more to spend per capita than boomers. When the economy recovers, they will face less competition among one another for jobs than baby boomers have. Thus, busters may advance more quickly.

Also, busters are staying single longer than the boomers did, and more of them are living with their parents well into their 20s. They're keeping their expenses low and building up bank accounts for their first apartment or house. Thus, busters are fast becoming prime targets for big-ticket items like cars, furnishings, appliances, and electronics gear, as well as the products and pursuits that have always interested young singles: beer, clothes, sports, and travel. But don't try to sell them with background music by the Doors, the Mamas and Papas, Phoebe Snow, or Jimi Hendrix. For all the busters care, that's Lawrence Welk music. They want their MTV.

Okies Heading Home

On the other side of the baby-boom generation is the mature market. Many in the 50-plus generation have not yet retired and are, in fact, at the height of their earning power. Just ahead of this small but affluent group are the parents of boomers who are retired or approaching retirement. Both older groups have fared reasonably well in their working years, because much of their careers came during periods of rapid economic expansion; and being from small generations, unlike the boomers, they advanced quickly and earned top dollar.

Furthermore, they bought their homes decades ago, before hyper-inflation. They've since seen their home equity skyrocket. In general, they're well fixed and ready to enjoy themselves. As the bumper sticker spotted in Florida says: "I'm spending my children's inheritance."

Some will realize tremendous windfalls by selling their homes, moving to less expensive areas, and banking the difference. For example, countless people living in southern California have sold their homes for $500,000 or more in recent years, then bought an equivalent home for one-half or one-third of the price elsewhere.

In fact, Oklahoma, which lost hundreds of thousands of people to California during the Dust Bowl and Depression, has seen many of these people come back home in retirement to live like kings and queens in the lake regions of the state. To encourage the return, one town in Oklahoma, Clinton, even advertised in California newspapers, telling expatriate Oklahomans about the financial benefits of moving back. (For more about mobility and residence, see Chapters 2 and 10.)

Other rural areas that have long struggled with farming and mining have begun aggressively promoting themselves as inexpensive but attractive alternatives for retirement or vacation homes. It's happening in the Ozarks, at the southern New Jersey shore, northern Michigan, parts of Appalachia, the Georgia mountains, coastal Mississippi, and central Florida. Typically, these places are still sparsely settled, near lakes, mountains, and woods, yet within a few hours drive of a major city on the interstate.

Balancing Lives

Convenience-oriented services help fulfill people's material needs. But the time constraints of a working society have opened other opportunities as well. Many services cater to people's desires—their psychological needs. Leisure is greatly desired, but increasingly hard to come by, as the typical American family goes off in several directions at the same time. With the growing number of two-career couples, frequently with different working and vacation schedules, plus children with schedules now as complex as those of Fortune 500 CEOs, the once-typical two-week summer vacation trip in the family sedan has gone the way of the DeSoto.

Hotels, airlines, and resorts have responded to the shifting demands and needs of a changing market by offering shorter vacation packages in addition to the more traditional ones. Weekend getaways and long weekend trips have become increasingly popular. The grand tour to Europe has shrunk from months to a few weeks, even days. Mountain Travel in El Cerrito, California, a pioneer in exotic adventure travel, such as climbing the Himalayas, still offers long trips. But it also offers a wider selection, including shorter adventures closer to home, like shooting the Colorado River rapids.

It's not enough to provide activities for the adults. Resorts and hotels now must consider the whims of their customers' choosy children, who have been weaned on computer games, soccer, and MTV.

Consumer market analyst Peter Moore, of Inferential Focus, has spotted a growing trend among hard-working people of all ages who are beginning to ease up, slow down, and enjoy themselves more. The 1980s was a time for working to advance one's career. Toward the end of the decade, it also became a time for rude awakenings: the stock market plunge, layoffs, downsizing, and stalled advancement. "Now they're trying to rebalance how they spend their time. We see a record number of people taking up the piano. People are going back into the garden; they're going to cooking school," Moore reports. "People are spending less time working."

Food companies and supermarkets are responding to everybody's belated interest in balanced nutrition with new products and new ingredients in old products: whole grains and low cholesterol being two popular attributes these days.

Getting back in shape is a big part of the new priorities. Some 15 million Americans run at least three days a week, including nearly 1 million aged 55 or older. In the Marine Corps Marathon, which attracts over 13,000 entrants each November, the biggest number of first-time marathoners are in their late 30s and 40s.

Marketers have also taken note of growing concern among busters, boomers, echo boomers, and others for the environment. StarKist touts its "dolphin safe" tuna. McDonald's scrapped its Styrofoam packaging in favor of recycled paper. Weyerhauser, the giant lumber and paper -

products corporation, now promotes itself as the "tree growing company," something it has always done to ensure its own survival, of course, but which is now seen as a selling point with the public.

Trends to Track; Questions to Ask:

- **Gerber.** One of the first to track demographic trends for marketing purposes, Gerber began by tracking diapers on clotheslines back in the 1930s. It has refined its methods significantly, but still uses demographic analysis in its planning. How are Gerber and other companies using demographics in marketing and product development? What will it tell you? What's the payoff?

- **Middle-Aged.** Now that the baby boomers find themselves in middle-age, how has this altered their consumption habits? What opportunities does this offer marketers? What are the appropriate products and services to aim at graying boomers?

- **Downscale.** In their rush to get a piece of the upscale market, businesses often ignore opportunities to be found in the downscale market. The median household income in 1990 was $29,943. A handful of smart marketers have done well by catering to the downscale. How; who; with what strategies and products; what's the payoff? Can downscale marketing survive; spread?

- **Generations.** Each generation has its own distinctive demographics, look, and style. How do these influence consumer trends? How can marketers best use demographic information to track the needs and tastes of various groups and effectively respond with the appropriate goods and products? Who's done it well; who hasn't? What lessons do those case studies offer?

- **Minorities.** One in four people in the U.S. is a minority. Each year, well over 600,000 immigrants (net) enter the country. What impact do these groups have on consumption patterns? Are special marketing techniques needed to reach them? How do their consumer patterns compare/contrast with other groups? Immigration and minority populations are projected to grow; how will this affect consumer trends?

- **Environmentalism.** Rising concern for the environment cuts across generational lines, although it is especially strong among baby boomers and baby busters. How have marketers responded in advertising, products, planning? How significant is the impact; is it a fad or a long-term trend?

- **Downshifting.** Americans, particularly boomers, are increasingly leaving the high-paid fast track, some voluntarily, some not, for more enjoyable, slower-paced, usually lower-paying jobs. Has this yet been felt in consumer markets? Does this present long-term opportunities and/or problems to marketers of goods and services; which ones?

- **Busters.** Long ignored by just about everybody, the baby bust is growing up. The generation right behind the baby boom, busters have been nicknamed "yiffies" by *Fortune* magazine—the "young, individualistic, freedom-minded, and few." Is this group worth targeting? How are they different from or similar to others? How can they be reached and with what?

SOURCES:

- The Census Bureau, Suitland, Maryland.
- Population Reference Bureau, Washington, D.C.
- Inferential Focus, New York, New York.
- Age Wave, Inc., Emeryville, California.
- Claritas, Alexandria, Virginia.
- Donnelley Marketing Information Services, Stamford, Connecticut.
- CACI, Fairfax, Virginia.
- The Futures Group, Glastonbury, Connecticut.
- Teenage Research Unlimited, Northbrook, Illinois.
- Langer Associates, Inc., New York, New York.
- SRI International, Menlo Park, California.
- Yankelovich Clancy Shulman, Westport, Connecticut.

10 Demography Meets Geography: Metro and Nonmetro Areas

Halfway between the separate metropolitan areas of Baltimore and Washington, D.C., lies the once, but no longer, sparsely populated Howard County, Maryland. For geographers at the Census Bureau, it is a crucial missing link.

Howard County's rapid growth in the 1980s filled in much—if not all—of the last open stretch between the two metro areas, which could cause them to merge and become America's newest megalopolis, or super-metro area.

The official decision will be made by the U.S. Office of Management and Budget (OMB) in 1992, based on 1990 census results involving population density and the volume of commuter traffic between the two areas. If this particular region qualifies as what the OMB calls a consolidated metropolitan statistical area (CMSA, for short), it will join the ranks of 21 existing CMSAs, including Greater New York, Los Angeles/Riverside, Philadelphia/Wilmington/Trenton, and San Francisco/Oakland/San Jose. But the region's more than 6 million residents have already made the decision, calling the corridor in which they live 'Washbalt,' or 'Baltwash,' depending on where they reside or where their sentiments lie.

To understand the geography of demographics, one must first understand the terminology of OMB and Census Bureau geography. Unlike school geography, which deals with such matters as a country's elevation above sea level, principal crops and capital cities, government geography deals in CMSAs, MSAs, PMSAs, central cities, nonmetropolitan areas, urbanized areas, census tracts, block groups, and others.

The most basic geographic areas in the U.S. are the four regions and nine subregions or divisions. The states assigned to regions don't always make vernacular sense. For example, Texas, the setting of countless western movies, is not in the West region; the Census Bureau puts it in the South, along with such seemingly northern states as Maryland and Delaware. Hawaii and Alaska are in the West, while the Census Bureau puts the Dakotas—two culturally western states—in the Midwest with Michigan and Illinois.

In some census reports, results are also included for the United States' various territories, possessions, and trusteeships, including the Commonwealths of Puerto Rico and the Northern Mariana Islands; and the possessions of American Samoa, Guam, and the Virgin Islands. These are listed separately from state and regional data, under the category "outlying areas."

Some things don't change. There have been 50 states since 1959. But the number of counties is not so static. After the 1980 census, 4 new counties were added to Arizona, New Mexico, and Alaska. Today there are 3,141 counties or county equivalents in the U.S. (county equivalents include Washington, D.C., the 64 parishes of Louisiana, and the 18 boroughs and 9 census areas of Alaska).

As mentioned in a previous chapter, census-takers count people by household when conducting a headcount. When it comes time to segregate households and the people inside them, the bureau does it two partially overlapping ways: by statistical areas and by political areas. This makes the data more widely usable for both businesses, which don't think in terms of political geography, and governments, from villages to the White House, which must plan and deliver services and govern by political boundaries.

For statistical areas, households are first totaled for census blocks, often street blocks, bounded by roads and other prominent physical features. Blocks are further aggregated into block groups, and census tracts— small, locally delineated statistical areas within a county, generally having stable boundaries. When first established by local committees, block groups and census tracts were designed to have relatively homogeneous demographic characteristics. Census tracts make up census designated places, or CDPs—densely settled population centers without legally defined corporate limits or corporate powers, defined in cooperation with state official and local data users.

When tabulated politically, the Census Bureau adds up census blocks, block groups, and census tracts this way: voting districts (VTD); incorporated places (political units incorporated as a city, town, or village); minor civil divisions (MCDs—legally defined subcounty areas called townships in many states); county or county equivalent, such as a Louisiana parish or Alaska borough; voting districts; congressional districts; and states, the District of Columbia, and outlying areas. There are also Alaska native regional corporations (ANRC) and American Indian reservations, and associated trust lands. Finally, there is the sum total, the United States of America.

Again, like Latin, census geography has an exception to every rule. The bureau publications, *Tiger: The Coast-to-Coast Digital Map Data Base* and *Census '90 Basics* give concise, thorough, understandable explanations of census geography and its applications. The history of the bureau's ever-evolving geography is discussed in *Census '80: Continuing the Factfinder Tradition.*

The geography is not arbitrary nor an idle exercise in minutiae. The various boundaries give the demographic statistics perspective and permit comparisons with one another and over time. This isolates and spotlights social and economic progress and problems, as well as consumer markets for services and products.

Some results from the 1990 census are published in printed reports down to the level of towns, cities, and unincorporated areas (CDPs), which is more than enough for most data users. Statistics by census blocks, tracts, and zip codes, are not in the bureau's printed reports. However, such rich and finely detailed data are of interest to marketers, reporters, and government planners, who can find it on the computer tapes and other computer products available for purchase from the Census Bureau, as well as a variety of private data companies.

The Metropolitan Advantage

In layman's terms, a Metropolitan Statistical Area (MSA) is a central city plus the surrounding suburbs and outlying cities economically and socially linked to it. An MSA is made up of counties. Metro areas can cross state lines, as in the case of metro New York, which includes parts of New York, New Jersey, and Connecticut; or Philadelphia, which includes some of Pennsylvania, New Jersey and Delaware; or metro Chicago, which also includes Gary, Indiana, and Kenosha, Wisconsin.

The OMB's precise definition of an MSA follows:

"Each MSA must include at least: (a) One city with 50,000 or more inhabitants, or (b) A Census Bureau-defined urbanized area of at least 50,000 inhabitants and a total MSA population of at least 100,000 (75,000 in New England). The standards provide that the MSA include as 'central county(ies)' the county in which the central city is located, and adjacent counties, if any, with at least 50 percent of their population in the urbanized area. Additional 'outlying counties' are included if they meet specified requirements of commuting to the central counties and of metropolitan character (such as population density and percent urban). In New England, MSAs are defined in terms of cities and towns rather than counties."

A consolidated metropolitan statistical area (CMSA) consists of two or more neighboring MSAs that have sufficient population, density, and urbanization in the border area between them and sufficient worker commutation from one metro to the other. The individual MSAs in a CMSA are called PMSAs (Primary MSAs). For example, the Los Angeles CMSA consists of four distinct PMSAs: Anaheim-Santa Ana, Los Angeles-Long Beach, Oxnard-Ventura, and Riverside-San Bernardino. The Chicago CMSA includes the separate PMSAs of Aurora, Illinois; Chicago; Gary, Indiana; Joliet, Illinois; Kenosha, Wisconsin; and Lake County, Illinois. By far the largest CMSA is Greater New York, which is made up of 12 PMSAs in a three-state area.

Two years after each decennial census, the geographers of OMB and the Census Bureau review the census results to see if population growth in the preceding decade has created any new metropolitan areas. One region that's been eagerly hoping to become an MSA is Rocky Mount, North Carolina, which grew 21 percent during the 1980s, more than double the national rate. But early indications from the 1990 census are that Rocky Mount's tally falls 103 people short of the magic MSA population threshold of 50,000. The city, believing it has topped that, has challenged the bureau's official first tally in hopes of getting it revised upward.

"The bottom line is money," says city planning director Joseph Durham. Under the federal government's Community Development Block Grant program, every certified metro area is guaranteed federal funds, based on population size and need, for things such as housing, infrastructure, and economic development projects. However, there is no such guarantee for cities with less than 50,000 people that fall in nonmetropolitan areas. These places must compete against one another each year for the limited funds set aside for small cities.

Another advantage to being designated a metro area is the prestige it confers. "It's moving up to the big leagues, a big psychological boost," explains Durham. "And it helps for marketing purposes."

Here's how: the Census Bureau and other government agencies publish much more demographic and economic data, rankings, and other information for metro areas than for nonmetropolitan areas. The reports that carry the more detailed metro data become important reference works, which are scrutinized closely and regularly by corporate leaders looking for new markets, places to relocate, and areas to expand their business. Metro data published by the Census Bureau are quickly picked up and widely disseminated by publications such as *Sales & Marketing Management* magazine, *Advertising Age*, and *American Demographics*, as well as dozens of private data companies.

If a place doesn't make the metro list, it runs the real risk of not being considered by corporate decisionmakers. The status—and stakes—are that much greater when one becomes a consolidated metro (CMSA), putting one in an elite group of only a few dozen super metros. If Washington and Baltimore qualify as a CMSA, the 8th and the 18th largest independent metros would join to become the fourth largest CMSA. "It gives us increased visibility...It puts us into the first cut, when you look at the top 5 markets in the nation, versus looking at the 8th and 18th," notes Robert T. Grow, executive director of the Washington/ Baltimore Regional Association.

In Census Bureau terminology, which is precise if not always mellifluous, an MSA's suburbs are often called "metropolitan areas outside the central city" or "balance of metro." This doesn't exactly summon up sylvan images of station wagons, chemically treated lawns, and heavily mortgaged three-bedroom single-family homes on quarter-acre lots. But then, the "metro area outside the central city" definition includes traditional suburbs as well as small cities outside—but economically connected to—the central city. In the Detroit PMSA, for example, the cities of Pontiac and Flint are in the metro area but outside the central city.

Lest we forget, there is also, a vast untamed region outside the boundaries of metropolitan areas, home to about one in five Americans. The

Census Bureau calls it nonmetropolitan. To the average person—and in the shorthand of headline writers—this is often translated into "rural," which is close, but not precisely correct.

The bureau has been using and refining and redefining its metro/ nonmetro categories since 1910. Yet, ever since the first census in 1790, it also has broken the population into rural and urban categories, which are similar but not identical to metro/nonmetro. Urban/rural, which has been used less and less in recent decades, does not offer the marketing flexibility that metro/nonmetro calculations do.

Urbanized areas are not as all-inclusive nor do they extend as far outward as metro areas. They focus more on the central city and its "closely settled areas," or inner-ring suburbs, whereas metro areas take in much more outlying territory including outer-ring suburbs, which the highway network today puts within commuting distance and shopping distance of the central city.

Under the urban concept, what is not urbanized is rural. This was an especially useful scheme up to the post-World War II explosion of suburbia. Before then, people tended to live either in cities or in rural America. In the first census of 1790, 95 percent of the country's 3.9 million residents lived in rural areas. Rural America was still the majority just prior to World War I, a reflection of this nation's strong farming tradition in its earlier years.

Where We've Been; Where We're Headed

America's industrial revolution and the jobs it created in major cities steadily lured tens of millions of people from rural areas to the cities. In 1990, one-third of the population lived in urban areas. By 1940, 56 percent did.

After World War II, with booms in the economy, babies, and housing, veterans who went through college on the GI Bill flocked en masse to sprouting suburbs across America. In 1948, when its first bungalows opened, 300 families moved into the pioneering New York suburb of Levittown, Long Island, in one day. No wonder—Levittown houses then sold for $7,900 with $100 down. The new suburban communities swiftly transformed the landscape and American culture, and, eventually, the economy.

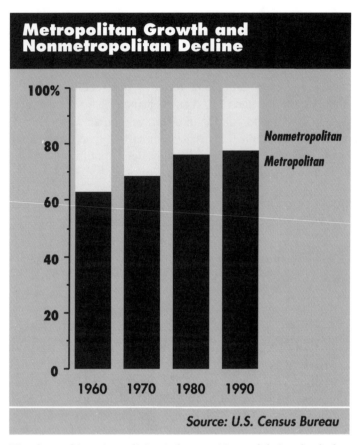

Metropolitan Growth and Nonmetropolitan Decline

Nonmetropolitan

Metropolitan

1960   1970   1980   1990

Source: U.S. Census Bureau

The share of Americans living in larger cities and their suburbs has been rising for decades.

As more and more people left the cities and truly rural areas for the burgeoning suburbs, the traditional urban/rural geography lost favor to the metro/nonmetro concept.

The metro geography was better at quantifying fluid reshuffling within a region. In 1950, just as the suburban rush was picking up steam, the U.S. population of 151.3 million broke down this way: 56 percent metropolitan (central city, 33 percent; suburban, 23 percent); 44 percent nonmetropolitan.

By 1990, metro areas accounted for 77 percent of the population (central cities, 32 percent; suburbs, 45 percent); nonmetro areas, 23 percent. Not only are people moving out of nonmetro areas, but as suburbs on the metro fringes grow ever outward, they envelop land that was previously nonmetro. As population density increases, areas tip from nonmetro into metro.

As of 1990, the nonmetro population was 56 million. Residents of central cities totaled 82 million; those in suburbia number 112 million. Between 1950 and 1990, the suburban population more than quadrupled, while the nonmetro share declined. What kept the population of central cities growing was immigration and higher fertility rates of city dwellers.

By 1990, half of the U.S. population lived in the 39 largest metro areas, each with a population over 1 million, according to the Census Bureau. In contrast, the 1950 census showed only 14 metropolitan areas with populations over 1 million; they had a combined population of 45 million, less than 30 percent of the U.S. population.

The biggest metro, by far, remains Greater New York, with 18 million people. It is followed by Los Angeles, with 14.5 million, and Chicago, with 8.1 million. As has been the case for several decades, most of the fastest-growing metros of the 1980s were in the South and West.

The Suburbanization of Minorities

While suburbia has long been largely lily-white, middle-class blacks have begun moving to the suburbs for many of the same reasons as white families. Surveys show that blacks have moved to the suburbs seeking better schools for their children, better housing and municipal services, lower taxes, and safe neighborhoods.

By the late 1980s, over one-fourth of all blacks lived in the suburbs, up from 17 percent in 1981. As recently as the early 1960s, suburbia was virtually closed to black families. Opening the way was the 1968 Fair Housing Act, subsequent litigation and enforcement of open-housing statutes, and the growing black middle-class.

Blacks now represent more than 7 percent of America's suburban population, but they are not evenly distributed for a variety of reasons including: steering by realtors, an unwelcoming attitude in certain towns, and a reluctance among many blacks to be the first to move into a white suburb. The majority of suburban blacks are concentrated in the older, inner-ring suburbs closest to the central cities. Many of these same suburbs are experiencing some white flight, just as cities did decades ago. Asians and Hispanics, who have faced fewer barriers in America's suburbs in the post-World War II era, are more widely dispersed than blacks.

Even as middle-class blacks and other minorities leave the central cities, the minority share of center-city populations has increased, because whites have left at a faster rate. Also, the minority city population is replenished through immigration and higher birth rates to a greater extent than the majority population. Many more blacks, Asians, and Hispanics still reside in America's central cities than in the suburbs.

By and large, central cities continued losing population during the 1980s. But the losses were slower than they had been in the 1970s, even in distressed places like Detroit, Cleveland, Buffalo, and Bridgeport.

Part of the slowing loss is a matter of "everybody who's going has gone long ago," leaving behind the poor and less mobile, who are mostly minorities, but also some folks of means who have opted to stay, often in high-rise townhouses with tight security.

Also easing the loss has been a discernible counter-flow of what some call "urban pioneers"—upscale singles and couples moving into neighborhoods with under-valued but handsome and often historic homes. This has been called "gentrification," a process that can stabilize neighborhoods and expand a city's tax base. But this can also uproot longtime low-income residents, typically renters, who can't afford the escalating rents as neighborhoods go upscale or coop.

Immigration is slowing the population losses in many central cities and causing some, like New York City, to actually grow after decades of decline. Bringing in entire families and creating new ethnic enclaves, immigration has helped revive struggling neighborhoods of central cities. It's happening in New York City; across the Hudson in Elizabeth, New Jersey; across the country, in San Jose; and in scores of cities in between.

Suburbs— Still the Land of Promise

There was a surprising "rural renaissance" in the late 1970s and early 1980s, first spotted by USDA demographer Calvin Beale. Urbanites were moving to nonmetropolitan areas, fleeing the pressures of city life and seeking the peace and quiet and other amenities of small-town life. But jobs did not come with them. Many newcomers suffered long commutes back to jobs in the city. The "rural renaissance" proved shortlived, perhaps undone by the aggravating commutes and rising gasoline prices. By the mid-1980s, nonmetro areas were losing population again.

Fueling much of the metro growth outside central cities has been the movement of not only people, but jobs, to suburbia. Between 1980 and 1990, employment grew by 20.5 million, to 122.6 million. Economist Nestor Terleckyj, who forecasts population and employment projections for NPA Data Services in Washington, D.C., calculates that 24 percent of the new jobs popped up in the counties in which central cities were located; 64 percent were in metro areas outside central-city counties; just 12 percent were in nonmetropolitan counties.

TREND-TRACKING TIP: Bright Lights, Big City, but Bigger Metros
A metro area is not a city; and a city is only part of a metro area, though the terms are often loosely used and confused, as is the term rural. If you've gotten this far and are not sure of their precise meanings as well as that of other Census Bureau geography, re-read this chapter because the geography is basic to understanding where demographic trends are—and are not—happening.

Why are so many jobs sprouting in metro areas outside central cities? Terleckyj credits the expanding highway network, which makes the outlying areas easily accessible to workers and customers from anywhere in the metro area, proximity to regional airports, affordable and wide-open land, and less red tape and crime than in central cities. It's also where a growing number of people—and therefore workers—now live.

Some have called these new employment centers "suburban cities," places like Stamford, Connecticut; Troy, Michigan; Naperville, Illinois; Mesa, Arizona; and Milpitas, California. Almost every state has them. In fact, there are often several suburban cities within a single metro area. University of Miami geographer Peter O. Muller notes: "The suburbs are no longer 'sub' to the urbs." The long prevailing metro configuration of one dominant central city is giving way to what Muller calls a "pepperoni pizza," a weakened central city surrounded by a galaxy of vibrant suburban cities.

Washington Post writer Joel Garreau calls them "edge cities: life on the new frontier" in his 1991 book of the same title (Doubleday). Instead of the old city's skyscrapers, low modern buildings sprout across the suburban landscape, separated from one another by green lawns and parking lots.

"The hallmark of these new urban centers is not street life, for usually there are few sidewalks. There are jogging trails around the hills and ponds of their characteristic corporate campuses. Shopping malls usually function as the village squares of these new urbs," writes Garreau. The awe-inspiring monuments of suburbia are not famed generals astride their horses, but "an atrium that shields trees perpetually in leaf at cores of corporate headquarters, fitness centers, and shopping plazas."

Garreau continues: "They are cities because they contain all the functions a city ever has contained, albeit in a spread out form that few have come to recognize for what it is. They represent the third wave of metropolitan development in this half century. First, we moved our homes out past the traditional idea of what constituted a city. Then we moved our marketplaces out to where we lived. Today, we have moved our jobs out to where most of us have lived and shopped for two generations. That has led to the rise of Edge City, and to profound changes in the ways we live, work, and play."

Not only people and jobs, but many of our institutions and even sports teams that previously tied us psychologically and emotionally to central cities have headed for suburbia. The Detroit Pistons now play in Auburn Hills, Michigan. The New York Giants long ago crossed the Hudson River to a stadium in the Meadowlands in East Rutherford, New Jersey. Somehow it just doesn't have the same ring—the East Rutherford Giants, former and future Super Bowl Champions.

A generation or two ago, people identified with the major city in their area, even when they didn't live within its confines. People now increasingly identify with their county or town and speak of the immediate area in which they live. This is useful to be aware of because it often gives a shorthand indication of one's demographics, lifestyle, and outlook.

In metro Detroit, people talk of living in historic Boston-Edison or Sherwood Forest, or the understated but elegant Pointes, or blue-collar downriver, or woodsy northern Oakland County. Many living in Detroit's suburbs now take a perverse pride in telling you that they have not been downtown in years.

In New York, the allure of proclaiming oneself a New Yorker has given way to people speaking of living 'down the shore,' in the Village, on the Sound, on the Island, up in Westchester, or out in Princeton.

In fact, people often don't think in terms of traditional broad geographic boundaries at all, much less the Census Bureau's definitions. Saying you live "down the (New Jersey) shore" pegs people as independent outdoor types with sand between their toes, who wanted to get away from the crowding of northern New Jersey. Residents of Hoboken (birthplace of baseball and Frank Sinatra) tend to be urban pioneers who are artsy types or professionals. If people say they live in Princeton, they probably don't and didn't attend the famed university, but they live and work near the booming high-tech Princeton corridor along Route 1, a condo paradise for upwardly mobile singles and young families. The older, more established families are found just a few miles off Route 1 in charming Tudor and Victorian homes in old historic villages, whose rural roads are experiencing gridlock.

While land is plentiful, congestion is also inevitable, with the influx of new residents and commuters on suburban and country roads. With population and job growth come increased demands for municipal services and the taxes to pay for them. The push of people and jobs outward is likely to continue, but at a decelerating rate, because of the aging of the population (older people are less mobile) and the overall slowdown in U.S. growth.

While there was increasing population concentration in the biggest metro areas during the 1980s, medium-sized metros may be gaining in appeal during the 1990s. Especially attractive are metros surrounding college towns and state capitals.

Trends to Track; Questions to Ask

- **Metro.** There are now 284 metro areas; 77.5 percent of the population lives in them. A steadily growing proportion of Americans live in metro areas. What are the different types of metros and why are they important? Explore the metro trends and their significance.

- **Suburbs.** A key building block of metro areas is their suburbs, which saw their population quadruple between 1950 and 1990. The suburbs are no longer 'sub' to the urbs, notes geographer Peter Muller. Why not? What's happening; what's causing the transformation? What impact is this having on the economy and society? What are the likely scenarios in the 1990s? How do the inner-ring and outer-ring suburbs differ?

- **Nonmetro.** If it's not metro, then it's nonmetro, according to the Census Bureau. What does that mean? Once where the majority of Americans lived, nonmetro areas now account for only 22.5 percent of the population. What's causing the drop; what are the political, economic, and marketing repercussions and ramifications?

- **Rural Renaissance.** In the late 1970s, there was a short-lived revival in rural America. What triggered it; why did it end? Describe the changes in the residents and economies there. What are the prospects for the future?

SOURCES:

- Census Bureau, Suitland, Maryland.
- Bureau of Economic Analysis, Washington, D.C.
- Department of Agriculture, Washington, D.C.
- U.S. Dept. of Transportation, Washington, D.C.
- National League of Cities, Washington, D.C.
- National Association of Counties, Washington, D.C.
- City & State magazine, Chicago, Illinois.
- NPA Data Services, Washington, D.C.
- National Association of Towns & Townships, Washington, D.C.
- Institute for Urban Studies, University of Maryland, College Park, Maryland.
- Rural Sociology Department, University of Wisconsin, Madison, Wisconsin.
- Geography Department, University of Miami, Coral Gables, Florida.
- Highway Users Federation, Washington, D.C.

11 Annual Checkup: Diagnosis of America's Health

In colonial times, the average life expectancy of a baby born in America was in the mid-30s. By 1900, it had risen to 47 years. And by 1990, life expectancy at birth had reached 75.4 years, according to provisional data.

Life expectancy is projected to rise another two years or so in the 1990s, thanks to further medical advances, improving diet, and healthier lifestyles. Nevertheless, the U.S. health picture is mixed, with clear achievements and glaring gaps, according to the latest government statistics. Runaway health-care costs are only part of the problem.

Although at a record high for this country, life expectancy in the U.S. is currently topped by more than two dozen nations. U.S. infant mortality is 9.1 deaths per 1,000 live births, a new low. Still, the U.S. ranks only 24th in the world in this basic health indicator.

In presenting *Health United States 1990*, Dr. Louis Sullivan, secretary of the Department of Health and Human Services (HHS), said the report "shows us that we have a good deal to be proud of, but much work yet to be done." Mortality from heart disease and stroke continued a long downward trend, but the overall death rate for cancer is higher now than 30 years ago. AIDS too clouds the future course of American health. While some analysts feel the spread of the AIDS virus has peaked, others expect it to spread still farther and have an as-yet unknown impact on life expectancy. At a press briefing in April 1991, Dr. Sullivan warned: "We are paying a shocking cost for poor health—a cost measured in lives lost prematurely, valuable human potential wasted, and an economic burden that is diverting an ever-larger share of GNP to health care." In 1988, some $540 billion, or 11 percent of America's GNP, went to health care, up from 5.3 percent in 1960. The U.S. spends a higher share of GNP than any other developed nation on health care. By contrast, Canada, with its much discussed national health-care system, spends 8.6 percent.

While medical advances and greater access to health care are important ways to improve the health and longevity of Americans, Sullivan calculates that premature deaths could be cut 40 to 70 percent through better diet, conscientious prenatal care, exercise, using seatbelts, not smoking, and not abusing alcohol or drugs.

Asian Americans enjoy the best health of any racial group, with the lowest mortality rates at all ages. No doubt this is partly due to the traditional Asian diet, which is low in red meat, but high in fish and vegetables. Also, Asian Americans have the highest household income and educational attainment of any U.S. group, both of which are positively correlated to good health. Asians also have fewer teen and out-of-wedlock births than other groups. Teenage and unmarried mothers tend to get less prenatal care and to have low-birth-weight babies, which increase the risk of infant mortality. Non-Hispanic whites trail Asian Americans in overall mortality rates, but are substantially ahead of blacks and most groups of Hispanics.

The key statistics from HHS:

- **Infant mortality (1985)**

Japanese Americans	6.0 infant deaths per 1,000 births
Chinese Americans	7.4
whites	9.0
blacks	18.7
American Indians	13.9
Mexican Americans	8.8
Cuban Americans	8.0
Puerto Ricans	12.3

- **Prenatal care (1988)**

Japanese Americans	86% of mothers receive prenatal care
Chinese Americans	82
whites	79
blacks	61

- **Prenatal Care (continued)**

    American Indians 58%
    Mexican Americans 58
    Cuban Americans 83
    Puerto Ricans 63

- **Death rates (1988)**

    white males 664 deaths per 100,000
    white females 384
    black males 1,038
    black females 593

- **Life expectancy at birth (1990 provisional)**

    whites 76.0 years
    blacks 70.3

    There are no comparable figures available for Asians and Hispanics. However, life expectancy in Hawaii, a state where Asians are the majority, was 77 years in 1980.

- **Health insurance coverage (1986)**

    Non-Hispanic whites 88% have health insurance coverage
    Asian Americans 84
    blacks 78
    Mexican Americans 65
    Cuban Americans 77

    More than 30 million Americans do not have insurance coverage.

Reeling in the Years

Age brings its rewards. The longer one lives, the longer one is likely to live. Although life expectancy at birth was only 60.4 years for today's 65-year-olds, when they were born, the mere fact of having survived so long means that they now have an average remaining life expectancy of 16.9 years, to the age of 81.9. This is true for all groups. Blacks and Hispanics who live to age 65 have subsequent mortality rates similar to whites. In fact, the death rate for blacks aged 65 and older was only minimally higher than white seniors, while the rates for Hispanic, Asian, and even American Indian elderly were actually better than those of their white counterparts. This suggests to many that life expectancy for various groups could be similarly long if the mortality disparities in infancy and young adulthood and their causes could be significantly lessened, if not eliminated. Unfortunately, these disparities remain great.

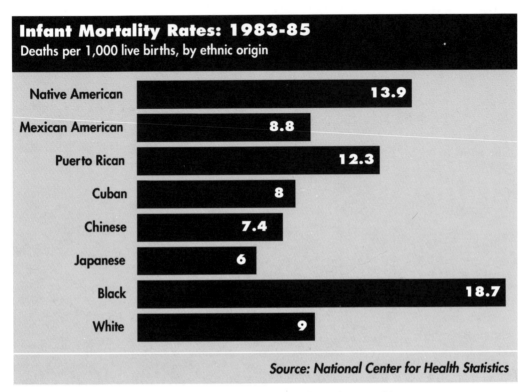

About one in 100 babies born in the U.S. dies before reaching the age of 1.

However, despite the headlines given to dramatic transplants and other life-extending surgery, gains in life expectancy after age 65 have actually been modest. While people who now reach age 65 can expect on average 16.9 more years of life, this represents an increase of only three years in the last four decades.

In general, the higher the educational attainment and income, the better one's health is. With educational attainment comes a greater appreciation of the value of moderate habits and regular checkups. And the higher income that often follows educational attainment provides the wherewithal for better medical care.

We have already seen that infant mortality is much higher among blacks. The late teens and young adult years are also a particularly vulnerable

TREND-TRACKING TIP: Great Expectations
Life expectancy is typically cited for a specific year. For example, the provisional life expectancy in 1990 stood at 75.4 years. This is the average length of life for a baby born that year. It does not mean that people of all ages living that year can expect to live to 75.4 years.

Life expectancy is also calculated for different age groups.

Gains in life expectancy have come in large part due to dramatic declines in infant mortality. Improvements in survival rates have been heavily concentrated at younger years, ensuring that more people than ever reach age 65.

period for many minorities, who have high rates of violent death. American Indians aged 15 to 24 have the highest death rate due to unintentional injuries. Their mortality rate is two to three times that of any other group. Indians also have the highest suicide rate. Homicide is the leading cause of death for black youths, and they have a death rate seven to eight times greater than that for whites and Asians. The homicide rate of Hispanics and American Indians is three times that of whites. These high mortality rates among the young depress overall life expectancy for most minority groups. Dr. James O. Mason, assistant secretary at HHS, says that the 1990 health report reveals "the tough problems—such as homicide and AIDS—that impact most on minorities and must be attacked more successfully if we are going to continue to increase overall life expectancy in the U.S. and not, in fact, slip backward."

There are substantial ranges in life expectancy and mortality rates among the states and regions, reflecting differences in racial composition, heredity, lifestyle, income level, environment, types of employment, and access to insurance. After Hawaii's large and long-living Asian population, the states that consistently have the highest life expectancy in the U.S. are Minnesota, Iowa, Utah, North Dakota, Nebraska, Wisconsin, Kansas, Colorado, and Idaho. All have small minority populations and reasonably clean environments. Income levels in these states tend to be above average, while many of the residents are of northern European stock, who are generally long-lived. In the case of Utah, there is the added benefit of the abstemious lifestyle of its majority Mormon population, who do not smoke or drink.

At the other extreme, life expectancy tends to be shortest in the Deep South, which has the lowest per capita income, and in industrial Midwestern states, which have the riskiest jobs. Both regions also have substantial minority populations.

The ten leading causes of death overall for all ages in descending order are: heart disease, cancer, stroke, accidents (half of which are motor vehicle accidents), chronic pulmonary disease, pneumonia/influenza, diabetes, suicide, chronic liver disease/cirrhosis, and kidney disease.

AIDS was the 11th leading cause of death in 1990, up from 15th in 1988. Federal government spending on AIDS-related activities totaled $2.3 billion by 1989, compared with $6 million in 1982.

In light of the aging population and the rapid growth in the minority populations, expenditures on health care in the United States are sure to grow steadily, as will the burden on government, employers, and families. By the late 1980s, more than 1.6 million Americans were living in nursing homes, an increase of 20 percent from a decade before. There are well over 26,000 nursing homes in the U.S. The number of patients and nursing facilities will jump appreciably in the coming decades as middle-aged boomers become senior boomers.

Currently, one in four Americans is overweight. Some 7 million people have been diagnosed as having diabetes; another 5 million people may have the disease and not know it. Health costs related to diabetes alone reached $20 billion by 1987.

In 1990, some 157,000 new cases of lung cancer were diagnosed—15 percent of all new cancers. Over one-quarter of the population suffers from high serum cholesterol.

Fourteen percent of Americans have some limitation of activity due to a health problem, ranging from 5 percent for those under age 18 to over one-third of those aged 65 and older.

On a given day, about 1 million people are in the hospital. The average stay for men is 7.1 days; for women, 6.2 days. There were a total of 34 million admissions in 1988, many of which were people who were admitted more than once. Yet, over 30 million Americans don't have health insurance.

Perhaps prodded by such disappointing statistics and/or in reaction to the excesses of previous decades, there is a discernible trend of individuals taking more interest in their own health, through better diet, more exercise, and healthier habits. Per capita consumption of poultry, fish, and fresh fruit is rising, while consumption of red meat and canned fruit has dropped. As many as 15 million Americans now run or jog at least three times a week, according to *Runner's World* magazine, and the number grows each year. Some 17 million people play tennis, up from 10.7 million in 1970. Forty-one million play softball, up from 16 million in 1970.

Half of all men and one-third of all women smoked in 1965. By 1987, these shares were down to 32 percent of men and 26 percent of women. Even more hopeful, the proportion of teens who smoke has dropped from 27 percent of boys and 24 percent of girls in 1974 to roughly 12 percent for both. The share of teens who have consumed alcohol has also dropped, but remains high.

On average, women live seven years longer than men, a reflection of the higher proportion of men who work in dangerous jobs, smoke, and drink. Furthermore, women are more likely to see a doctor more frequently. On average, American women have 6.1 contacts with a physician in a given year, of which 3.7 are office visits. The balance is roughly evenly split among telephone contact, hospital visits, and other. Men have only 4.7 contacts per year with a doctor, of which 2.7 are office visits; telephone contact, 0.5; hospital, 0.7; other, 0.7.

Women's more frequent physical contacts are due in part to care during and immediately after pregnancy. Not surprisingly, there are numerous contacts for infants and young children, which drop off between ages 5 and 17. Contact then starts rising for adult women in the child-bearing years and continues rising. Not until the mid-60s do men have more physician contacts than women. The highest level of contacts for both men and women come after age 65.

Whites have one more physician contact per year than blacks do, 5.6 versus 4.7. But blacks average 11 contacts annually at age 65 and over, compared with 8.7 for whites.

Altogether, 23 percent of Americans have not had contact with a doctor in over one year. The proportion is slightly higher for men than women, and slightly higher for blacks than whites.

Employers, too, are learning the benefits of managing risk and stress. Also, studies clearly show that fitness improves worker productivity and attitude. While companies struggle to manage the rising cost of health-care benefits, a fast-growing number is getting involved in so-called wellness programs. By the mid-1980s, one-third of U.S. companies sponsored some sort of fitness program for employees, ranging from a little corner set aside for noontime aerobics to fully equipped gyms. Many also offer programs to quit smoking, with some employers paying the cost of the course if successfully completed. The Washington Business Group on Health expects more than 90 percent of companies to offer some kind of wellness program by the year 2000.

But improving health and increasing life expectancy could prove to be a double-edged sword, because it creates a larger older population, for whom chronic health problems and frailty mount. One of the fastest-growing segments of the population is the 85-and-older group, projected to jump from 2.9 million in 1988 to 4.6 million in 2000 and 8 million in 2030. That's sure to add to the burden of the health-care system.

However, some forecasters believe that the growing emphasis on fitness and exercise could significantly lessen the number of chronic problems that many elderly people suffer from and decrease the months or years of extreme illness and immobility. "The big debate is whether older means sicker or healthier," acknowledges futurist Clem Bezold, executive director of the Institute for Alternative Futures and co-author of *The Future of Work and Health*. "I believe that we can be older and healthier by adjusting our lifestyles and communities. Our lifestyle change includes diet and exercise; and changing our communities means reducing social and personal isolation and giving older persons more meaningful opportunities to contribute. All of those things can contribute to lower morbidity, even as we push out the margins of how long we live."

RATES: Mortality or death rates are computed for individuals and for causes of death. For analytical purposes, rates are also calculated by age, sex and racial groups to identify patterns of vulnerability. To determine the mortality rate for a particular cause, take the total number of deaths due to that cause in a year and divide by the total population, then multiply by 100,000. In 1988, this yields a death rate from heart disease of 166.3 deaths per 100,000 population. To compute the overall death rate, take the total deaths in a given year, divide by the population, and multiply by 100,000. This gives a total death rate of 535.5 deaths per 100,000 population.

Trends to Track; Questions to Ask:

- **Life Expectancy.** Americans born in 1990 can expect to live 75.4 years, an increase of some 35 years since the turn of the century. Yet some 20 other nations have longer life expectancy. Why? What accounts for the progress as well as the gap with other countries? What are the differences by race and sex? What causes the differences; can they be eliminated? Will life expectancy continue to rise? What impact will that have on the economy, health-care system, families, society?

- **Infant Mortality.** Despite significant improvements here, the U.S. lags behind some two dozen countries in infant mortality. Why is infant mortality still so high in the U.S.; can the rates be brought in line with other western nations; how? What are the differences by race, sex, and region? What are the implications and repercussions of the nation's infant mortality rate?

- **Mortality Rates.** Death rates have been declining for heart disease and stroke but rising for cancer. Why? What are the trends for the other leading causes of death? What role does lifestyle and diet play in mortality trends, and can there be further improvements? How do rates compare and contrast among racial groups? Who's the healthiest and why; least healthy and why?

- **Wellness.** One-third of all U.S. companies by 1985 offered fitness programs for employees. By the year 2000, the majority of firms are expected to have some sort of wellness program. What's causing the rapid growth in the field? What are the costs and benefits to companies and workers?

- **Oldest Old.** The 85-and-older population is expected to grow more than 50 percent between 1988 and 2000, reaching 4.6 million. The numbers will grow even faster after that. How does the growth rate of this group compare with others, and why is it growing so rapidly? What demands does this place on society, and is society prepared? What will the lives of the oldest old of the future be like?

SOURCES:

- U.S. Dept. of Health and Human Services, Washington, D.C.
- National Center for Health Statistics, Hyattsville, Maryland.
- Centers for Disease Control, Atlanta, Georgia.
- U.S. Census Bureau, Suitland, Maryland.
- American Medical Association, Chicago, Illinois.
- *Journal of the American Medical Association,* Chicago, Illinois.
- *New England Journal of Medicine,* Boston, Massachusetts.
- Select Committee on Children, Youth and Families, U.S. House of Representatives, Washington, D.C.
- Institute for Alternative Futures, Alexandria, Virginia.
- World Future Society, Bethesda, Maryland.
- Children's Defense Fund, Washington, D.C.

Part II

· · · · · · · · · · · · · ·

Trend Tracking

12 A Billion Here, A Billion There: Avoidable Mistakes

"Household Income Jumps 53 Percent in Last Decade," reads the headline in the morning paper.

"Average Income Plunges Since 1980," trumpets the headline in the rival afternoon gazette.

They are both correct, and they are both incomplete. The first story focused on current dollars, which is like comparing apples and oranges because it ignores the impact of inflation. The second story dealt in constant dollars, which takes inflation into account. The unsuspecting reader who sees only the first story would be left with a false impression. The reader who saw both stories would be confused.

Clearly, statistics confound, infuriate, and perhaps frighten a lot of people who forgot much of what they learned in school. The fact remains that one doesn't have to be a rocket scientist to understand and effectively use statistics, although you may need a crash refresher course in basic arithmetic and a few dos and don'ts.

Some dos:
- Be aware of the source of the statistics, its reputation, and the validity of the numbers.
- Know what the statistics are quantifying and how they were computed.
- Double- and triple-check your own arithmetic where possible, as well as any statistics given to you over the telephone. A lot of zeroes get dropped and numbers transposed when taking dictation.
- In comparing statistics, be sure to determine whether any numeric or percentage changes are statistically significant or not.

- In surveys and polls, find out how big the sample is and how it was selected. Is it big enough to be valid? Be aware of the margin of error.
- Read all footnotes. The tiny print can save you from botching up the numbers.

Some don'ts:
- Don't assume anything. Ask questions about the numbers, their source, and the methodology until you understand and trust them.
- Don't mix apples and oranges, such as median and mean, or constant and current dollars.
- Don't forget to put statistics in context; by themselves they can be meaningless, or worse, misleading. For example, don't simply focus on a numeric increase or decrease, but also include the percentage change and how both compare with previous periods.
- Don't be satisfied with just one set of statistics when additional data are available. No matter the subject being gauged, there are often several different statistical measurements. Consider as many as possible.
- Don't rely on charts or graphs for a fix on the precise numbers. They are prone to distortion, often exaggerating changes. Get the statistics that generated the charts and make your own judgment.

Benjamin Disraeli said: "There are three kinds of lies: lies, damned lies, and statistics." The late Senator Everett Dirksen (R-IL) once observed: "A billion here, a billion there, and pretty soon it starts adding up to real money." Economist and statistician Robert S. Reichard writes in his 1974 book, *The Figure Finaglers:* "The newspaper columnist writing about inflation will undoubtedly choose those types of prices that show a sharp advance—and conveniently forget to mention any areas where prices are stable or even declining. Similarly, the hard-sell TV commercial will quote all sorts of irrelevant statistics to convince you that brand A is far and away the best brand on the market."

Admittedly, statistics can be numbing and intimidating. They can also be used to prove practically any point. But the person who takes the extra few minutes to scrutinize the numbers closely can differentiate the truths from the lies and has a tremendous advantage over those who simply scan the numbers uncritically and toss them about undigested.

Grade-School Math: The Key to Deciphering Demographics

It is my contention that anyone with a sound command of grade-school math can capably handle most of the statistics found in reports, surveys, and polls produced by the government, think tanks, universities, business, and special-interest groups. A refresher course in simple math and its pitfalls follows.

Let's compute the percent change in the U.S. population between 1980 and 1990. In 1980, the U.S. resident population was 226.5 million (the exact numbers are at right). By 1990, the population reached 248.7 million. First, calculate the numeric change over the decade, which was 22,164,068. This is the numerator to be divided by the baseline or starting population, in this case the 1980 population of 226,545,805. The result is .098, or an increase of 9.8 percent.

$$\begin{array}{r} 248{,}709{,}873 \;(1990) \\ -\,226{,}545{,}805 \;(1980) \\ \hline 22{,}164{,}068 \end{array}$$

$$\frac{22{,}164{,}068}{226{,}545{,}805} = .098$$

Many people find it harder to compute percent declines, though it works the same way. The city of Detroit saw its population fall from 1,203,368 in 1980 to 1,027,974 in 1990. The numeric difference is a decline of 175,394 people. Divide this by the starting 1980 population. The result is -.146, or a drop of 14.6 percent.

These calculations are called percent changes over time. Another type of percentage frequently used in demography is ratios, comparisons of different groups or values at the same point in time.

To illustrate this, let's compare the 1990 earnings of women and men. The median earnings of full-time year-round workers that year were $27,866 for men and $19,816 for women. The comparison can be stated two different ways. Women earn 71 percent of what men do, which is calculated by dividing women's earnings by men's, yielding a ratio of 0.71; or 71 percent. Stated the other way, men earn 141 percent of what women do, which is arrived at by dividing men's earnings by women's. Either comparison can also be expressed as a ratio. The female-to-male earnings ratio is 0.71; the male-to-female earnings ratio is 1.41.

Having mastered the computing of percent, people often get into trouble misinterpreting what the percents show. Over half of all women are now in the labor force. Many people take this to mean that women, who are more than half the population, also represent more than half the labor force. They are, indeed a slight majority in the population, but they are definitely not a majority of the nation's workers. By 1990, 57.5 percent of women aged 16 and older were in the work force, but they were only 45 percent of workers.

With regard to poverty, two-thirds of America's poor in 1990 were white. However, only 10.7 percent of all whites were poor. Both factual, but easily misinterpreted.

In dealing with percent, always double check what the percent is actually showing. Never assume. As in the case of working women, ask: Does the percent show the proportion of all women who work, or the proportion of the total labor force that women constitute? Similarly, with poverty, does the percent show the proportion of a group in poverty or what they represent of all people in poverty?

Some who may avoid the uncertainties of percent changes may yet be emboldened to plow ahead and confuse averages. There are actually several kinds of averages that people too often use interchangeably, even though they mean very different things. The two most common averages are mean and median. There are also the less used but helpful mode and midrange.

Mean is what most people think of when they say average. Mean is computed by summing all the values under scrutiny and dividing by the number of values. Mean is a good indicator of the average when the variables fall within a finite range—say test scores, which can range from 0 to 100, but tend to range from the 50s to the high 90s. The mean of the test scores of nine students with marks of 98, 92, 85, 80, 77, 73, 73, 73, and 68 is 79.9. That's a fairly accurate gauge of the various scores.

Another average is the median, which is simply the midpoint, or the middle value of a range of values. In this case, it is 77. Half of the scores fall below that number, and half are above.

Midrange is a type of average derived by adding the lowest and highest numbers together and dividing by two. In the above series, the midrange is 83. Mode is most useful in a large collection of numbers with a relatively small range. It is the number that occurs most frequently: in this case, 73.

Means can be subject to wild distortion by an especially high or low value. This is likely to occur when one end of the series is finite, but the other end is infinite, as in the case of income.

Let's compute the mean income in a hypothetical neighborhood, where eight new moderately priced homes have been built on property that was sold off by the millionaire living on the still sprawling estate across the way. The annual incomes of the families in the eight new homes are $42,500, $45,100, $51,220, $59,900, $63,000, $67,500, $78,200, and $81,300. The annual income of their millionaire neighbor is $675,000 plus stock options and deferred compensation. The mean income of all nine households is $129,302, which is clearly misleading.

Where one or a few values are unusually high or low, it's better to compute the median. In this case, the median is $63,000, which is a much better reflection of the income level of the neighborhood.

In policy debates, labor negotiations, and such, opposing sides typically use the type of average that is most beneficial to their position. Be on the alert for that and ready to challenge numbers. Demand supporting evidence.

When the subject is income, comparisons are frequently made over time. The first question to ask is: are the numbers reported in current or constant dollars? It makes a big difference. Too often, reporters and analysts leap to mistaken conclusions by comparing current dollars, not realizing that impressive income increases are due largely to inflation.

Current dollars measure what the dollar is valued at in a particular year. In contrast, constant dollar measurements take inflation into account and put dollar amounts for each year on a level playing field. In this way, any shifts found are due to increased productivity or pay raises, without the distortion of inflation, and are called changes in "real" dollars.

Also be aware that when the numbers under scrutiny are projections, they are based on certain assumptions. Typically, forecasters produce several series of projections, using different sets of assumptions. The end results of the various forecasts can vary widely, depending on which assumptions are used.

In its 172-page *Projections of the Population of the United States, by Age, Sex, and Race: 1988-2080*, the Census Bureau offers 30 separate projections, each with a different mix of assumptions about births, deaths, and immigration. In a classic understatement, the text of the report concedes: "One complication in using these projections is that there are 30 alternative series."

While anything is possible, some of the underlying assumptions are improbable, such as the ones assuming annual net immigration of 300,000—less than half what it is now—or life expectancy 13 years longer than it is now, or birth rates higher than they have been in over two decades or lower than they have ever been.

The reason that the bureau produces so many forecasts with so many different assumptions and combinations of assumptions is that "the history of population has shown that unforeseen events can rapidly modify the demographic environment," the report explains. "The actual future population is never identical to the projected population."

While the bureau doesn't recommend any one series, its middle series is the one given a bit more attention in the report than most others. Most users of the study tend to focus on the middle series, too, because its assumptions are based on recent trends. But there are just no guarantees in the world of projecting.

When using projections, no matter the source, be aware of the underlying assumptions and remember that there may be other projections by the same source using different assumptions. Unless the analyst proffers one set of projections as preferred, they all have equal weight. A projection is not a prediction. A prediction is a firmer forecast of a likely occurrence or evolution of a trend.

Keeping Track of the Zeroes

Whether it's this year's national income or population, aggregate numbers can swell into the many millions and billions, which is a lot of zeroes. Oftentimes, however, government or private reports drop the last three digits. Footnotes and headings advise readers that the numbers are in thousands meaning that they need to add three zeroes to obtain the actual numbers.

When getting statistics over the phone, always be sure that you understand the correct magnitude. It's all too easy to get millions and billions mixed up and to lose track of decimal points. Better yet, have the needed data faxed or mailed to you, so nothing gets lost in the translation.

It's also highly advisable to check over any calculations done by colleagues, unless you're confident they can do basic math. Painful experience shows that too many bright people can't, including a terrific editor of mine, John P. Reilly—also known as "The Chief," who once wrote a headline for a story on the skyrocketing cost of new commuter railcars in Connecticut. The story clearly stated that costs had risen 50 percent, yet the headline inexplicably proclaimed: "Cost of New 'Cosmo' Cars Doubles." The editor, a wordsmith and first-rate newsman, was an admitted basket case when it came to arithmetic. Amazingly, no one— not even the railroad—called to point out the error.

Another more common mistake among headline writers and rookie armchair analysts of stock-market reports is to assume that the doubling of a base amount is a 200 percent increase, which it is definitely not. Think about it. If the value of a stock or the price of a product, initially worth $100, doubles to $200, the increase is $100, or 100 percent—not 200 percent. A 200 percent increase would have been to $300.

A Brand-New, All-Time Record High

While such blunders are honest mistakes, a common practice in news stories, advertising claims, and business analyses is to exaggerate or overstate the numbers. Ever hungry for an angle to trumpet, reporters, editors, analysts, and marketers of all sorts are constantly transforming minor blips, aberrations, or even statistically insignificant change into major new trends or whopping increases, when they are neither new nor whopping, whatever whopping is. Part of the problem lies in using vague, unsupportable descriptors. Who's to say what constitutes a "sharp" drop or a "widespread" shift?

On the other hand, those who don't pay attention can draw incorrect conclusions even if they don't use unfounded adjectives. In the Census Bureau's income and poverty report of 1989, the number of people in poverty totaled 31.5 million, or 12.8 percent of the population. Some reporters touted this as a marked improvement over the previous year, because the numbers dropped from the 1988 poverty rate of 13 percent, or 31.7 million people.

Overlooked by many was the Census Bureau cautionary note that the changes were "not significantly different." Given the margin for error in the 1989 results of plus or minus 900,000, or plus or minus 0.3 percentage points, it was possible that the 1989 poverty picture was worse than in 1988.

Nevertheless, the 1989 numbers are revealing and valid in and of themselves, because they estimate the situation at a point in time, within a small range of variance. They may also indicate a stabilization of the poverty rate in recent years. To fully assess trends, it's best to compare change over an extended period of years or decades, rather than one year to the next. Like steam locomotives, most demographic trends don't hit top speed from a dead stop; they build up momentum over a long period.

Also, beware the over-used superlative: the "most" this or that, "a first," or an "all-time high." Every time the Census Bureau issues its population breakdowns, the media make headline news of the fact that women are a majority, not a minority. But, it's not news; females have been a majority in the U.S. for a long time.

U.S. population figures are also frequently reported as having reached "a new record high." Again, this is hardly big news, since the population of the U.S. has always been growing. Every day it hits a new high. (The exception is where you see record highs cited in this book, of course.)

In straining to find superlatives to hang on numbers, one runs the risk of overlooking their true significance. In the case of the U.S. population, the significant fact is that while the total is a new high and increased by 22 million last decade, the rate of growth has been slowing steadily.

Whatever the statistic under scrutiny, it helps to look at it from two or more angles to put it in perspective. In the case of U.S. population growth in the 1980s, one would definitely get the wrong impression by simply looking at the numeric increase of 22 million. On one level, it's impressive, almost as many people as live in all of Canada. But to fully appreciate what's happening, one should compare that increase against previous decades as well as compare proportional changes. This reveals that the numeric increase began declining after 1960, while the percent gain of 9.8 percent is the second smallest in two centuries. Only during the Depression of the 1930s did population grow more slowly.

While the Census Bureau has been keeping tabs on population growth since 1790 and fairly reliable statistics exist from Colonial times, many series of statistics have only been kept for surprisingly limited periods. For example, weather data have been collected for less than 100 years; attitudes on abortion have been surveyed nationally and consistently only since the early 1970s; while data on Hispanics have been truly comparable just since 1980.

In the case of Hispanics, prior to 1980, the Census Bureau's count was based on Spanish surnames, place of birth, and/or Spanish spoken at home. Since then, the Census Bureau's Hispanic count has been based on self-identification, which yields a much higher total.

The moral of the story is that when claims are made for record this or all-time that, even assuming the assertion is valid, the record pertains only to that period for which data have been collected, not since the beginning of time. Be sure to find out what the starting point is, especially with survey questions.

In polling by Gallup, Harris, the National Opinion Research Center, and others, questions are constantly added and dropped from surveys. Question wording also changes, which may or may not make current results comparable to previous responses. When dealing with polling and survey information, ask the survey takers how far back the results are comparable. In any survey, the length of comparability can vary from question to question.

Method Is Everything

While many demographic data derive from the Census Bureau's actual headcount of the entire population in the decennial census, other important data are gathered in the bureau's Current Population Survey (CPS). The biggest of its kind, the ongoing CPS nearly 56,000 households nationwide every month. In addition to the CPS, there are countless surveys and polls done by researchers at think tanks, universities, political parties, and special-interest groups to gather sociological, marketing, and political information. Typically, these surveys and polls are published with footnotes or appendices that detail their methodology. The footnotes and appendices—too often ignored should always be read to avoid misinterpreting the numbers or blowing them out of proportion.

The enormous size of the CPS sample combined with the profession-alism and nonpartisanship of the Census Bureau make the CPS very reliable, with a small margin of error. However, reliable surveys by other organizations are conducted with as few as 500 respondents. The key is to get a representative sample. But even with the best intentions and techniques, the smaller the sample, the bigger the margin for error. Sometimes surveys and polls can be dead wrong, as embarrassed political pollsters found out during the 1988 presidential race.

The Bush landslide followed repeated polls showing a close race, with many polling pundits predicting a Dukakis victory. Red-faced pollsters blamed voters for lying to them. Others said that the results demonstrated the volatility of the electorate, the complexity and impenetrability of voters' thinking, and the limitations of polls.

A poll or survey's sample size, the wording and order of questions, and circumstances of the interview, as well as the respondent's mood and ambivalence, can all influence results.

Questioning Survey Questions

In attitudinal polls, research has shown that respondents often have difficulty classifying complex feelings with a simple yes or no answer. It's also been shown that respondents sometimes give the 'politically correct' answer—the one they think the interviewer wants to hear, especially on sensitive issues. Respondents with this tendency are known among researchers as "yea-sayers." Then there are always those who simply lie.

While the media often do not report all the questions and answers, the astute reader of polls and surveys will review the entire survey where possible to get the fullest view and understanding of the results. Partial results can yield an incomplete understanding. For example, polls have repeatedly shown that a majority of Americans support the availability of legalized abortion. That's true enough, as far as it goes. However, the same surveys often also find that about half of all Americans believe abortion should be legal only in certain circumstances, which casts the results in a more complex and revealing light.

A common and valid technique to uncover shifts in attitudes or demo-graphics is to compare the latest poll, survey, or census results against earlier data. It's essential, though, to first determine if both current and older data are comparable. Usually, there's no problem, but methods, definitions, and the questions asked often change over time. Sometimes it's just a matter of terminology. What the Census Bureau now calls married-couple families used to be "husband-wife" families. As long as you know what's what and who's who, you can safely make the comparison.

Changes occasionally make it impossible to make comparisons. Check the footnotes or with the author of a study to determine if current statistics are comparable to previous years.

Improvements in counting and better cooperation can also skew numbers and complicate comparison. The 1990 census counted 1,959,234 American Indians, an increase of 38 percent from 1980. That's three to six times faster than the growth rates for blacks and whites. Census officials and Indian leaders believe much of the Indian "growth" was due to better counting, more promotion of the census within the Indian community, and a growing pride and willingness among Indians to identify themselves as Indians, where before they may have been reluctant to do so.

Numbers that stand out like this should set off alarms and prompt questions. Usually, there is a valid and interesting explanation that gives the numbers added dimension, as with the Indian statistics. Other times, the explanations expose soft or bogus numbers that are best avoided.

As part of determining a study's methodology, also examine the background, funding, agenda, and potential biases of the organization doing the research. While the Census Bureau rightly prides itself on its objectivity and impartiality, some researchers clearly have agendas that tie into their research. Democratic pollsters obviously root for Democratic candidates, just as GOP pollsters root for the Republicans. During negotiation time, management has one set of income and employment figures; the unions, another. Advocates for the homeless have estimated the homeless population as high as 3 million people and more. At the other extreme, published estimates of the homeless have been as low as 250,000 and quickly dismissed as preposterous.

A research organization's agenda does not necessarily invalidate its research results. But its agenda or political affiliation and such are relevant facts that the statistics user should keep in mind in weighing the numbers. When using such research in articles or reports, it's important to clearly state the background of the data source, as well as methodology, so that everyone can reach his or her own informed conclusions.

Sometimes the conclusion should be that the methodology is dubious and the statistics should be ignored, as was the case when a group of businessmen favoring the expansion of a local Connecticut road surveyed opinions, among motorists stuck in rush-hour traffic. Local newspapers dutifully reported that respondents overwhelmingly supported the expansion of the clogged country road. But said one expansion opponent of the survey's question: "That's like asking a guy in an old jalopy if he'd like a new Mercedes."

SOURCES:

- *Statistical Abstract of the United States* and the Current Population Survey, U.S. Census Bureau, Suitland, Maryland.
- *Population Handbook,* Population Reference Bureau, Washington, D.C.
- *The Insider's Guide to Demographic Know-How,* by Diane Crispell, American Demographics Books, Ithaca, New York.
- *Elementary Statistics,* by Mario F. Triola, Benjamin Cummings, Menlo Park, California.
- *Everyday Math Made Easy,* by Peter Davidson, McGraw-Hill, New York, New York.
- *Statistics Without Tears,* by Derek Rountree, Charles Scribner's Sons, New York, New York.
- *The Figure Finaglers,* by Robert S. Reichard, McGraw-Hill Book Company, New York, New York.

13 Books to Use for Number News: Organizing a Demographics Reference Library

Now that you've completed your crash course in Demographics 101, it's almost time to dive in and start crunching the numbers, but not just yet. First, here are some tips on organizing your demographic reference library and network of contacts.

Whether you're a journalist, marketer, planner, or just plain interested, a few well-stocked shelves of essential reference books and reports and a Rolodex filled with the right names puts you at a tremendous advantage in obtaining and deciphering the numbers. One thing to keep in mind is that some general references provide historic data. As the Census Bureau's assistant director Peter Bounpane says, "To know where you're going, first you have to know where you've been."

The obvious place to start assembling reference books and contacts is at the Census Bureau. If you're anywhere near the Census Bureau, do what I did in 1977; go there for a visit. And bring a suitcase, because you may return with about 20 pounds of books and reports.

> **TREND-TRACKING TIP: Mailing Lists to Get On, Not Off**
> Publications from the Census Bureau, other government agencies, and many private organizations are typically free to the media, while others have to buy them. But nonmedia types can usually get on mailing lists for announcements and press releases without charge. To save the price of purchasing the more expensive reports, always check in with the local library or the nearest university library, which usually sub-

scribe to major reports from the Census Bureau and other government agencies. If not available there, see if the staff can get it on loan from another local library, the state government, or the nearest government repository library.

Your first stop at the Census Bureau will be the Public Information Office (PIO). The PIO staff fields hundreds of inquiries daily. They know their census material and the researchers at the bureau. If the PIO can't answer a question, it can direct journalists and other callers to the appropriate expert who can.

Get to know the people in the PIO and gain their trust, especially if you plan to call frequently. Your contacts there can prove invaluable in the future in getting you through the maze that is the Census Bureau, by giving you a "heads up" on upcoming reports, keeping you apprised of bureau developments, and putting you in immediate touch with the right people among the 3,500 staffers at headquarters and another 3,500 scattered across the country.

Be sure that the PIO has *your* direct telephone number, fax number, and mailing address, so it can stay in touch with you, too. Get on the bureau's mailing list for releases and announcements of upcoming reports. Journalists should also ask to be added to the list to receive complimentary copies of bureau reports and books.

Those visiting the headquarters should request a tour and to meet some of the bureau's top researchers, always remembering to inquire about what they're working on and what reports they have coming up that might be of interest. For those who can't manage to get to the Washington area, consider a trip to the regional bureau office or data center nearest you. Even though they'll be relaying information from Census headquarters, it is always helpful to know the local contacts.

Bear in mind that the Census Bureau is a vast agency with many of the nation's leading authorities in various demographic, sociological, and economic specialties. Just as at the ballpark where you can't tell the players without a program, so too at the Census Bureau. For reference, a copy of the bureau's six-page "Telephone Contacts" is invaluable. It lists more than 200 bureau demographers, economists, sociologists, and statisticians by specialty. Keep this close to your office telephone and use it during your visit as a checklist of the people you want to see.

As you meet people, or later when you get to know them better over the telephone, try to politely extract their home phone numbers, because assignments and urgent questions don't always neatly pop up between 9 and 5. In asking for a home telephone number, I always preface the request by assuring them I will use it sparingly and not too late at night.

In the back of my mind is the memory of when I was a cub reporter at *The Detroit News* and covering a ballot issue on transportation. Vote returns were neck and neck. Counting went into the early morning hours, forcing me to call the bill's sponsor at 2 a.m. and again at 4 a.m. to get his assessment of how things were going. But that was politics; I don't recall ever calling a demographer later than 9:30 or 10 at night.

During initial visits or follow-up telephone contact with analysts at the Census Bureau or anywhere, inquire about any outside research or articles they are working on, in addition to their duties at the bureau. It's not uncommon for government researchers to do articles for outside journals. For example, articles by Census Bureau analysts occasionally turn up in such places as the Population Reference Bureau's series of *Population Bulletins*, or the Population Association of America's quarterly *Demography*.

While the logical place to start a conversation with a researcher is talking about his or her own work, I always wind up by asking if they know of research by any colleagues that might be noteworthy and conclude by soliciting any suggestions or leads they might have. I do that the first time I meet a researcher and during every subsequent telephone conversation. The story suggestions and angles demographers come up with can be impressive, and often better than the ones editors or managers dream up.

One can easily spend an entire day or two at the Census Bureau. Must-see offices include the Marriage and Family Branch, Income and Poverty Branch, Economics Branch, Aging Population, Race Statistics, Hispanic and Other Ethnic Population Statistics, Marital Status and Living Arrangements, Metropolitan Areas, Migration, Education, Fertility, and State and Local Estimates.

Essential Reading

Releasing hundreds of reports a year, the Census Bureau is one of the nation's biggest publishers. And some of its titles rank up there with any other best-sellers. Everyone is strongly urged to get a copy of the latest *Statistical Abstract of the United States*, the Census Bureau's perennial best-seller, published its 112th edition in 1992. For trend trackers, it is probably the most-referred-to book there is—1,000-plus annually updated pages of current and historic facts and figures from the Census Bureau and hundreds of other sources.

There are over 1 million statistics in the abstract, covering population, agriculture, economics, education, elections, employment, the environment, government expenditures and taxation, health, income and poverty, law enforcement, manufacturing and trade, recreation and travel, with selected international statistics, as well as addresses and telephone numbers of key sources.

Another special book from the Census Bureau is the annual *Census Catalog & Guide*, which lists all of the bureau's publications and products, tentative availability date, price, and ordering instructions. Most individual printed reports cost less than $10; some, like the annual *Statistical Abstract*, cost upwards of $30 or more. The *Census Catalog & Guide* itself is $15. Data are also available in more expensive computer formats (see Chapter 17).

Nonjournalists can place orders for individual reports and books, or subscriptions for series of reports, by contacting the bureau's Customer Services; telephone (301) 763-4100. In addition to Customer Services, reports and books are also available from two dozen Government Printing Office bookstores located in major cities and found in the Yellow Pages under "federal government." GPO bookstores are also listed in the *Catalog*, as is the 50-state network of State Data Centers, which sell copies of Census Bureau reports and other products in computer form.

State Data Centers are themselves another gold mine of data from private sources and other government agencies, in addition to the Census Bureau. Many such centers, which are usually an office of state government or at a university, also produce their own statistical abstracts, modeled after the Census Bureau's, and publish various demographic and economic reports, as well as population and age projections for their counties and state.

Another important contact for business users of census data are the Business/Industry Data Centers located in many states. "Participants receive economic data and related assistance and training from the Census Bureau and other federal agencies to further economic development in their States and to assist businesses and other users of economic data," notes the *Census Catalog & Guide 1991*. The catalog carries the addresses of the Business/Industry Data Centers.

While it has branch offices and affiliated data centers across the country, the Census Bureau's headquarters in Suitland, Maryland, is only 15 minutes from Capitol Hill in Washington, D.C. The mailing address, however, is: U.S. Department of Commerce, Bureau of the Census, Washington, DC 20233.

Highly Placed Unimpeachable Sources

Those who venture to Washington, D.C., might as well also pop into the Department of Labor's Bureau of Labor Statistics, the Department of Education's National Center for Education Statistics, and the U.S. Department of Agriculture, all in the district proper; and the National Center for Health Statistics in nearby Hyattsville, Maryland.

Other important potential sources in D.C. include various think tanks and special-interest groups, including the Population Reference Bureau (specializing in U.S. and world demographic research and information); Worldwatch Institute (global perspective on implications of rapid population growth); and Joint Center for Political Studies (domestic social/economic trends and public policy, with a focus on the impact on minorities). Big-think outfits like Brookings Institution and American Enterprise Institute, among others, cover the socioeconomic waterfront, gauging implications from neighborhoods to the world.

But for later trips on the road or future phone calls, there are certainly many fine think tanks across the country to bear in mind, such as the Roper Center for Public Opinion Research, Storrs, Connecticut; National Opinion Research Center, Chicago; Center for Continuing Study of the California Economy, Palo Alto, California; and Hoover Institution, Palo Alto. A helpful directory listing over 12,300 think tanks and research institutes of various types is the *Research Centers Directory*, published by Gale Research Inc., Detroit, which is available at most major libraries.

At each of these places, follow the same strategy outlined for the Census Bureau. If you can't visit in person, grab the phone and start dialing. While you miss the face-to-face contact, you can actually cover a lot more ground and faster by phone, plus you don't have to tip all those cab drivers.

At each subsequent agency or think tank, get on its regular mailing list and find out straightaway if there are any different procedures and contacts for journalists versus other data users, such as educators, planners, marketers, and entrepreneurs. And be sure to promise—or threaten—that you'll be back in touch, regularly.

Don't forget the universities and colleges. Some of the leaders in demographic research include Arizona State, Brown, Florida State, Georgetown, Harvard, Pennsylvania, Penn State, Princeton, University of Michigan, University of Chicago, and the various state universities in California. But at almost any college, there is usually somebody in the social sciences department doing some kind of demographic or related research that might be of interest. Most colleges, as well as private and government agencies, have lists of experts like the Census Bureau's "Telephone Contacts" sheet. Get as many of these lists as you possibly can.

One quick way to find out who's who in the world of academic demography and where they are is by checking the membership directory of the Population Association of America (PAA), located in Washington, D.C.; telephone (202) 429-0891. The PAA is the professional association of demographers. The directory, which sells to nonmembers for $40, lists about 3,000 demographers and researchers in related fields.

Another useful, albeit expensive, directory is the annual *Encyclopedia of Associations*, published by Gale Research. The 1992 three-volume set, which sells for $320, lists more than 22,000 organizations. No matter the subject, trend, hobby, or malady, there is at least one—and probably several—organizations dealing with it and possibly producing research of interest to those tracking demographics for news, marketing strategies, policy implications, or planning purposes.

As 19th century French writer and critic Alexis de Tocqueville is quoted as saying in the *Encyclopedia*'s introduction: "The Americans of all ages, all conditions, and all dispositions constantly form associations.... Wherever at the head of some new undertaking you see the government of France or a man of rank in England, in the United States you will be sure to find an association."

In the *Encyclopedia*, you will find the American Farm Bureau Federation, National Association of Home Builders, National Association of Latino Elected and Appointed Officials, the Small Towns Institute, the Appalachian Regional Commission, and many, many more. If you can't afford the directory, you'll likely find it in your company library or at the local public library. See the sources listed at the end of this chapter for other helpful directories.

Other possible sources of demographic research and expert analysts might be found, to your surprise, at public utilities, transportation and shipping companies, advertising agencies, marketing firms, labor unions, religious denominations, and the tax and planning departments of local and state governments. Unless you have a lead, the best place to start to find the right person to talk to in any of these organizations is the public information office, also known as the communications office, public relations, public affairs, or press relations office. If you strike out, ask for the marketing, planning or research department. With each public information officer and researcher you talk to, encourage them to call you at any time at the office or home—collect if necessary—with any tips or story ideas. And always be sure to be added to their regular mailing list for releases and reports.

With a few cranky exceptions, I've found that most demographers are quite eager to discuss their work, although sometimes hesitant to talk on the record with reporters. Still, with some prodding and assurances of fairness, demographers do open up about their research. Here's my theory why.

Demography and Its First Cousin Come of Age

Demography and its first cousin, sociology, are comparatively new disciplines, looked down upon by some in academia as pseudo-sciences. Sociology has been knocked as "the science of the obvious." In times of tight budgets and cutbacks, the social sciences are often where university administrators cut first. This has triggered a siege mentality in many demographers and an eagerness for acceptance and respect, which, for many, came first in the "real" world, as business and the media scrambled to understand trends and turned to demographers for answers.

The attention from the press and business world has raised the profile of and respect for demography among the public and, grudgingly and belatedly, in academia. To fuel further attention and hopefully ever greater credibility, demographers are talking up their work with the reporters they've come to know and trust.

It works to the benefit of everyone involved. Reporters get the stories. Researchers get the ink or broadcast time that gets their names and research before the public, establishing them as experts. That, in turn, can lead to calls from businesses seeking consultants, think tanks needing research specialists, or scholarly journals seeking articles. News clips can help when demographers come before their peer review board for faculty tenure, ask their boss for a raise, or apply to a foundation for a research grant.

After talking to each new demographer or other helpful source, I put their names and telephone numbers in my Rolodexes—three ways—by their name, name of their organization, and their area of expertise. I'm running out of Rolodexes, and will soon have to add three more to the three now filled to capacity.

Within a few weeks of initiating contacts with researchers and their information offices, a building and never-ending flood of mail will hit your desk: press releases and reports from the Census Bureaus and other sources. Wading through the mail is the start of my day, and it can take 15 to 30 minutes or more. The mail can be an excellent source of leads for news stories, marketing strategies, investment and entrepreneurial opportunities or problems, policy implications, and general talking points.

You'll find that a lot of press releases and reports you receive are embargoed. They carry a publication date before which nothing can be published. The reason for the embargo is to allow a few days for delivery of the report and give everybody an even start.

To Scoop or Be Scooped

The mails being what they are, reports or press releases might arrive after the embargo date. This may not matter to a lot of trend trackers. But it can leave journalists empty-handed and an editor screaming, "We've been beat." Semper paratus!

Releases and reports that aren't embargoed are for immediate publication, which has its advantages and disadvantages. It's great if the report is being issued not far from where you are; you just swing by and pick it up. It's not so great if the report's being issued in Washington, D.C., and you're working for the *Astabula Bugle* in the *Bugle*'s only newsroom in Astabula.

Whether it's an embargoed story arriving late or something for immediate release, there are a few ways to avoid being scooped. In no particular order, they are:

• Get the report or release faxed or delivered pronto. Pay for it, if necessary. If the report is too long, settle for the press release and report summary.

• If the fax machine is broken or your office doesn't have one, get a public information officer for the organization releasing the report to dictate the release and major findings to you. Then ask to be put through to the researchers involved in the study.

• Releases and reports are usually printed up days or even weeks before they're issued. Call and explain your difficulty in getting material in a timely fashion. Tell them of your keen interest in the report. Then ask for an 'advance' advance copy and promise to honor the embargo.

• Better yet, convince the powers that be to give you an exclusive and let you jump the gun. It's possible. After gauging the initial interest or lack of interest elsewhere and based on the clout of your publication or organization, researchers have been known to permit select reporters or other trend trackers to break an embargo on a report. They might agree to it in return for the promise of prominent play in a publication or some other medium.

- Fire up your computer and program your modem to tap into CENDATA, the pay-for-access computer database that carries official Census Bureau releases and report summaries as they're released. Of course, that's assuming you have a computer. Material is available via CENDATA at the same time it would be available in printed form. (See Chapter 17 for more on computer access to demographic data.)

The mass media are also important sources of demographic data and should be followed closely. Especially thorough in their demographic coverage and worth reading are the *New York Times*, the *Washington Post*, the *Wall Street Journal*, the *Los Angeles Times*, the *Christian Science Monitor*, *USA Today*, and the Associated Press. Among the popular magazines are *Time, Newsweek, U.S. News & World Report, New York, Business Week, Forbes, Fortune, Money, Advertising Age*, and especially *American Demographics*.

Publishers Weekly, the trade magazine for the book publishing industry, is important because of its listing of books to be published in the coming months, including ones on demographic and other sociological topics. Each week, several dozen books are reviewed, and each quarter, *Publishers Weekly* highlights several hundred more books to appear that publishing season.

Almost all newspapers subscribe to one or more of the wire services, such as the Associated Press, United Press International, and Reuters. Some other businesses too, especially brokerage houses and Fortune 500 firms, have paid to gain access to a news wire. If your firm does have a news wire ticker, I would recommend periodically scanning it to keep abreast of news and on the alert for demographic news.

The Associated Press and other wires are routinely fed reports and releases by all government agencies, as well as major universities and think tanks. In addition to reading the wires for their stories, also check the wire services' daybook and budget. The daybook is a 24-hour schedule of upcoming events: press conferences, release of reports, press availability, photo ops, etc. A place, time, contact person, and telephone number are given for each entry.

The budget is a twice-daily summary of the major stories that will be distributed within the next 12 hours. Each story is described in a paragraph, with pertinent facts.

Another excellent source of demographic information is the annual meeting of the Population Association of America. The meeting is held each spring. The registration fee is $65 for members, $80 for nonmembers, and no charge for the media.

Several hundred demographers attend the conference, so it's a great place to meet them face to face and expand your network of contacts. Hundreds of research papers are presented during the three-day conference. The only problem is that several papers are presented in different rooms at the same time. If you can't attend, make contact with the authors of the papers that are of interest to you. For the price of a polite letter of request and a self-addressed stamped envelope, you can usually get the papers you want.

Also, stay in regular contact with the professional organizations in related fields, including the American Sociological Association, the American Statistical Association, the Association of American Geographers, and the World Future Society, and consider attending their annual conferences as well.

SOURCES:

- All current, major reports from the Population Division of the Census Bureau, Suitland, Maryland including: *Statistical Abstract of the United States; City County Data Book; Projections of the Population of the United States 1988-2080; Money Income and Poverty Status in the United States; Household and Family Characteristics.*
- *Telephone Contacts,* Census Bureau.
- *Health United States,* National Center for Health Statistics, Hyattsville, Maryland .
- *Monthly Labor Review,* U.S. Department of Labor, Washington, D.C.
- *The Condition of Education, Volumes I-II,* U.S. Department of Education, Washington, D.C.
- *Directory of Members— Population Association of America,* PAA, Washington D.C.
- *The Encyclopedia of Associations*, Gale Research Incorporated, Detroit, Michigan.
- *The Insider's Guide to Demographic Know-How,* American Demographics Books, Ithaca, New York.
- *The Capital Source,* National Journal Inc., Washington, D.C.
- *Futures Research Directory,* World Future Society, Bethesda, Maryland.
- *The United States Population Data Sheet,* Population Reference Bureau, Washington, D.C.

14 Tell It to Sweeney: Communicating Demographic News

"There's no one right way to write a story," *Detroit News* editor Lionel Linder once gently advised me as he handed me one of my early demographic pieces, with suggested revisions and the clear implication that I had found at least one wrong way to write that particular story.

The one wrong way to handle a demographic story is to load it down with too many dry statistics and throw them at the reader undigested. Do that and you run the risk of overwhelming the reader, if not putting him or her to sleep. The same holds true for marketing analysis, corporate planning, consultants' reports, and government forecasting.

The most effective way to communicate demographic trends and their implications, as I've discovered through years of trial and error, is to use the statistics sparingly, blending them together with lively narrative, forward-looking analysis, and explanations from appropriate experts.

Since a demographic story is a people story, an essential ingredient is the experiences, anecdotes, and observations of some of the 'real people' who are a part of the particular trend under scrutiny. They draw in the reader.

That's sound advice for writing most any news story, not just demographics, and advice that editors at the legendary *New York Daily News*, once the nation's largest circulation daily, repeatedly relayed to their reporters. "Tell it to Sweeney; the Stuyvesants will take care of themselves," became the command to *Daily News* reporters. Roughly translated, it meant to write for, not down to, regular folks by writing about their concerns, their hopes, and their lives, and by putting them into the stories.

Often, the comments of 'real people' are as perceptive and usually more colorful than those of experts. That was certainly the case in a 1990 *USA Today* cover story I did on the more than 100 million Americans with annual household incomes below $25,000.

I quoted several people from Joplin, Missouri, where folks get by fine on less than $25,000. One man, a lab technician, told me: "I heard talk about people in big cities having dinner for $400. My God, $400! We could eat for six months.... We don't live high on the hog. We still live good." A Joplin auto mechanic said: "Most of my jeans I buy at Wal-Mart. To me, they're the same jeans—just 20 to 30 bucks less. My boy's just the opposite. He likes the high-dollar stuff. He'll go out and pay $70 for a pair of tennis shoes, which to me is stupid."

Informative, revealing, and colorful comments from everyday men and women enliven any demographic report and serve as a nice counterpoint to the often dry, but necessary remarks of experts. Real people are living the trends; they know better than anyone what's going on and what the impact is.

Making Statistics Palatable and Compelling

By delving into the grassroots repercussions of demographic trends and citing real-life examples, the statistics reporter can make even the seemingly driest data understandable, palatable, and compelling to the average reader, who is eager to know how these trends affect him or her.

For example, take the annual vital statistics report from the National Center for Health Statistics, which consists of 20 pages of numbers, including birth and fertility rates and monthly birth totals. Few people will wade through a story or speech that notes that the live birth rate in 1990 was 16.7 births per 1,000 women aged 15 to 44, an increase of 3.1 percent from 1989. At best, they might utter a "gee whiz" upon learning that the total number of births reached 4,179,000, the highest number in 27 years.

But most people would probably eagerly read a story where the focus was shifted to the causes and repercussions of rising births and the families, communities, and economy affected by these births. The data immediately come alive.

Here's the real story behind the numbers. Births in 1990 were the latest installment of what's called the echo baby boom, which has been underway since the late 1970s. Many career women of the original baby boom are now racing their biological clocks to make up for lost time. Many are having a first child in their 30s. Others are deciding to go ahead and have that second child, after insisting that one would be "it." In recent years, boomer parents have been joined by the younger baby-bust generation entering its own prime childbearing years.

A story on the trend hits home with the reader or viewer when it's explained that the echo boom is fueling growth in the convenience industry, causing school districts to reopen schools they had closed only a decade ago and hire new teachers, stimulating sales for everything from baby carriages to children's clothes, repopulating aging neighborhoods with young children, and putting added pressure on employers to offer childcare for working parents.

Indeed, less is more when it comes to statistics in such a story. One or two numbers might appear at the top of the story to set the stage, and then at appropriate points in the body of the story to quantify and validate assertions made by the author or other sources, perhaps wrapping up with a projection. Rather than clutter up the story and distract the reader, additional statistics might be found in accompanying charts or tables.

Some of the best written and most deftly edited trend stories are found in the pages of the *Wall Street Journal*, a pioneer in this type of explanatory journalism. The *New York Times*, *Detroit News*, *Los Angeles Times*, *Christian Science Monitor*, *Chicago Tribune*, *Philadelphia Inquirer*, *USA Today*, and the news weeklies are other periodicals that pay special attention to not only reporting demographic news, but making it understandable and relevant. Each has its own style and rules.

At these publications and throughout journalism, there are numerous types of stories and approaches. The permutations that preoccupy some editors can get confusing and in the way of sensible reporting. For the demographic reporter or business analyst, all research and writing should be analytical and explanatory. To simplify matters and for the purposes of examining techniques, we'll divide demographic stories into two broad categories: hard news and enterprise. While comments here are directly applicable to journalists, they also pertain to nonjournalists who must decipher and repackage demographic information in speeches, advisory memos, summary reports, and strategic plans.

Hard News and Racing Headlines

The hard-news story focuses on breaking news: a new demographic report, the latest annual statistics, testimony at a congressional hearing, publication of a hot book, etc. Whatever it is, new information has just become available, on short notice or no notice at all.

The stories tend to be reactive, quickly produced, responding to the event. That's when the demographic reference library and well-stocked Rolodex™ come in especially handy for quickly gathering pertinent background information and analysis.

Other times, though, there is some advance warning of a hard-news story, through a report or press release that arrives with an embargo or publication date a day or two hence. With the report or press release in hand, the reporter has precious extra time—a day or two—to gather background information, find and interview the right people, and properly develop and write the story.

In some cases, the new data on, say, income and poverty, are scheduled for release at an upcoming press conference. While the precise results are not yet available, the subject matter is known. Outside experts can often speculate with some accuracy on what the general findings will be. In the case of annually released data, general trends are often already apparent. So as not to be caught flat-footed, a reporter can do advance work, even writing background portions of the story, known as "10th add." Some paragraphs can be ready in reserve, based on an increase in poverty, while alternative paragraphs can be written, assuming a decline in the poverty rate.

Once a report is released or comments made at a press conference, the story can be "topped off" with the new information and paragraphs added, deleted, or changed from the "10th add" file as needed.

That's what I did with the Census Bureau's income and poverty report of 1988. Wanting a new angle, I decided to focus on the often-ignored rural working poor. Several days before the report was released, I interviewed experts and several impoverished families in Kentucky's coal-mining region and wrote up the results as an incomplete story. The day the poverty report was released, I got the newest numbers and additional comments from Census Bureau analysts and others and folded that material into the largely written article.

The story, as it appeared in *USA Today* on October 19, 1989, began: "Far from the slums of big cities, far from public view, live the forgotten poor of rural America. Still hidden by lush foliage along rutted, dirt roads are the people of the Appalachian Mountains..." Next came the new poverty statistics for various groups and regions.

Some hard-news demographic stories work with a lyrical lead like that one, but given space constraints and the emphasis on immediacy, you often must start with a summary or statistical lead.

The summary lead concisely describes the trends at work and puts them into context. Here's an example:

The U.S. is growing ever more racially and ethnically diverse, a cultural transformation fueled by immigration and higher minority birth rates, new census figures show. Blacks grew twice as fast as whites in the past decade. Asians are growing fastest, while Hispanics scored the biggest numerical gains among minority groups. Minorities now represent one-fourth of the U.S. population.

A more narrowly focused statistical lead spotlights the most important development and quantifies it. For example, most newspapers on December 27, 1990, ran page-one stories on the then-new 1990 census results that began something like this:

The United States gained 22.2 million people during the 1980s, up 9.8 percent—a rate slower than in recent decades, according to newly released results of the 1990 census. Just five states in the South and the West accounted for two-thirds of the growth, which brought the total U.S. resident population to 248,709,873 ...

In a hard-news story, additional news details typically follow in descending order of importance. But hard news is more than merely assembling a string of related facts. Even with tight news holes and deadline pressure, the properly crafted hard-news demographic story should have perspective, analysis by the author and others, and a sense of where trends are headed. If space and time allow, there should also be a few quotes from one or two 'real people.'

This is not reporting in the traditional triphammer style of the five Ws: who, what, when, where, and why. To grab and hold the reader, you have to answer the tougher question: So what? What does it mean to the reader? What does it mean to the future?

Structuring the Enterprise Story

Unlike hard news, the enterprise story is not reactive, but initiated by the reporter, whose enterprise pulls together information from disparate sources. Instead of responding to a specific event or study the way a hard-news story does, the enterprise piece often works in reverse by starting with a premise or trend that is then examined, quantified, and illuminated through various evidence, observation, and example.

Enterprise stories are typically much longer than hard-news stories, allowing more room and freedom to explore, interpret, and fully develop the topic at hand and determine its meaning. The stories are more colorful than standard news stories, with more quotes and detail. They also take longer to research and write and often involve hitting the road for an up-close look at the trend and to meet the people caught up in it. Going to the scene of the action to interview people and see for oneself allows a reporter to add color, rich detail, and a sense of place to a story.

With more space, the writer has the option of various types of leads, ranging from a short direct statement of fact to leads that might open with an anecdote or description of a scene that quickly captures the essence of the trend. An example of the direct approach can be found in a *Detroit News* piece I did on the trend of young adults returning to the parental nest. It started:

The family home, which sons and daughters dream of escaping as they mature, is luring back a rising number of young adults. Similarly, others are staying put with mom and dad longer than earlier generations did.

In a 1990 Gannett News Service story on seniors who spend winter vacations down south, I decided on a scene-setter lead that touched the senses. It began:

February traffic is a rainbow of out-of-state license plates, sure signs of the annual snowbird migration across America's Sunbelt. Southward flock millions of frozen Northerners...

An effective and frequently used technique for opening an enterprise story is to focus on a person or two in a situation carefully selected for its connection to the trend under scrutiny. In a 1989 *USA Today* enterpriser on retired "Okies" returning to Oklahoma after decades of working in California, my lead focused on one woman who made the return journey. The lead describes her looking through a photo album and remembering the Dust Bowl that forced her family to head west in the 1930s. The wind was fierce, the heat searing on the long drive to California in 1937, she recalls now from the comfort of her new air-conditioned Oklahoma house.

Whatever the lead, the objective is to hook the reader and get him or her to read on. There may be a colorful quote or two right at the start that advances the story. Then quickly comes the 'nut graph' or 'significance paragraph,' that sets out the importance and relevance of this story and trend.

In the story on young adults flocking back to the nest, the significance paragraph notes that high rents, tight budgets, and high levels of divorce are fueling the trend, which presents new challenges and opportunities to the entire family. This is followed by appropriate statistics from the Census Bureau, along with a quote from a bureau analyst, explaining the causes and implications of the trend.

In the snowbird story, the significance paragraph notes that the retiree influx causes some grumbling among locals about "condo commandos" and traffic jams. But the vacationers spend billions of dollars in the various Sunbelt resort towns, and the real-people touch was added by a quote from a retiree who noted: "If it wasn't for snowbirds, Florida's economy would still depend on picking oranges."

By this point, the story has established where we've been and where we are now: two crucial ingredients for determining where we're going. The balance of the story should address and fully develop the issues and points, and resolve the questions previously raised. Throughout, the story should weave together the author's own analysis with that of experts and the comments, experiences, and anecdotes of the real people charted by the statistics. It's in the body of the story that statistics often logically and most effectively go to quantify the assertions made earlier or to set up a new area for exploration.

At the *Christian Science Monitor*, which regularly tracks trends in its news columns, reporters practice what they call "problem-solving journalism." Rather than merely report on problems, *Monitor* articles go the extra step to examine the options and prospects for solving the problems. So should any reporter doing an enterprise story on demographic trends, which typically come with opportunities as well as challenges and the inevitability of change.

Finding Real People

Roscoe Born, who wrote many enterprise stories at the *Wall Street Journal* and later was a founding editor of Dow Jones' *National Observer*, believes that quotes play an important role in crafting effective enterprise stories. "There should be a balance to the eye that puts the reader into quotes just about as often as narrative," says Born. "It should be a verbatim quote, the actual words that the person said, not just 'Yesiree, Bob,' but an informative quote that advances the story."

While breaking up the tedium of plowing through long blocks of narrative and background, a quote also "gives some immediacy and breaks up the tone of the story. The voice becomes different. It lends authenticity," adds Born, author of *The Suspended Sentence: A Guide for Writers* (Scribners, 1986), which is based on his tenure in the mid-1980s as the "word doctor," or writing coach, at the *Detroit News*.

One of the biggest challenges in writing demographic stories is finding the right real people to quote. Unlike the so-called experts who are found in all sorts of directories, there's no handy list of people caught up in trends, such as career women belatedly launching families, young adults who move back to the parental nest, retirees wintering in Florida, transplanted Okies returning home, or families moving back into cities. So how and where do you find them, especially when you're on deadline?

Some strategies that have worked for me:

- Start by asking friends, relatives, colleagues, even strangers, if they know any people who fit the bill. But don't stop there. Keep trying to extend the network of people farther away from yourself and your immediate circle. You want to avoid basing a story on merely the observations of a small group of people who are basically just like yourself.

- Check any clips files or online bibliographic services available to you for articles that have already appeared on your subject. People quoted could be sources for your story or leads to other people.

- Go to where the trend is happening in a big way and start talking to people on the street corner. Even if they're not right, ask them if they know anybody who is.

- If you can't travel to where it's happening, work the telephones. Call the logical places where the people you need would go. For example, contact hospitals and corporate offices for leads on older career women having babies, real-estate offices and moving companies for people moving, and bridal shops and caterers to catch up with the half of newlywed couples that involve at least one person remarrying.

- If the fad has lasted long enough to become a trend, there is likely to be an association, lobbying group, or self-help organization related to it. Such groups are listed in *The Encyclopedia of Associations*. Call the appropriate group and ask to be put in touch with some of their members.

- Go through the telephone book and start calling people at random. The strike-out rate for this technique is high. Many people may brush you off, thinking you're trying to sell them something, but occasionally such calls can lead to good sources. Blind calls to mom-and-pop coffee shops and restaurants often pay dividends.

- If all else fails, call a clergyman. In fact, call several. They know their flock and what they're up to. If you approach them the right way, clergymen can prove very helpful.

Finding real people is the hard part. Once a reporter has gained their confidence, most people are flattered and eager to talk about themselves. What they say—and how they say it—can make a story stand up and sing. Sometimes as challenging as finding real people to interview is getting usable, good quotes from demographers, sociologists, economists, and other experts.

Johnny Carson once joked about the difficulty of interviewing a certain type of monosyllabic guest, who occasionally turned up on his late-night show. Carson would labor to come up with probing questions to draw the guest out and trigger a lively conversation. But the questions prove too good and detailed: the guest can add nothing more, but an abrupt, deafening yes or no. Carson thinks up another probing, perceptive question, eliciting only yep or nope, sometimes just a nod. Again and again. Finally, he'd be saved by turning to Ed to do an Alpo commercial.

Some demographers I've interviewed must have previously been guests on the "Tonight Show;" I've had the same experience, getting just a yes or no, which does not make for lively quotes. I'll rephrase the question, hoping for better luck. It helps to shorten the questions, leaving some detail out that must then be provided in the answer; don't make it so easy for the person to get away with just yes or no.

To get more material and hopefully better quotes on a particular point, keep the interviewee talking. Even when the reporter understands what someone has just said but doesn't like how it was said, he or she can play dumb and ask that the answer be repeated but in a simpler, more easily understood way. Or come right out and ask the person to rephrase the answer in a more colorful way, noting that it improves his or her chances of getting quoted in the story.

A variation of the yes-no syndrome is the eager-to-please interview subject who agrees with everything the reporter says, but adds very little more. In those cases, I finally say: "Please, I can't quote myself. Give me your thoughts on this issue or trend. How would you explain it to someone unfamiliar with the facts?"

Some people talk fast and in long bursts, making it tough sometimes for a reporter to get everything down. That's why it helps to have a tape recorder rolling. Sometimes, you just have to ask that the person being interviewed slow down just a bit or repeat something. Say: "This is good stuff, and I don't want to miss anything. You're getting ahead of me a bit, would you please just slow down?"

One trick for catching up with a runaway quote is to quickly ask a throwaway question, the answer to which you're not the least bit interested in. While the interviewee is responding, you're working from memory on wrapping up the answer to the previous important question.

When demographers and other academics start to slip into jargon, the writer needs to catch them quickly, before it's too late. At a press conference, one sure sign of jargon is when the pencils stop writing, and the tape recorders are clicked off. There is also usually a glazed look in the eyes of the assembled journalists. Those who lapse into academese, whether unintentionally or by design, increase their odds of either being misquoted, misunderstood, or not quoted at all.

Whether one-on-one or at a press conference, the perpetrator of the jargon must be quickly but gently reminded he or she is speaking to journalists, not fellow academics. Keep it simple, direct, with concrete examples, and preferably snappy quotes. After all, the journalists are struggling to understand a complex topic so they can translate it and make it palatable for their readers. In other words: "Tell It to Sweeney."

Working Your Sources; Pitching Ideas

While some stories are written today for publication this afternoon or tomorrow, many stories I've done began days or weeks before with the germ of an idea.

Ever on the lookout for story ideas to pitch to editors at the *Detroit News*, later at *USA Today*, and now at *American Demographics* magazine, I call my major sources weekly—places like the Census Bureau, the National Center for Health Statistics, the Bureau of Labor Statistics, and the House Census Subcommittee—to find out what's coming out in the next few weeks.

A daily check of the mail might take 15 to 20 minutes. I read at least three newspapers daily and several magazines and newsletters a week to keep abreast of the news and uncover reference material, budding trends, possible sources, and leads for future stories of my own.

Based on my calls, mail, and just plain snooping around, I work up a tentative running schedule of reports, press releases, press conferences, congressional hearings, etc. This leads to a separate constantly changing list of ideas and proposals for both hard news and enterprise stories.

In addition to the routine communication with various editors over the years, I've gotten into the habit of sending my immediate editor an informal memo of story proposals every three or four weeks, containing one or two dozen story ideas, each described in a paragraph. Typically, the editor identifies the ones he or she likes and ranks them in the order to be done. Some ideas are rejected, others go on the back burner, while some are ignored without comment. Three or four weeks later, I go back with another memo containing new ideas and some reworked proposals from months before.

Start pitching stories to your editor. The more proposals you pitch, the more stories you'll do based on your own ideas, rather than chasing something the editor cooked up, often to please his or her superiors.

Make sure the story proposals are a mix of hard news and enterprise pieces, and hold onto all memos. (In writing this chapter, I checked my files and unearthed story proposals from 10 and 15 years ago.) Stories bypassed or rejected from one memo can be tried again in a few months with a new twist. Many editors will give the go-ahead after previously rejecting an earlier version of the same idea. Or, wait awhile, and when the coast is clear and the office politics permit, try the idea on another editor, perhaps in another department.

One of my early sweet revenges was to have a feature story on rugby accepted by a friendly editor and published in a sports magazine several months after another editor at the same magazine savaged the story in a rejection slip he dashed off in red crayon. I still have the rejection slip. I've kept it, along with the published article, as a reminder that rejection is not terminal but can be a positive motivating force that goads you into redoubling your efforts.

Just as it is okay to revive a rejected idea or story, it is also perfectly acceptable to return to the subject of a story several months later. One editor I worked for years ago once said: "If it's worth doing, it's worth doing again and again." But it requires a fresh look; you can't merely regurgitate the same facts, conclusions, and quotes to make the same points. A good rule of thumb is to wait six months—supposedly just beyond the outer reaches of a reader's ability to recall an individual article—before returning to the same story for an update.

SOURCES:

- *The Suspended Sentence: A Guide for Writers,* by Roscoe Born, Scribners, New York, New York.
- *The Elements of Style,* by William Strunk Jr. and E. B. White, Macmillan Publishing Company, Inc., New York, New York.
- *Precision Journalism: A Reporter's Introduction to Social Science Methods,* by Philip Meyer, University Microfilm International, Ann Arbor, Michigan.

15 It May Be Black and White, But Is It Right? Evaluating and Analyzing the News

- "Increase in religious membership slightly outpaces population growth," read the headline in the *Star Ledger* over the Reuters story, based on a National Council of Churches survey. Less than three weeks later, *The Washington Post*'s religion page ran an Associated Press report on a Gallup poll, headlined "Religious Affiliation Declining."

- After decades of blanket coverage of the boom in working women, the media suddenly reversed field, and in the spring of 1991 trumpeted a budding trend: worn-out moms quitting those jobs to return to their young kids, according to *USA Today*, the *Washington Post*, and the nightly news. The stories were prompted by research by the Department of Labor showing that 72.8 percent of women aged 25 to 34 were in the labor force in January 1990, down from 74 percent the year before.

- An interesting Crain's *Chicago Business* article on population shifts in the Windy City and its suburbs reported that "among minorities, Hispanics formed the fastest-growing group."

- Opting for a different slant on the pressing homeless issue, a network news reporter advised viewers that estimates on the homeless actually understate the problem. Not included, he explained, are the potentially homeless—the millions of baby busters who, unable or unwilling to pay for their own apartments, have returned home to live with mom and dad, or never bothered to leave.

All interesting, but the readers of these stories should proceed with caution.

The seemingly conflicting stories on religions are not conflicting at all, which makes them confusing for sure. The first one was based on a survey of 219 religious bodies, finding membership rose to 148 million. The story on declining religious preference came from a Gallup poll of 3,233 adults. The studies are looking at two separate issues. Actual membership, which includes children as well as adults, can certainly be rising even as Gallup finds a drop in the proportion of adults with a specific denominational preference. [Read carefully in tandem, the stories are revealing. But reading only one story could give one a misleading impression.]

Mark Twain, who was around to read his first obituaries remarked, "reports of my death are greatly exaggerated." So too are reports of career women now quitting their jobs to stay with the kids. A small shift in statistics from one year to the next does not a trend make. Such a shift could be statistically insignificant, an aberration, and/or influenced by factors not readily quantifiable.

A week after the *Washington Post* reported the dip in working women aged 25 to 34, the paper's Outlook section ran a piece titled "The Trend That Wasn't." The second story quoted experts who viewed the dip as temporary and blamed it on the recession. A Labor Department economist pointed out that the department's own recent projections show that a rising proportion of women, including those 25 to 34, will be in the labor force this decade.

Crain's *Chicago Business* article was largely factual, crammed with solid news and analysis, except for one common error. Hispanics are not the fastest-growing minority group in metro Chicago, or in the nation; Asians are. What likely causes the confusion is that Hispanics scored the biggest numerical gains of any minority group in the 1980s and are projected to surpass blacks as America's largest minority group sometime around 2015.

Reporting on the homeless is a vitally important but especially difficult assignment to cover. It's an emotional subject, where a lot of opinion passes for fact. Anecdotes are frequently used to fill the gaps between shaky statistics, which vary wildly and are often unscientific and of questionable origin. The range of homeless population estimates quoted in the media runs from 250,000 to 3 million and more. Complicating the problem is the lack of agreement on just what constitutes true homelessness.

By no stretch of a fertile imagination, however, are young adults who live with their parents homeless. They're warm, fed, and likely living under a roof in privacy and the security of their old room. They're also doing what young adults did generations ago. Instead of wasting money on overpriced apartments, they're paying little or no rent and quickly building up their savings accounts to one day venture out on their own.

These illustrations point out the hazards of staying informed about demographics—or any topic—by uncritically relying on the news media, especially a sole source. The fact of the matter is: news articles, particularly those written on tight deadlines, are often incomplete, imprecise, and sometimes contain errors. The correction columns in newspapers and magazines are the proof. There are often sweeping generalizations drawn from specific cases, exaggeration, and use of inappropriate data to quantify something.

Then there's the matter of shading and tone. Most journalists strive for objectivity. But some others, practicing what used to be called "new journalism," believe in having a point of view and taking an advocacy stance, which can lead to the highlighting of one set of factors or statistics over another. That's certainly the case with many columnists, especially in the editorial pages.

Columnist and trend-tracker Ben J. Wattenberg devoted a book to what he perceived as examples of garbled and misinformed journalistic interpretation, entitled *The Good News Is The Bad News Is Wrong*. Needless to say, he didn't endear himself to erring colleagues. Yet, the book was an interesting exercise and provocative reading for journalists and their audiences.

It is not surprising that some stories are vague or contain occasional errors. News is history on the fly. Reporters and editors are under constant and unforgiving pressure to produce news stories to fill the news hole and air time. There is no letup, prompting journalists to look everywhere for stories, including at themselves.

Some trend stories start with journalists noticing changes in their own lives and those of their neighbors. Assuming that it's happening else-where if it's happening to them, reporters proceed to produce enterprise stories that sometimes wind up quoting friends or friends of friends.

Many years ago, someone once warned me about the writings of a leading social analyst, still on the scene today: "He changes his mind, and he thinks he's started a new trend." If it's truly a trend early in the making, there may be no firm statistics available to quantify it. That places the burden on anecdotes to support the story. Sometimes it works; sometimes it doesn't.

Such stories can be revealing glimpses when they include the experiences of a cross-section of people. But they don't always work when the evidence and anecdotes are gathered from a small circle of friends and acquaintances, because journalists do not constitute a representative sample of the U.S. population. Particularly at the major media outlets, the educational and income levels of reporters and editors are higher than the national average, and their politics tend to be more liberal than those of the average American.

Always check to see if the people quoted and cited in a story are demographically diverse. If not, you may be reading a story about lifestyle changes among the reporter's Thursday night poker group.

But That's Not What I Wrote—Honest!

While mistakes and omissions are often assumed to be the fault of the reporter whose name appears at the top of the story, it can just as often be the work of the editor or editors who slice and dice a story as it gets through the editing meat-grinder. But it's the bylined reporter who gets the complaining calls, as was the case with friend and award-winning science writer Hugh McCann, who years ago did an intriguing article for the *Detroit News* about a computer experiment.

Three Stanford graduate students in the late 1970s used their newly acquired, high-powered computer to take pi out to the 15-millionth decimal place, much farther than ever before, to see what would happen to the sequence of numbers, which begins 3.14159.... Previous research had found that beginning at the 710,150th digit, there comes an intriguing string of seven consecutive 3s. The Stanford students spent years seeing if there were any other surprises the farther out they took pi.

Reporter McCann, who is also a published novelist, wrote a bright engaging story that explained the experiment in simple but compelling detail and built up suspense as to the outcome. He waited until the last few paragraphs to report the Stanford results.

Unfortunately, readers never got to learn what happened, because an editor, in his haste to trim the story to fit the space allotted to it by yet another editor, used an old and risky trick. He cut the story from the bottom up, on the theory that the least important information and extraneous detail are left for last.

McCann's story, as published, stopped dead, missing the last crucial paragraph, prompting an avalanche of puzzled calls from readers wondering what the heck happened in the experiment. McCann responded by sending out copies of his offending article, with the excised closing paragraph typed out and taped onto the bottom. The reattached paragraph explained that the Stanford project was abandoned after two years of computations, having uncovered no new, unusual sequence of repeating numbers beyond the 710,156th place.

Mistakes and overblown assertions can also be introduced by editors who are unfamiliar with a particular topic, but are determined to punch up a reporter's prose and presentation. Such changes are often made after a reporter has completed a story and gone home.

The media are engaged in an unending race with one another to get to stories first and to capture the biggest audience possible, which makes for aggressive reporting on a growing number of issues and beats. As society has grown more complicated and many problems have become more pressing, there has been a corresponding proliferation of researchers, self-help organizations, and special-interest groups focusing on these problems.

In searching for solutions, they are producing mountains of statistics— some solid and some not so solid. From think tanks to Capitol Hill, data are routinely used to forcefully prove points or promote policy agendas. That's not to say that the numbers are inflated, unscientific or invalid, rather that they should be double-checked for validity and completeness. And when published or broadcasted, statistics should be used with care, always citing and explaining who the source is.

Trends are fascinating stuff and often not as neat or as simple as reported, even in the stories I myself have written over the years. That's why it behooves the serious trend-tracker to use news reports, even original research papers, and analysis by the experts as the starting point for one's own search for the meaning of the trends.

The risk of errors and omissions is not limited to news stories. The original demographic studies themselves can be flawed by sample size, methodology, vagary, incompleteness, honest mistakes, exaggeration, and ideology.

The Demographic Detective

People determined to stay on top of the demographic news and to put it to good use need grounding in the basics, a practiced eye, and a probing skeptical mind. While difficult at times, the search for solid demographic information and knowledge can also be fun. It's like playing detective. And as any seasoned detective knows, you must methodically follow procedure:

- The more news sources you turn to on a particular demographic development, the fuller the picture you have and the deeper your understanding. Never rely on just one news account. It could be wrong or incomplete. Mass media offer a first glimpse of events. Don't stop there. Using leads gleaned from press accounts, track down the original research on which the press accounts are based.

- Know the background and agenda—if any—of the organization or individual that did the original research. While the Census Bureau and other government agencies rightly pride themselves on their objectivity, some research organizations do have agendas and use findings to advance their point of view. This doesn't necessarily invalidate their work, but it's important to keep in mind.

- In addition to knowing the agenda of the source of a study, it's important to know the methodology used and any limitations of the data. Always, always search for and read the appendix or fine print for the important details on methodology that are typically left out of a story. In dealing with surveys and polls, determine the size and representativeness of the sample, how sample members were selected and interviewed, and what the refusal rate was. And look at the margin of error. If these details are not included or not available upon request, consider it a bright caution light.

- Even if the statistics are sound, scrutinize claims of their significance and be ever wary of the use of superlatives. In the chase for scoops and to make a story sing, some reporters, editors, and headline writers occasionally succumb to exaggeration or focus on an insignificant shift in numbers rather than report it as the more boring "no significant change."

- Turn to other research on the same subject to build on, compliment, or refute the original research. In all reading, be curious and skeptical. Look for the gaps as well as the unanswered questions and unasked questions. Dig for the answers; look for the connections.

- Just because you are reading or hearing something reported today, never assume that this is the newest news on the subject. It might not be. Academics, being a slow methodical bunch, often take years to publish their analysis. Example: Professor X releases his just-completed analysis of the Census Bureau's five-year-old migration computer files, even though the Census Bureau has since updated that information. As late as 1988, people outside the Census Bureau were still publishing research based on the the 1980 census. Politely ask of any and all researchers: Is this the latest information available?

- You can never be too sure, even with primary sources. The Census Bureau, National Center for Health Statistics (NCHS), and other government agencies often scoop themselves. Example: NCHS will publish preliminary birth data for 1991 in mid-1992, showing a drop in births. Then it releases its updated final numbers for 1990 a few months later, showing a jump in births for that year. The preliminary numbers for 1990—close, but not exactly like the final—were released a year earlier. The casual newspaper reader is subjected to a roller-coaster of the trends. To avoid that, compare preliminary with preliminary, final with final. Never mix the two, or else prepare for a ride on the Coney Island Cyclone.

- If you have any questions or want to discuss an article or topic, pick up the telephone and call the reporter or researcher in question. At the worst, he or she may hang up on you. But if you are polite, and avoid shouting or calling on deadline, you stand a good chance of getting what you need. For the price of a telephone call and a compliment if justified, you have developed a contact to go into your Rolodex™. In closing a conversation, ask for names of other people knowledgeable about the subject in question who you might call.

- Always hold onto press clips, scholarly papers, and related material for future reference. The clips themselves become an invaluable resource.

Deadline Every Minute

The demographic news in the paper or on radio or television is often reported by the wire services. Even if it is being delivered in modulated tones by a million-dollar anchorman, he may only be reading a reworked version of a story sent across the country by AP, UPI, or Reuters. That is what's known in the business as "rip and read"—the stories have been ripped right off the wire service printers.

Unable to staff every event and chase every story, suburban and metropolitan newspapers and broadcast outlets increasingly rely on wire copy for many stories, especially from faraway places. While a broadcast listener or viewer may not always be able to spot a wire story, a reader can, because such stories are usually preceded by a credit.

With bureaus, staffers, and stringers scattered around the world, the wire services perform an invaluable service by reporting objectively, widely, and quickly. A book on the history of the United Press is titled *Deadline Every Minute*, reflecting the speed with which wire services report the news and compete to be first.

One drawback is that some wire reports, which are often written in less than an hour, skim the surface and rely heavily on just a few sources, sometimes just a single source. Thus, important points can be missed or angles not fully developed. Also, because of tight space, newspapers that use wire stories are permitted to trim them, losing more detail.

The wire services provide newspapers and their readers an important "heads up" on news, a quick read, and fast leads. But the serious trend tracker should follow these leads by reading stories on the same news event in major papers and magazines that do in-depth demographics reporting. These include: the *New York Times*, the *Wall Street Journal*, *Los Angeles Times*, *USA Today*, *Christian Science Monitor*, *Chicago Tribune*, *Miami Herald*, *Philadelphia Inquirer*, *Boston Globe*, as well *U.S. News & World Report* and the other news weeklies, and the monthly *American Demographics* and *The Numbers News*.

Such articles typically blend findings from the primary source (the study and its author) with secondary sources (related material from other studies and quotes from other analysts).

Since demographic trends often influence politics and policy, one should also read the political magazines and what used to be called "journals of thought," for interpretation, if not the latest news, of demographic trends. From the conservative *National Review* and the neoconservative *Commentary* to the currently moderate *New Republic* and on to the *Nation* on the left, political journals and other periodicals can provide a second, albeit politically filtered, view of the rushed reporting of the daily press and news weeklies.

And while one might feel most comfortable with those sharing one's own political perspective, it's stimulating and revealing to read the slant from another camp. While it would never be conceded in a debate, the other guy occasionally has some recommendation or program that merits stealing. Even if one vigorously disagrees with another's appraisal, that irritant can help clarify and strengthen one's own analysis.

For demographic topics of special interest, it is highly advisable to get the original study that triggered the media coverage. Either borrow a copy from a major library or get your own copy by writing or telephoning the source. There may be a small charge for nonjournalists.

Addresses and telephone numbers of major demographic sources can be found in various directories, available at most libraries, including: the *Federal Yellow Book*, the *Capital Source*, the *Encyclopedia of Associations*, the *Directory of Members*—Population Association of America, and the *Insider's Guide to Demographic Know-How*.

U.S. Bureau of the Senses

Reports produced by the Census Bureau and other government agencies are also available on computer tapes, CD ROM, or via CompuServ or DIALOG links to CENDATA (more details to come in Chapter 17). University and major metropolitan libraries often have standing orders for major government reports, which arrive somewhere between days and weeks after publication. It may take more hunting to find reports from private sources, especially other than the major ones.

In their search for a statistic, an expert, or a copy of a demographic report, many people wind up calling (301) 763-4040. That is the Census Bureau's Public Information Office (PIO) and a good place to start a data search, even if it's the wrong place to get the data.

Each weekday, hundreds of calls pour into PIO from around the country and around the world. Callers range from journalists, planners, marketing analysts, and business executives to school children doing reports and adults in bars trying to settle a bet.

"Sometimes we get calls from people who say, 'Send me the census,'" reports Mark Mangold, a veteran information officer. He jokingly adds: "We could send it, if they've got an empty tractor trailer to come pick it up."

The decennial census takes months to conduct and years to publish the results. Census data becomes the new baseline for much demographic research done by other researchers both within and outside the government. So it's logical that people often write or call the bureau first with their questions.

The name of the agency gets a little garbled sometimes. Letters have been addressed to Bureau of the Sensors, Bureau of the Consensus, Bureau of Defenses, Bureau of the Censors, and even Bureau of the Senses, notes retired bureau staffer Judith Cohen in *American Demographics* magazine.

Still, the letters get through and get answered, as are all of the telephone calls. If the needed reports or experts are not there at the Census Bureau, the experienced public information staff can often direct callers to an appropriate source elsewhere.

Other important sources to keep in mind, when trying to locate a specific expert or to match up a trend with an appropriate analyst, are the Population Association of America, the American Association of Geographers, and the American Sociological Association. These and other professional organizations maintain computerized lists of their members, by area of specialization, for referral purposes.

SOURCES:

- *Telephone Contacts*, Census Bureau, Suitland, Maryland.
- *The Statistical Abstract*, Census Bureau, Suitland, Maryland.
- Population Association of America, Arlington, Virginia.
- *The Insider's Guide to Demographic Know-How,* 2nd edition, American Demographics Books, Ithaca, New York.
- *The Federal Yellow Book,* Monitor Publishing Co.; Washington, D.C.
- *The Capital Source*, National Journal Inc., Washington, D.C.

16 Pitching Proposals: How to Get Your Demographic Studies Covered by the Media

The new federal study on the economy was only mildly interesting and passably newsy. Determined to generate maximum exposure, the veteran press information officer handling the study decided to give it to only one reporter—who happened to be from a very influential newspaper.

The reporter was told he could have a 24-hour jump on everybody else. Seeing the prospects of an exclusive and hearing the feet of competing reporters behind him, the reporter accepted the offer and raced into print with a story, igniting a second round of articles a day later by all the other reporters playing catch up. When those other reporters complained to the publicist, he apologized, saying there had been an unintended slipup. To assuage a reporter at the next most important paper, the publicist promised her a head start on the next report, guaranteeing that it would also get extensive coverage.

The publicist in question has since retired from government service, though his gambit has been used effectively by others before and since. But one can do it only so many times before reporters wise up and demand a fair start for all, even as they individually try to get reports and information leaked to them.

There are, of course, other, less risky ways of disseminating information and generating media attention. Some nonjournalists, especially those who may be dealing in business or academic research, may think their work is too obscure or specialized for a general audience. But it doesn't have to be. Consider:

- A 1978 University of Michigan survey to gauge the public's level of resistance to surveys found that a majority of people actually like being surveyed. The results appeared in newspapers across the U.S. The *Detroit News* liked the results so much, it unintentionally ran two stories on the study by different reporters in different sections in one week.

- An archaeologist who studied middle-class trash to uncover clues to diet and health habits shared his findings with the federal government. The Scripps-Howard News Service, in turn, shared the results with hundreds of client papers.

- A team of psychologists conducted an experiment and found that joggers speed up when they feel they're being watched. The findings appeared in *Psychology Today*. Editors at the *Detroit News* saw the findings there and did their own story on the study, which got picked up by the Scripps-Howard News Service, ultimately winding up in *Long Island Newsday* among other papers.

- The Metropolitan Life Insurance Company studied the mortality rates of 2,300 prominent career women and learned that successful career women live longer than women on average. Met Life scooped the media by publishing the results in its own quarterly *Statistical Bulletin*, which goes free of charge to libraries and media. Once the bulletin was mailed out, the study was all over the wires and evening news.

- A Nashville-based manufacturer of tire gauges did a survey of 150 motorists to find out what they had in their car glove compartments (none had gloves). The most common items were maps, insurance and registration papers, sunglasses, and tissues. Apple cores and a stale sandwich also turned up. Over a three-year period, the funny results were repeatedly published as reporters stumbled across previous stories of the results. "It's like a bad penny, it keeps coming back," says somebody familiar with the survey.

Admittedly, none of these stories is the stuff of Pulitzer Prizes. Yet, each proved to have news value, evidenced by the ink and air time they got with just a little effort.

Getting Good Ink, and Your Name Spelled Correctly

The next time you're involved with research for your department, manufacturing company, or ad agency, you might suggest to the boss that the results be sent to the media as well as its intended audience. If there are proprietary data in the research, they can be left out of the press release and summary of findings, usually without eliminating the news value. In such cases, one would first have to get the permission of the client or research sponsor to distribute the edited material to the media. But this is done all the time. Sponsors are likely to grant approval, because it's a way of getting their names before the public.

For those who might be inclined to ignore a reporter and his requests for data or interviews, one word of advice: Don't. It's in your self-interest to talk to reporters, at least some of the time. Researchers who shun the media only embolden reporters to get at the research some other way. If you're not explaining your research to them, reporters will likely draw their own conclusions and/or go to other researchers to interpret your data. The others get quoted, and possibly get the credit. And they and the reporter may misinterpret your findings.

At least when the researcher is involved in preparing press releases and talking with reporters, he or she has a measure of control. If skilled at being interviewed, the researcher can focus the discussion, provide the correct interpretation, and ultimately get the rightful credit for the work. Assuming the resulting media attention is fair and favorable, the value of getting publicity for the results is worth the effort. While there are no guarantees, favorable media publicity can boost reputations and goodwill, which in turn may well lead to promotions, raises, tenure, expanding sales, and new business.

The University of Michigan, one of the nation's finest universities and research institutions, believes enough in the benefits of publicity that it maintains a 14-member media relations office. (That's in addition to the sports information office.) Media relations staffers are in regular contact with reporters and editors from the mass media, as well as the scholarly and technical journals. The department constantly produces and mails out press releases, using mailing lists keyed to specific research areas and based on reporters' stated interests or beats. In 1985, it also began transmitting releases electronically via computer directly to major media at the university's expense.

If your organization has a press or public information staff, contact them. They can be of assistance in promoting a report. Let them know that you also stand ready to assist them, by granting interviews, drafting press releases, whatever.

Do-It-Yourself P.R.

While it helps, an in-house publicity department isn't essential to getting media attention. Do-it-yourself publicity can work just as well. All you need is a typewriter, a telephone, fluency in the English language, and something newsy to say. A not insubstantial number of the demographic stories I've done over the years originated with a telephone call from the researcher alerting me to his or her work and suggesting coverage.

Before setting the publicity blitzkrieg in motion, it is important for the researcher to write the study in the mother tongue—plain, direct English. It's a wonderful language, when used correctly. Jargon, over-blown language, and manufactured pseudo-scientific words and phrases should be avoided. They obscure meaning, raise the risk of misinter-pretation, and antagonize readers.

(I myself take a perverse pleasure in such self-important, contorted, and muddled prose. While I deplore it, I also collect examples of it. Among my favorites are: 'personalized motor transport,' which is what one researcher insisted on calling a car; and 'condominiumize'—the alleged verb for condo conversion.)

You're finished writing the study; now what?

The next phase is to decide on a publicity strategy. The options:

• **Scope.** You can go narrow, or wide, or in between. The target can range from a single media outlet to all of them. In between, the choices include: specialty publications, such as scholarly, trade or business magazines; regional publications; daily or weekly newspapers; weekly news maga-zines; and radio and TV variations of all of the above.

• **Trigger.** The media attention needs a trigger: a telephone call to the right reporter, a press release, the completed study, a press conference, or any combination thereof.

• **Original Article.** An alternative to the press release is for the research-ers to write up the findings in an article for a specialty or general-interest publication. That becomes the announcement for the study; other reporters will take their cue from it. That was the case with the *Psychology Today* study on joggers and the Met Life mortality study.

How wide the focus of a publicity campaign should be depends on how much attention you're interested in and realistically how wide the interest might be. Try to objectively assess your study's news value and appeal.

Read your study, not as its author, but as an editor looking for a good story. Can you honestly say that your study is newsworthy? One way to check is to mention it to friends and acquaintances in conversation. Summarize its findings and value quickly; gauge your listeners' response. Did you hold their interest; did they want to know more? If so, then you may have a newsworthy study. In the celebrated bygone era of The Front Page, the exclamations that editors sought from readers were: "Gee whiz!" Or, "Omigosh!" Another way to test your study's news value is to show it to a trusted colleague who has had some experience with the media. What is his or her assessment?

If you opt to write up the study findings in an article for publication, the first step is to submit a story proposal to the editor. The proposal should be an engaging concise letter stating the theme of the article, the material it will cover, and the findings and conclusions it will contain. The first paragraph or two of the well-written proposal often winds up being the lead of the resulting story. The proposal should also explain the story's reader appeal, the relevance of the data, and the writer's qualifications to do the story.

Writer's Market, published annually by Writer's Digest Books, lists several thousand periodicals, describing their editorial needs and submission and writing-style requirements. It's crucial to be familiar with the style and needs of a publication before submitting a proposal or story to it.

To head out blindly is to invite rejection, as I once did as a fledgling freelance writer many years ago. Hoping to crack the market of city magazines, I wrote to several, including *Buffalo* magazine, proposing articles on such topics as: urban renewal, gentrification, big-city politics, etc. *Buffalo* sent back a brief courteous rejection slip, advising: "Your ideas are not appropriate for a magazine concerned with the American bison."

Those who want to launch their publicity blitz by sending their research to a reporter or two should choose the favored reporters carefully. To do that, read the publications and follow the news broadcasts to see who is capably and regularly covering your general topic and thus would likely be interested in your research. Then begin contacting them in descending order of the importance of their publications or broadcast stations.

The Middle Ground Where Sources and Reporters Meet

Don't be shy about calling a reporter. Calling may feel awkward the first few times, but keep in mind the facts of a journalist's life: reporters depend on sources. Reporters, in the eyes of their editors, are only as good as their last story. The demand to fill the news hole or air time is constant. Reporters cannot dig up all the stories themselves, so they depend on—and welcome—suggestions and material from sources.

In the initial telephone or face-to-face contact, the researcher should quickly outline the study and its news value, offer it to the reporter, and attempt to gauge the level of interest. Usually, a reporter will agree to at least look at something that falls into his or her beat. It is an enticement to a reporter to offer material on an exclusive basis or with a 24- to 48-hour jump on everybody else.

Limiting distribution to one reporter or a handful of reporters is a gamble. They may or may not bite. In general, the more reporters that the press releases go to, the greater the odds and the greater the play. Whenever possible, even in a mass mailing, material should be sent to specific individuals, rather than simply to the publication or some vague destination within, such as "the editor" or "news department." It is permissible, even advisable, to send the same material to more than one person at a particular news outlet, increasing the odds that one of them will pick it up.

If it's unclear to whom you should address your study, call the publication. Ask for the newsroom. Explain you have an upcoming report on such-and-such. Who would be the logical person to receive it? Newsrooms field calls like this all the time, including collect calls from penitentiaries and asylums, but if you stick to your guns, you will get an answer.

Also check in with colleagues outside your organization who have been involved with similar research in the past and have contact with the news media. Ask them for names of reporters, editors, and producers who might be interested in your subject. Additional leads to appropriate editors and reporters can be found in the *Editor & Publisher Yearbook*, the *Gale Directory of Publications & Broadcast Media*, as well as *Writer's Market*. As you assemble names from contacts and reading, develop an address and telephone list for future mailings and calls, including notations on any special interests or tidbits to give you an edge.

High on the list of press contacts should be the names of the appropriate editors and reporters at the wire services, including the Associated Press, United Press International, and Reuters. If the wire services pick up your report, it can conceivably wind up going to 1,600 daily newspapers in the U. S., and more overseas.

The AP and Reuters are headquartered in New York City and UPI in Washington, D.C. All three also have bureaus in major cities around the country. Contact the bureau in the major city nearest you. Check telephone information or the *Editor & Publisher Yearbook* to find out where that is.

In addition to the news wires, there are several supplemental services like the Scripps-Howard News Service, the Copley News Service, the New York Times News Service, and the Los Angeles Times-Washington Post News Service, among others. Don't overlook them. They service many hundreds of papers with features, columns, and analytical stories, and are particularly interested in trend stories and articles that interpret the news.

A mass mailing should also include publications known for their longstanding demographics coverage: the *New York Times*, *Wall Street Journal*, *Los Angeles Times*, *Washington Post*, *USA Today*, *American Demographics*, *U.S. News & World Report*, *Time*, and *Newsweek*.

The Press Release

Having worked up a list of potential contacts, which will be refined and added to with each subsequent report, it's time to work on the press release.

A press release is a summary of the major findings of a report, which may or may not accompany the press release. Take care writing a press release. It's probably one of a dozen or two that a reporter gets each morning, and one of a hundred that reaches an assignment editor every day. They will all be read, but in probably just 15 to 30 seconds each. So, the press release must be effectively written to quickly communicate the major news and key findings and sufficiently pique the reader's interest to the point where he or she will want to know more.

Press releases, printed on letterhead, should have the name and telephone number of a contact person at the sending agency or company, as well as the name and number of the author/researcher involved in the study. The release should also carry at the top a release date: either for immediate release or a few days hence. Immediate release catches people ill-prepared and puts those with late mail delivery at a disadvantage. The benefit of an embargoed release date is that it gives everyone an even start and a little extra time to do advance background research and interviewing.

A headline should introduce the press release, which should read like a tightly written, comprehensive news article. The release's opening paragraph is either a summary lead that outlines the major findings or a more focused statistical lead that spotlights and quantifies the major finding. Major trends should be put into historical context where possible, by comparisons to changes/rates in previous years or decades. Other findings follow in descending order of importance. The source of the research, the principle author, funding, and other pertinent background information should also be presented in a paragraph high up.

An example of a well-written press release that hit all the highpoints was one released by the Census Bureau to accompany its *Marital Status and Living Arrangements: March 1990* report. The report itself has less than 12 pages of text and 88 pages of statistics. Buried in there are many wonderful stories, but finding them takes a practiced eye and a few careful readings. The two-page press release provides a precise roadmap for quick navigation and actually ticks off story angles in various bullets. It reads:

America's young adults are delaying marriage and continue to live at home with their parents, according to a March 1990 survey by the Commerce Department's Census Bureau.

The survey, which does not reflect results of the 1990 census, found that 77 percent of persons aged 18 to 24 had never been married. About two-thirds of those 19.6 million never married were residing with their parents.

The estimated median age at first marriage was 26.1 years for men and 23.9 years for women, up from 23.2 years and 20.8 years in 1970.

Delayed marriages and high divorce rates since the 1970s have affected the living arrangements of children, the survey showed. Seventy-three percent of those under age 18 were living with both parents in 1990, compared with 85 percent in 1970. The proportion living with one parent doubled over the period from 12 percent to 25 percent.

Eighty-seven percent of children in one-parent situations were living with their mother in 1990.

Other survey highlights:
- *The proportion of women aged 30 to 34 who had never married nearly tripled, from 6 percent in 1970 to 16 percent in 1990.*
- *Some 36 million men and 43 million women had never married or were currently widowed or divorced.*
- *There were 2.9 million unmarried-couple households in 1990, an increase of 80 percent over 1980.*
- *Of all adults, 8 percent were currently divorced and had not remarried.*
- *Five percent of children under age 18 lived in the home of their grandparents.*
- *Of the non-institutional population aged 85 and older, 23 percent lived with a spouse and 47 percent lived alone.*

The release gives the reporter a good sense of what is in the study and what the news is, and has hopefully whetted the reporter's appetite to dive into the report for more detail. Each bullet could be the topic for a separate story. Taken together, they are fascinating pieces in a portrait of the American family in upheaval.

Listed at the top of this particular press release is the name of demographer Arlene Saluter, the author of the Census Bureau study, who was available by telephone for individual interviews about her findings. As it turned out, that particular press release and report received wide media attention, with stories running on the wire services and TV and in the major daily newspapers. Some reporters phoned the study's author directly to liven up their stories with her comments, which were not carried in the release.

In fact, the only thing lacking in the Census Bureau press release was some quotes. Good, lively, and informative quotes in a press release can often grab the reader's eye and improve the chances of media coverage. Comments from the study's author on the findings and their implications inform the reporter of the story possibilities. Quotes also give the reporter or editor reading the release a gauge as to how colorful and quotable the source might be in a live interview.

Whoever writes the press release, and often it's written by the author of the study, should be sure to avoid the jargon that researchers often slip into. Despite the aversion of some researchers to interpret their findings, it is important that they have something illuminating to say in the press release and to say it in a lively fashion. Any comments and speculation about the future direction of trends and their impact strengthen the release and its appeal to the reader.

As with the Census Bureau release shown on page 207, an efficient style used in many press releases is to use bullets in the lower part of the release to highlight other findings in the report. The release should also put the research in context and give the qualifications of the author as an expert.

Editors and reporters rely on press releases to tip them to the news. Journalists are often very busy, frequently juggling several assignments, and are sometimes unfamiliar with a subject. The press release has to point them in the right direction and make clear what the news is and its value, even going so far as to give hints as to possible story angles.

It is especially helpful to reporters to receive the entire study along with the press release, as well as a separate sheet of charts. For media people to recreate charts, they need the actual numbers that were used to generate the graphics.

The Press Conference: Coffee Is Served

One effective way to boost a report and accompanying press release is to present them at a press conference. Of course, there's the risk that no one will come. It has happened, even to top newsmakers.

While his press conferences are usually standing room only, the Reverend Jesse Jackson was no doubt surprised at a particular 1990 press conference he called to discuss the savings and loan crisis, but to which only one reporter came. The reporter, from the *Wall Street Journal*, wound up doing an amusing story on the amazing—for Jesse Jackson—occurrence of practically nobody showing up to hear what he had to say.

The press conference can be used as the exclusive platform to unveil a new study. More typically, however, it is run in tandem with the mail distribution of the study and press release. After a thorough presentation of the findings by the author of the study, he or she and other appropriate people involved should stick around to field questions and give one-on-one interviews, which are especially important to TV and radio broadcasts. To the individuals and organizations wanting the ink, the press conference offers the possibility—never the guarantee—of greater media attention and author control of the discussion.

Press conferences should always be scheduled with the reporters' deadlines in mind. Mid-morning or early afternoon are generally best. That allows enough time for TV reporters to complete their editing for the evening news and for print reporters to make the next day's first edition.

Advance notice of at least a few days should be given for press conferences. Press kits should be available, including the study, press release, appropriate charts and background material, and biographies and glossy black-and-white photos of key players. To generate as much publicity as possible for the sponsoring agency, it helps to have a banner with its name above the podium or a readable crest on the front of the lectern, to be captured by the TV and still cameras. And it doesn't hurt to have coffee, donuts, or sandwiches on hand for rushed reporters who must eat on the run.

Notices of the press conference can be included in the mailings of the study and press release. Also, if possible, try to get the press conference listed on the "day book" of the wire services. The day book is the daily listing of upcoming events of interest to reporters, produced by the Associated Press, United Press International, and Reuters. The day book, which is distributed to the clients of the wire services, includes a summary paragraph on the press conference with its location and the name and telephone number of a contact person. To get your client listed, contact the wire service bureaus, starting with the Associated Press in the nearest major city.

Assuming you've successfully negotiated the first hurdle and reporters have actually shown up for the press conference, the next challenge is to get everyone to focus on the important aspects of the findings. One old, if not venerated, way to do that is to plant a question or two among friendly reporters. But given the growing appeal of demographic research, there should be no shortage of pointed questions and little need for priming.

Controlling the Interview

Whether at a press conference or when a reporter telephones with some questions, it is important for the interviewee (you) to maintain as much control as possible. Obviously, that's nearly impossible if Sam Donaldson is in attendance, but always worth striving for.

For starters, never speak off the top of your head or ramble on. Always try to anticipate the questions that reporters will ask and know what you want to say, preferably something succinct, intelligent, and quotable. Offer cogent, colorful examples where appropriate.

You do not have to speak in prepackaged sound bites, but don't ruin your chances for good exposure by droning in leadenous compound, complex, run-on sentences, either. The aim is to get your message across. The way to do it is to speak directly, with authority, in a lively fashion, that makes people want to listen or read what you have to say.

If you get sidetracked, or an additional thought occurs to you some minutes after completing an answer, interject. Say something like: "Before answering the next question, I want to go back to the earlier one to add these further thoughts…"

If you don't know what to say or are not sure of your facts, never, never wing it. If you end up being wrong and your error ends up in print, you won't look like an expert. When you are not sure of an answer, turn to a dependable colleague to jump in, or tell the reporter that you will double-check to make sure and get back to him or her. Then do it promptly.

In talking with reporters, speak clearly but not too fast. People who speak too quickly increase the risk of being misquoted, especially if the reporters are taking notes without a tape recorder. But even a tape recording can garble words if they are spoken too quickly. At a press conference, without breaking the crystal or windows, speak up in a firm voice that can be heard in the back of the room. Tape recorders cannot always pick up what mumblers have to say.

During the give-and-take of an interview or press conference, you may find the discussion veering away from important points you want to get across. You must refocus the discussion. No matter what the next question is, answer it appropriately, but also slip in the information you want covered. Or simply hold off the next question, by saying: "Before we get to more questions, there are a few points that I want to bring into the discussion..."

Where possible, play editor by gently suggesting what the hot news is and possible story angles. You might even suggest additional sources to call to further develop the story.

When things are winding down, encourage reporters to call back if they have any follow-up questions or if they want to double-check some facts and figures. That protects you; it also protects them.

At the conclusion of an interview, never attempt to set conditions, such as: "Call me before you quote me," or "I want to read whatever you write before it goes into print." First off, you can't set rules after the game's been played. Second, few if any reporters would agree to such conditions, even at the outset. If you have any requests or ground rules, the time to set them down is before the cameras and tape recorders start rolling.

Some people have an aversion to being tape recorded. As they say in the FBI and CIA, a recording precludes "deniability" down the road. Assuming that you are not passing state secrets, however, it is usually in a reporter's and interviewee's mutual interest to tape record an interview, especially in a demographics discussion where there are a lot of statistics and some of the explanations are complicated. Using a tape recorder ensures that all the information is preserved and that quotes will be accurate.

SOURCES:

- *Editor & Publisher Yearbook*, Editor & Publisher, New York, New York.
- *Gale Directory of Publications & Broadcast Media,* Gale Research Inc., Detroit, Michigan.
- *Writer's Market*, Writer's Digest Books, Cincinnati, Ohio.
- *Media Marketing: How to Get Your Name & Story In Print & On the Air*, by Peter G. Miller, Harper & Row, New York, New York.
- *Power and Influence: Mastering the Art of Persuasion,* by Robert L. Dilenschneider, Prentice Hall Press, New York, New York.

17 Getting Stats Fast and First: Computer Access to the Census and Other Databases

Instead of patiently waiting for the mailman to deliver the Census Bureau's latest printed report, you can scoop the bureau and reporters everywhere by going right to your computer to get census data.

In response to increasing demand and uses, the Census Bureau and other government agencies now make their data available in several electronic formats, including online services, compact discs, and computer tape.

The advantages:

- **Access.** Online databases, computer tapes, and compact discs offer much quicker access to the data, sometimes weeks, even months, before reports are printed, released, and distributed.

- **Analytic Capability.** Data in all three formats can be massaged and crunched to varying degrees for custom analyses.

The disadvantages:

- **Lack of Historic Data.** Electronic data often do not include comparisons to previous years, as found in printed reports. To do so, one has to buy previous computer tapes (and make sure they have comparable geography), go to a private vendor who has done the comparisons, or make reference to the printed reports.

- **Cost.** The appropriate computer hardware and software are needed to access and use computerized data properly. The data alone can cost hundreds of dollars, while the hardware costs run into the thousands.

- **Expertise Required.** While going online is a relatively simple matter, diving into compact discs or computer tapes can require a great deal of computer ability, patience, and time. You can't bluff your way through the computer tapes, as a Washington, D.C.-based trade association discovered. The association, which shall remain nameless, used census tapes to prepare its own report on trends in its industry at the county level. Readers were amazed at how good business was. Unfortunately, a miscue in the programming had doubled all the numbers.

Then there's the time that *USA Today* scooped everybody, including the Census Bureau, with its front-page exclusive on America's center of population, based on its own analysis of the 1990 census computer tapes. It placed the nation's midpoint in a farmer's field in Crawford County, Missouri. But several months later, when the Census Bureau got around to publishing its own calculations, the actual spot was five miles away in a barely accessible forest.

These two stories are intended not to dissuade anyone from making use of census computer data, but rather to caution all who use them to be fully prepared. Don't rush, know what you're doing, and know when and where to get help.

High-Tech 1990 Census Data

Help with the Census Bureau's various computer products and formats is a telephone call away, to the bureau's Data User Services Division (DUSD), at (301) 763-4100. DUSD, which fields calls from the media and public, is the place to go to learn about the contents of individual computer products and to place orders. Some people have standing orders; others order individual tapes or compact discs.

The 284-page *Census Catalog & Guide 1991*, available from DUSD or the Government Printing Office, lists the tentative release schedule and price of census reports in both printed form and various computer formats. The catalog also provides a crash course in computer data options.

The master computer tapes from the 1990 census are known as Summary Tape Files (STF) and have designations ranging from STF-1A to STF-4D, each with different information. STF-1A through STF-2C have data from the short-form census questionnaire that was sent to all

U.S. households and include population counts by age, race, sex, Hispanic origin, and marital status, along with selected housing data. Data are available for the nation, states, metro areas, congressional districts, counties, towns, and cities, and in some cases down to the block level. (See Chapter 10 for definitions of census geographic areas.) STF-3 and STF-4 releases include the more detailed social and economic data that were collected from the "long-form" census questionnaires sent to one in six households. These include educational attainment, citizenship, migration, fertility, work experience, income, and more detailed housing information.

Block-level data from STF-1A and STF-3A will be available on microfiche, which cannot be manipulated. The bureau is preparing several special computer tape files to be released in 1992 and 1993, including a "County-to-County Migration File." Many of these data will never be published in printed form because the cost and magnitude of such publications would be prohibitive. While each 1990 census release has been available first on computer tapes, compact discs will probably become more popular, because they are easier to work with. With a compact disc reader, which costs several hundred dollars, a researcher can download data from the disc into a personal computer for use. In contrast, a tape drive costing several thousand dollars is needed to download data from a computer tape.

Some of the 1990 census STF releases will be available on compact disc. Census data broken down by zip code will be available on tape and possibly compact disc and online, which will make them popular with marketers. "There is growing interest at the desktop level in census computer products," says Kurt Metzger, a senior research analyst at Wayne State University's Center for Urban Studies. "A lot of people were interested in the mainframe tapes, primarily because they were out so much earlier than printed reports and other computer formats. But the whole idea of CD-ROM is going to push machine-readable data to the forefront, because of the ease of access." CD-ROM is shorthand for Compact Disc-Reader Only Memory.

In addition to ordering computer products directly from the Census Bureau's Data User Services Division, they can also be ordered from any of the state data centers found in all 50 states. The centers, often located at a state university or a department in state government, have been designated by the Census Bureau as the repository for census data in that state. A full list of the addresses and telephone numbers of the state data centers can be found in the *Census Catalog & Guide 1991*.

The 1990 census results are the new baseline for much social science and economic research, where until recently analysts have been operating with ten-year-old data from the 1980 census. Now that new data are available, researchers in state government, at universities, and in the private sector are working overtime to crunch and interpret those numbers for planning, scholarly, and marketing purposes. For those without the money or resources to do computer analysis themselves, this provides another avenue to the census findings. Let others do the work for you. Check with the state data centers as well as the social science departments of area universities to find out who's crunching the census data, what they're looking for, whether the results are available to others, and on what terms.

Even those who have the census computer tapes and are doing their own analysis should ask around to find out who at the universities, in state government, and in the private sector are also analyzing the tapes. While they may be working from the same database you are, they may be focusing on different combinations of data or levels of geography that yield yet another angle on the results.

For example, in 1991, the Census Bureau published population counts for towns and cities broken down by race and Hispanic origin. A quick look at the numbers shows that the suburbs overall experienced a significant influx of minorities during the 1980s. However, some researchers looking at the same data down to the block level have found that blacks are not evenly distributed, but rather heavily concentrated in certain suburban neighborhoods, particularly in older inner-ring suburbs. Asians—and to a lesser extent Hispanics—are more widely dispersed in suburbia.

Still other researchers crunching Summary Tape Files have added income and educational attainment to their analysis of population shifts. Adding those two variables shows that suburban blacks often have higher levels of income than white residents of the same immediate area, and that some upper-income black professionals are bypassing inner-ring suburbs for developments on the metro fringes.

In addition to its own standard reports, the Census Bureau does some customized analysis of its data, known as special tabulations, for paying customers. Many of the customers are states or counties trying to plan for the future, or corporations hoping to spot new trends and marketing opportunities within regions, including where to put new malls or restaurants. After someone or some organization has ordered and paid for a special tabulation, that information becomes available for purchase by others 18 months later. To find out what special tabulations are available, check with DUSD.

Another invaluable source of census and other government and private sector data is the Missouri Institute for Computer-Assisted Reporting (MICAR). Established at the University of Missouri's School of Journalism in 1989, the institute runs seminars and offers assistance to reporters and editors using any kind of database for journalistic purposes. MICAR has its own library of government and other databases and has developed software that lets newspapers and broadcasters use computer tapes without mainframe computers. MICAR's staff can also offer technical help and leads to reporters needing assistance.

Similar programs are run at Syracuse University, the Transactional Records Access Clearinghouse, and Indiana University School of Journalism's National Institute for Advanced Reporting.

With the proliferation of and demand for computerized data from the Census Bureau and elsewhere, an entire industry of private consultants and data-crunching firms has sprung up. The *Insider's Guide to Demographic Know-How*, published by American Demographics Books, lists over 75 such private firms, including CACI Marketing Systems, Claritas/NPDC, Datamap, Inc., Market Statistics, NPA Data Services, Inc., and the WEFA Group. Numerous organizations have retained these and other firms to crunch census data and other databases for them.

Keeping Up

Interest in government data has reached the point where users have formed several organizations to lobby, and to swap ideas and contacts. The Association of Public Data Users (APDU) was organized in 1975 and is based at Princeton University's Computing Center. The 350 members include marketers, academics, private corporations, planning agencies, government, and individual researchers, all bound by their interest in government data. The association holds an annual meeting in Washington, D.C.

For many journalists, planners, and business people, the Census Bureau's computer tape files are too much data, too much expense, and too much trouble, despite the advantages. Another way to stay on top is through CENDATA, available by computer through two information vendors, CompuServe and DIALOG.

CENDATA carries a daily list of printed reports released that day, along with a backlist of available reports. CENDATA's menu system is user friendly, and the bureau contends it does not require any special training. "Economic time-series data generally are online within an hour of their release to the media; other data are transmitted via CENDATA on a flow basis—in some cases, weeks before the printed report's appearance," notes a bureau announcement on the CENDATA service. "Users can reformat and import (data) into other applications programs after downloading to disk or printing."

In addition to 1990 census data, CENDATA also carries statistics on manufacturing, agriculture, business, construction and housing, foreign trade, government revenues and expenses, manufacturing, and international data. Press release summaries of the findings in each report can be immediately called up. In some cases, there are also extracts of Summary Tape File data for larger geographic areas like states and counties.

The Census Bureau has published several booklets that clearly explain the features of its various computer data products. The booklets include: *Hidden Treasures: Census Bureau Data and Where You Can Find It*, *Census '90 Basics*, *Census ABC's*, and *TIGER: The Coast-to-Coast Digital Map Database*.

TIGER is a census acronym for Topologically Integrated Geographic Encoding and Reference system, a digital map database that automates the mapping and related geographic activities required to support census and survey programs. An invaluable tool for marketers, TIGER itself doesn't contain census data. However, with the appropriate software, it permits spatial analysis of census statistics. TIGER, which includes all 50 states, has minute details down to roads, railroad tracks, and rivers.

TIGER, along with population density and other demographic data, are used to help locate everything from new shopping malls and restaurants to auto plants, hospitals, and schools. TIGER was also essential to the reapportionment and redistricting processes, which are the first and constitutional duties of each decennial census.

The Census Bureau has also set up a billboard that allows anyone with a personal computer and modem to message the bureau directly with inquiries. In addition to the Census Bureau, many other government agencies make their data available on various electronic formats. State data centers also have information on what is available from other agencies.

The monthly ten-page *APDU Newsletter* from the Association of Public Data Users carries briefs on new computer databases available from various government agencies and private sources, including nonprofit institutions and corporations.

The Insider's Guide to Demographic Know-How (American Demographics Books), by Diane Crispell, provides a rundown of some of the more interesting databases and the various formats in which they are available. Other directories of databases, available in most libraries, include: *The Directory of Online Databases*, Gale Research, Detroit; and *The Federal Database Finder*, Information USA, Inc., Kensington, Maryland.

There is an ever-growing list of databases, many thousands, available to anyone with a computer and the know-how to use it, for the price of the software and access time.

Here is a sampling of what's out there:

- Consumer Expenditure Survey, Bureau of Labor Statistics.
- National Assessment of Education Progress, Integrated Postsecondary Education Data Systems, and National Education Longitudinal Survey, all from the National Center for Education Statistics.
- Assorted health, hospitalization, birth, death, marriage, and divorce data, from the National Center for Health Statistics.
- American Housing Survey, Department of Housing and Urban Development; demographic and economic data on immigrants by zip code, Immigration and Naturalization Service.
- National Crime Survey, Bureau of Justice Statistics.

From other agencies, databases are available on motor vehicle accidents, air and water quality, traffic flow, on-time and late arrivals by scheduled airlines, and visits by foreign tourists.

Many of these and other databases are available directly from government agencies in several formats, including nine-track tape, CD-ROM, and online. Slater Hall Information Products, in Washington, D.C., also offers assorted government databases on compact disc with retrieval software.

Instead of going out and buying a nine-track tape, floppy disk, or CD-ROM to plug into your computer setup, going online allows you to plug your PC into a database by telephone via a modem. There are more than 3,000 online databases, many offering current as well as archival material. Among the assorted databases accessible online are newspapers, magazines, trade journals, bibliographies, dissertations, stock prices, residential and commercial real estate sales, lawsuits and their disposition, pending and enacted legislation, address lists broken down by demographic variables, demographics by zip code, industrial production and sales, retail and wholesale data, commodity prices, and press releases from everywhere. Some of the major online services are CompuServe, Congressional Quarterly, DIALOG, Dow Jones News Retrieval, and Mead Data Central, LEXIS•NEXIS.

In addition to the subscription fee, the user pays for access by the length of time connected to the database by telephone. After going through the menu and retrieving the precise data desired, you download it into your computer's memory for crunching and for future reference.

SOURCES:

- *Census Catalog & Guide 1990,* Data User Services Division, Census Bureau, Suitland, Maryland.
- Association of Public Data Users, Princeton, New Jersey.
- *The Insider's Guide to Demographic Know-How,* American Demographics Books, Ithaca, New York.
- Missouri Institute for Computer-Assisted Reporting, University of Missouri, Columbia, Missouri.

18 The Top-Ten Countdown: Trends to Track in the 1990s

As the 1990s unfold and we fast approach the magical 21st century, here are the ten trends a panel of one—your author—has decided are most important to track.

In no particular order, except for number one, they are:

10. Half a dozen states in the Sunbelt will continue to account for three-quarters of the population growth in the U.S. (Arizona, California, Florida, Georgia, Nevada, and Texas). They will also get a big chunk of the new jobs. As boom spots in those states mature, they will develop urban problems long seen in older Rustbelt cities. Water will become an increasingly hot Sunbelt issue and could alter growth patterns.

9. Suburbia will continue to spread ever outward and lead central cities and nonmetro areas in population growth. Not only people, but jobs, will increasingly head for the suburbs, which will no longer be subservient to the cities. Suburban issues will become dominant on regional agendas, because suburban coalitions will have more votes than cities in state legislatures and Congress.

8. Members of the baby bust, the much smaller generation right behind the baby boomers, are entering their 20s and starting to flex their economic muscles. Marketers and media will begin to pay attention. As a smaller group, they will be at an advantage in buying their first homes, because of the oversupply of starter houses left behind by baby boomers. Busters will also face less job competition from each other than do the boomers.

7. The family, battered by decades of divorce and rearrangements, will enter a period of relative stability, if not calm. People will marry later, and hopefully be better prepared financially and emotionally. Divorce will level off or drop. The importance of the family is being rediscovered.

6. Immigration will account for a rising share of population growth in the 1990s, with more than three-quarters of the newcomers coming from Asia and Latin countries. The majority will settle in the Sunbelt. They will also help repopulate and revitalize older urban centers.

5. Blacks will remain America's largest minority through the 1990s, but may be surpassed by Hispanics around 2015. Blacks and Hispanics overall will narrow the income and educational gap with whites, although a large minority underclass will remain. Asians, although much smaller in number, will garner attention because they will remain the fastest-growing group, with the highest educational attainment and household income.

4. Elementary and secondary schools (K-12), after seeing enrollments decline in recent decades because of the baby bust, are growing again, as echo boom babies advance through the school system. Enrollment is also becoming ever more racially and ethnically diverse, adding new challenges and opportunities at a time when the importance of quality education is greater than ever. Colleges will scramble to find new teachers, while trying to upgrade their curriculums and turn out better-prepared graduates.

3. Retirees and people downshifting from their first careers will be looking for vacation and retirement getaways. A growing number will bypass Florida and Arizona and head for less crowded and less expensive spots like the Ozarks and Appalachia. A new generation of boom spots will emerge beyond metro areas, around lakes and forests, but within a few hours' drive of the big cities. Also, we will move ever closer to water, the most precious natural resource.

2. Women workers will continue to increase their share of the work force. Whether pursuing career goals or working because they must, women will place special demands on employers for child care, flex-time, and part-time work. Employers will respond to keep good workers happy

and productive. Expect more people to work at home. While the work force ages, the minority share will grow, with the fastest growth among Hispanics and Asians. Employers and workers will increasingly confront language barriers and widely varying skill levels. This will put a greater burden on employers to train new workers and upgrade the skills of experienced workers.

1. The baby boom has sprouted gray hairs and is now smack in middle age. Because of their massive numbers, boomers will continue igniting trends for the rest of their lives. They will make sure that health care and Social Security are front-burner issues, and they will turn the heat way up.

And finally, here is the most important statistic in all of demography: 3,017,634,040. No, that's not the population of the world, but rather the telephone number of the public information office at the Census Bureau.

Give them a call: (301) 763-4040.

Appendix I

. . . .

Source Addresses and Telephone Numbers

Appendix: Source Addresses and Telephone Numbers

Age Wave, Inc.
1900 Powell Street
Emeryville, CA 94608
(415) 652-9099

American Association of
  Marriage and Family Therapy
1100 17th Street, NW, 10th Floor
Washington 20036
(202) 452-0109

American Association of Retired Persons
601 E Street, NW
Washington, DC 20049
(202) 434-2277

American College Testing
P.O. Box 168
Iowa City, IA 52243
(319) 337-1000

American Council of Education
One Dupont Circle, Suite 800
Washington, DC 20036
(202) 939-9300

American Demographics
P.O. Box 68
Ithaca, NY 14851
(800) 828-1133

American Enterprise Institute
1150 17th Street, NW
Washington, DC 20036
(202) 862-5829

American Jewish Committee
165 East 56th Street
New York, NY 10022
(212) 751-4000

American Medical Association
515 North State Street
Chicago, IL 60610
(312) 464-5000

American Sociological Association
1722 N Street, NW
Washington, DC 20036
(202) 833-3410

American Statistical Association
1429 Duke Street
Alexandria, VA 22314-3402
(703) 684-1221

Americans for Generational Equity
415 D Street, NE
Washington, DC 20002
(202) 686-4196

Asia Society
725 Park Avenue
New York, NY 10021
(212) 288-6400

Association of American Geographers
1710 16th Street, NW
Washington, DC 20009-3198
(202) 234-1450

Association of Governing Boards of
  Universities and Colleges
One Dupont Circle, Suite 400
Washington, DC 20036
(202) 296-8400

Association of Public Data Users
Princeton University Computing Center
87 Prospect Avenue
Princeton, NJ 08544
(609) 258-6025

Battelle Memorial Institute
505 King Avenue
Columbus, OH 43201-2693
(614) 424-7906

BrainReserve, Inc.
1 Madison Avenue
28th floor
New York, NY 10010
(212) 481-8580

Brookings Institution
1775 Massachusetts Avenue, NW
Washington, DC 20036
(202) 797-6000

Bureau of the Census
Washington, DC 20233
(physically located at 4600 Silver Hill Road,
Suitland, Maryland)
(301) 763-4040

Bureau of Economic Analysis
U.S. Department of Commerce
1401 K Street, NW
Washington, DC 20230
(202) 523-0777

Bureau of Economic and Business Research
221 Matherly Hall
University of Florida
Gainesville, FL 32611-2017
(904) 392-0171

Bureau of Labor Statistics
U.S. Department of Labor
441 G Street, NW
Washington, DC 20212
(202) 523-1913

CACI
1100 North Glebe Road
Arlington, VA 22201
(703) 841-7800
(800) 292-2240

Center for American Women and Politics
Eagleton Institute
Rutgers University
New Brunswick, NJ 08901
(908) 828-2210

Center for Continuing Study of the
  California Economy
610 University Avenue
Palo Alto, CA 94301
(415) 321-8550

Center for Demography and Ecology
4412 Social Science Building
University of Wisconsin
Madison, WI 53706
(608) 262-2182

227

Center for Migration Studies
209 Flagg Place
Staten Island, NY 10304
(718) 351-8800

Center for Population Research
231 Poulton Hall
Georgetown University
Washington, DC 20057
(202) 687-6807

Center for Population Studies
Harvard University
9 Bow Street
Cambridge, MA 02138
(617) 495-2021

Center for the Study of Popular Culture
Bowling Green State University
Bowling Green, OH 43403
(419) 372-2981

Center for the Study of Population
Florida State University
654 Bellamy Building
Tallahassee, FL 32306-4063
(904) 644-1762

Center on Budget and Policy Priorities
777 North Capitol Street, NE, Suite 705
Washington, DC 20002
(202) 408-1080

Centers for Disease Control
1600 Clifton Road, N.E.
Atlanta, GA 30333
(404) 639-3311

Children's Defense Fund
122 C Street, NW, Suite 400
Washington, DC 20001
(202) 628-8787

Claritas/NPDC
201 North Union Street
Suite 200
Alexandria, VA 22314
(703) 683-8300

College Entrance Examination Board
Educational Testing Service
Rosedale Road
Princeton, NJ 08541
(609) 921-9000

Conference Board
845 Third Avenue
New York, NY 10022
(212) 759-0900

Council for the Advancement and
  Support of Education
11 Dupont Circle, Suite 400
Washington, DC 20036
(202) 328-5900

Data User Services Division
Customer Services Office
U.S. Bureau of the Census
Washington, DC 20233
(301) 763-4100

Department of Agriculture
Population Section
Economic Research Service
1301 New York Avenue, NW, Room 340
Washington, DC 20005
(202) 219-0535

Department of Commerce
14th Street and Constitution Avenue, NW
Washington, DC 20230
(800) 424-5197
(202) 377-2000

Department of Health and Human Services
200 Independence Avenue, SW
Washington, DC 20201
(202) 619-0257

Department of Labor
200 Constitution Avenue, NW
Washington, DC 20210
(202) 523-4000

Department of Transportation
400 7th Street, SW
Washington, DC 20590
(202) 366-4000

Donnelley Marketing Information Services
70 Seaview Avenue
Stamford, CT 06904
(203) 353-7000

East-West Center
Population Institute
1777 East-West Road
Honolulu, HI 96848
(808) 944-7444

Editor & Publisher
11 West 19th Street
New York, NY 10011
(212) 675-4380

Election Data Services
1225 I Street, NW, Suite 700
Washington, DC 20005
(202) 789-2004

Forecasting International, Ltd.
1001 North Highland Street
Arlington, VA 22201
(703) 527-1311

Gale Research, Inc.
835 Penobscot Building
Detroit, MI 48226
(800) 877-4253

George Gallup Organization
47 Hulsich Street
Princeton, NJ 08542
(609) 924-9600

General Accounting Office
441 G Street, NW, Room 7049
Washington, DC 20548
(202) 275-2812

Allan Guttmacher Institute
111 Fifth Avenue
New York, NY 10003
(212) 254-5656

Louis Harris & Associates, Inc.
630 Fifth Avenue
New York, NY 10111
(212) 698-9600

Heritage Foundation
214 Massachusetts Avenue, NE
Washington, DC 20002
(202) 546-4400

Hispanic Policy Development Project
1001 Connecticut Avenue, NW
Suite 310
Washington, DC 20036
(202) 822-8414

Hudson Institute
5395 Emerson Way
Indianapolis, IN 46226
(317) 545-1000

Immigration and Naturalization Service
U.S. Department of Justice
425 I Street, NW
Washington, DC 20536
(202) 376-3066

Inferential Focus
200 Madison Avenue, Room 1904
New York, NY 10016
(212) 683-2060

Institute for Alternative Futures
108 North Alfred Street, 2nd floor
Alexandria, VA 22314
(703) 684-5880

Institute for Public Policy Studies
440 Lorch Hall
University of Michigan
Ann Arbor, MI 48109-1220
(313) 764-3490

Institute for Research on Poverty
1180 Observatory Drive, Room 3412
University of Wisconsin
Madison, WI 53706
(608) 262-6358

Institute for Social Research
University of Michigan
426 Thompson Street
Ann Arbor, MI 48109-1248
(313) 764-8363

Institute for Social Research
UCLA
Los Angeles, CA 90024
(213) 825-4321

Institute for Urban Studies
University of Maryland
1119 Lefrak Hall
College Park, MD 20742
(301) 405-6790

Internal Revenue Service
111 Constitution Avenue, NW
Washington, D.C. 20224
(202) 566-4024

Joint Center for Housing Studies
Harvard University
79 John F. Kennedy Street
Cambridge, MA 02138
(617) 495-7908

Joint Center for Political Studies
1301 Pennsylvania Avenue, NW, Suite 400
Washington, DC 20004
(202) 626-3500

Joint Economics Committee
U.S. Congress
G-01 Dirksen
Washington, DC 20510
(202) 224-5171

Langer Associates, Inc.
19 West 44th Street
New York, NY 10036
(212) 391-0350

Missouri Institute of Computer
  Assisted Reporting
120 Neff Hall
School of Journalism
University of Missouri
Columbia, MO 65211
(314) 882-0684

National Association of Counties
440 First Street, NW 8th floor
Washington, DC 20001
(202) 393-6226

National Association of Home Builders
15th and M Streets, NW
Washington, DC 20005
(202) 822-0200

National Association of Latino
  Elected & Appointed Officials
708 G Street, SE
Washington, DC 20003
(202) 546-2536

National Catholic Education Association
1077 30th Street, NW, Suite 100
Washington, DC 20007
(202) 337-6232

National Center for Education Statistics
U.S. Department of Education
555 New Jersey Avenue, NW
Washington, DC 20208-5650
(800) 424-1616, (202) 219-1395

National Center for Health Statistics
U.S. Department of Health & Human Services
6525 Belcrest Road
Hyattsville, MD 20782
(301) 436-8500

National Council on Aging
409 Third Street, SWSuite 200
Washington, DC 20024
(202) 479-1200

National Council of Churches
475 Riverside Drive
New York, NY 10115
(212) 870-2227

National Education Association
1201 16th Street, NW
Washington, DC 20036
(202) 833-4000

National Institute for Advanced Reporting
School of Journalism
Indiana University ES 4104
902 West New York Street
Indianapolis, IN 46202-5154
(317) 274-2774

National Journal Inc.
1730 M Street, NW
Washington, DC 20036
(202) 857-1400

National League of Cities
1301 Pennsylvania Avenue, NW
Washington, DC 20004
(202) 626-3000

National Opinion Research Center
University of Chicago
1155 East 60th Street
Chicago, IL 60637
(312) 753-7500

National Urban League
500 East 62nd Street
New York, NY 10021
(212) 310-9000

Northeast Midwest Institute
218 D Street, SE
Washington, DC 20003
(202) 544-5200

NPA Data Services
1424 16th Street, NW, Suite 700
Washington, DC 20036
(202) 265-7685

231

Office of Population Research
Princeton University
21 Prospect Avenue
Princeton, NJ 08544
(609) 258-4870

Population Association of America
1722 N Street, NW
Washington, DC 20036
(202) 429-0891

Population Reference Bureau
1875 Connecticut Avenue, NW, Suite 520
Washington, DC 20009-5728
(202) 483-1100

Population Resource Center
15 Roszel Road
Princeton, NJ 08540
(609) 452-2822

Population Studies Center
University of Michigan
1225 South University Avenue
Ann Arbor, MI 48104-2590
(313) 998-7270

Population Studies and Training Center
Brown University
Box 1916
Providence, RI 02912
(401) 863-2668

Public Information Office
Bureau of the Census
Washington, DC 20233
(physically located at 4600 Silver Hill Road,
Suitland, Maryland)
(301) 763-4040

Rand Corporation
P.O. Box 2138
Santa Monica, CA 90407-2138
(213) 393-0411

Roper Center for Public Opinion Research
University of Connecticut
341 Mansfield Road, Room 421
Box U-164
Storrs, CT 06269-1164
(203) 486-4440

Runzheimer International
Runzheimer Park
Rochester, WI 53167
(414) 534-3121

Rural Sociology Department
350 Agriculture Hall
University of Wisconsin
Madison, WI 53706
(608) 262-1510

Select Committee on Children,
   Youth and Families
U.S. House of Representatives
385 House Office Building , Annex 2
Washington, DC 20515
(202) 226-7660

Social Security Administration
Baltimore, MD 21235
(800) 772-1213

Sociology Department
University of Chicago
1126 East 59th Street
Chicago, IL 60637
(312) 702-1234

Southwest Voter Research Institute
403 East Commerce Street
Suite 260
San Antonio, TX 78205
(512) 222-8014

SRI International
333 Ravenswood Avenue
Menlo Park, CA 94025-3493
(415) 859-4324

Statistics Canada
Ottawa, Ontario
Canada K1A 0T6
(613) 951-8116

Stepfamily Foundation
333 West End Avenue
New York, NY 10023
(212) 877-3244

Subcommittee on Census and Population
Committee on Post Office & Civil Service
608 HOB Annex 1
Washington, DC 20515
(202) 226-7523

Sunbelt Institute
409 3rd Street, SW, Suite 202
Washington, DC 20024
(202) 554-0201

Superintendent of Documents
U.S. Government Printing Office
Washington, DC 20402
(202) 783-3238

Teenage Research Unlimited
601 Skokie Boulevard
Northbrook, IL 60062
(708) 564-3440

Towers Perrin
245 Park Avenue
New York, NY 10167
(212) 309-3400

Transactional Records Access Clearinghouse
478 Newhouse II
Syracuse University
Syracuse, NY 13244-2100
(315) 443-3563

United Nations Population Fund
United Nations
220 East 42nd Street
New York, NY 10017
(212) 297-5000

United States Catholic Conference
3211 Fourth Street, NE
Washington, DC 20017
(202) 541 3000

United States Conference of Mayors
1620 I Street, NW
Washington, DC 20006
(202) 293-7330

Urban Institute
211 M Street, NW
Washington, DC 20037
(202) 833-7200

Urban Research Institute
University of Louisville
426 West Bloom Street
Louisville, KY 40292
(502) 588-6626

U.S. Chamber of Commerce
1615 H Street, NW
Washington, DC 20062
(202) 659-5000

WEFA Group
401 City Avenue, Suite 300
Bala Cynwyd, PA 19004
(215) 667-6000

Woods & Poole Economics
1794 Columbia Road, NW
Washington, DC 20009
(202) 332-7111

World Future Society
4916 Saint Elmo Avenue
Bethesda, MD 20814
(301) 656-8274

Worldwatch Institute
1776 Massachusetts Avenue, NW
Washington, DC 20036
(202) 452-1999

Yankelovich Clancy Shulman
8 Wright Street
Westport, CT 06880
(203) 227-2700

Zero Population Growth
1400 16th Street, NW, Suite 320
Washington, DC 20036
(202) 332-2200

Appendix II

· · · · · · · · · · · · · · ·

Glossary
of Terms

Glossary

Adjustment. A major controversy surrounding the 1990 census—and the subject of pending litigation—was the decision by then Commerce Secretary Robert Mosbacher to not statistically adjust the results upward to compensate for the people missed. He maintained that there is no guarantee that adjusted counts would be more accurate than the original numbers, and they could be less accurate, especially below the state level.

Average. There are several kinds of so-called averages. The most common type is mean, which is derived by adding together all the values, then dividing the total by the number of units. (See page 156 for more specifics.)

Baby Boom. 77 million people were born between 1946 and 1964, comprising the generation known as the baby boom. Women on average had 3.7 children during this period. Making up 31 percent of the U.S. population, baby boomers are forever igniting trends and are a prime target for marketers. The boom peaked in 1957 when 4.3 million babies were born; it ended after 1964, when births dropped below 4 million and kept plunging.

Baby Boomlet (see Echo Baby Boom).

Baby Bust. After the last baby boom year of 1964, births began to drop, plunging to a low of 3.1 million in 1973 and hovering around that level through 1976. This is the baby bust generation, totaling only 41 million. During this period, the typical woman had just under two children. Keeping births low: newly liberalized divorce laws, introduction of the Pill, legalization of abortion, and the women's movement, which sent growing numbers of women into college and the work force. As a small generation, busters in theory have less competition among themselves for jobs than did the more numerous boomers.

CD ROM (Compact disc, read-only memory). This is one of the computer formats through which 1990 census data are available. CD ROM versions of census reports are available for purchase directly from the Census Bureau or through its 50-state network of state data centers.

CENDATA. This online computer file contains electronic versions of Census Bureau reports, which can be accessed by modem through CompuServe or DIALOG.

Census. Formally known as the decennial census, the U. S. census is the actual enumeration of the entire country, conducted every 10 years by the Census Bureau in years ending in zero. The Constitution requires a census for the purpose of reapportioning the 435 seats in the U.S. House of Representatives, and for local redistricting. The results are also used in policy and business planning, and as part of formulas that distribute over $45 billion annually in federal funds. Results from each new census are hungrily awaited by countless researchers, because the numbers set the new baseline for much of the scholarly and policy research in the social sciences and government. The first census was conducted in 1790, under the direction of Thomas Jefferson. Even then there were complaints about people being missed. Among the vociferous complainers was George Washington.

Census Bureau. A part of the Commerce Department, the Census Bureau is the federal agency that conducts the census every 10 years in years ending in zero, and the ongoing Current Population Survey. Census data are vital to congressional reapportionment and redistricting, as well as public and private planning and allocation of federal funding. The bureau was not established as a permanent agency until 1902. Prior to that, a temporary organization was set up every decade and then shut down after completion of the count and publication of its results.

Current Population Survey. In addition to the decennial census, the Census Bureau also conducts the ongoing Current Population Survey as a means of gathering intercensal data, providing a sense of changes occurring between censuses. The CPS, as it is commonly called, is conducted monthly at some 56,000 households, which constitutes a representative national sample.

Demography. Sociology was once called the science of the obvious. If that's so, then demography, sociology's first cousin, is the science of taking the obvious to its less than obvious conclusions. Demography is the statistical study of people, quantifying changes in how people live, work, and play.

Echo Baby Boom. In the late 1970s and through the 1980s, births began rising again in what's been tagged the Echo Boom, also known as the baby boomlet. Women continued to have small families as they did during the baby-bust years, but what causes births to shoot up is that many women who started families in the late 1970s were themselves from the original baby boom, so there were more of them around to have children. As of 1990, births had reached 4.2 million higher than in 1964—the last year of the original baby boom. The echo boom is likely to slope off soon. Births should begin falling in the early 1990s as the massive baby boom passes out of its childbearing years.

Family Household. Two or more people who are related by blood, marriage or adoption, and living under the same roof constitute a family, as defined by the Census Bureau and demographers in general.

Hispanic Origin. As with race, Hispanic origin is a matter of self-identification. Hispanic is an ethnic grouping, derived from a Spanish-speaking culture. Hispanics can be of any race, although the majority identify themselves as white.

Household. The people who live in a dwelling—apartment, condo, house, or mobile home—comprises a household. Households are divided into two basic types: family households, in which at least one other person is related to the householder, and nonfamily households, in which a person lives alone or with nonrelatives.

Householder. Reference person by whom many household characteristics are measured, including household type.

Immigration. Immigration is the movement of people into a country, including both legal immigrants and illegal or undocumented immigrants. Emigration is the movement of people out of a country.

Life expectancy. Usually computed from year of birth, life expectancy has risen steadily with the passing years, as diet, lifestyle and medicine have improved. To take these advances into account for older age groups, remaining years of life expectancy is also computed for various age groups, typically in 10-year cohorts. For example, men aged 65 in 1987 had an additional 14.8 years of life expectancy; women, 18.7 years.

Mean. The most frequently used average and what most people mean when they say average, it is derived by adding together all the values or numbers, and then dividing that total by the number of values—or numbers—added together.

Median. A type of average, median is that middle number or point at which half of units fall above, half below. For example, the 1990 U.S. median household income of $29,943 indicates that half of households have higher incomes, half have lower.

Metropolitan Area. A central city of at least 50,000 population, plus the surrounding suburbs and cities that are economically and socially linked to the central city combine to form a metro area, for a minimum total population of 100,000. The Office of Management and Budget is the final arbiter of metro areas. There are currently 284 metropolitan statistical areas. By 1990, 77.5 percent of the population was living in a metropolitan area (central cities, 31.3 percent; suburbs, 46.2 percent). The metro areas and their component counties and cities are listed in the Census Bureau's annual *Statistical Abstract*.

Migration. Relocation from one residence to another is called migration. Two-thirds of the migration within the U.S. is within the same county. The so-called Sunbelt has been the destination of the majority of migrants during the last two decades. While immigration and emigration refer to international movement, migration usually refers to moves within a country.

Natural Increase. The excess of births over deaths is population growth due to natural increase. It does not take migration into consideration.

Nonmetropolitan Area. The area that is not defined as metropolitan. The 22.5 percent of the population outside metropolitan areas are living in nonmetro areas. (See **Metropolitan Area**)

Population Association of America. A professional association of demographers with over 2,800 members and based in Washington, D.C., the PAA holds an annual meeting at which hundreds of research papers are presented on the latest academic demographic research.

Population Change. Population changes—up or down—are the net result of four factors: births, deaths, immigration, and outmigration.

Poverty. Everybody at one time or another feels that he or she is poor, but the federal government is the ultimate judge. Based on an annually adjusted market basket, which includes food, transportation, utilities, and housing; the government comes up with an annual poverty threshold. Those with income below the threshold are considered officially poor. The threshold varies depending on the size of the household; the threshold for a family of four in 1990 was $13,359.

Race. You are what you say you are. Race is often a matter of self-identification—filling in the blank on a survey or census questionnaire. Choices include: white, black/African American, Asian or Pacific Islander, American Indian, and Other. Note that Hispanic is not included among the races; it is an ethnic category.

Replacement Level Fertility. For a couple—and a nation—to merely replace themselves; they must have 2.1 children per couple. The 0.1 children bonus counterbalances those who die before reaching reproductive age themselves. During the baby boom era of the 1950s and early 1960s, couples had well over three children per couple. In the 1970s, fertility dropped below replacement level. If maintained for over a generation, the U.S. population would ultimately begin shrinking, which some Census Bureau population projections suggest. However, this could be more than counterbalanced by immigration, which in recent years has been running at over 600,000 annually. And fertility rate in recent years have hovered around the replacement level of 2.1.

Statistical Abstract. Perhaps the most important reference book published by the Census Bureau is the annual *Statistical Abstract of the United States*, which contains not only the latest census results on dozens of subjects, but also historical statistics for comparisons, updated data from the Current Population Survey, and data from other government and private sources.

Summary Tape File. Data from the 1990 Census are released in both printed reports and electronic format, including computer tapes. The later are known as Summary Tape Files, with designations ranging from STF-1A to STF-4D. The advantage of the STF files is that they contain much more data detail and for smaller areas of geography than found in the printed reports; some STF tapes go down to the census block level. The disadvantage is that they require a lot of time-consuming number crunching and formatting, and there are no historical comparisons, as found in many printed reports.

Undercount. Despite the best efforts of 350,000 enumerators who worked months attempting to count everyone in the U. S. in the 1990 Census, some people were missed. This is called the undercount. After double-checking its own work through the Post-Enumeration Survey or PES, the Census Bureau estimated that it missed 2.1 percent of the 1990 population, or 5.3 million people.

Index

(See also the Glossary and Sources)

* indicates table or chart

income trends 113
migration trends16-17, 20, 125-126
population growth 26
vernacular 140-141
religion 67-68
retirement:
Social Security 95-96
migration 22-23, 125-126, 224
rural population 135

S

smoking 149
Social Security 5, 95-96
spending patterns 121*
states: 223
data centers 168-169
death rates and life expectancy 147
population change 1990-91 18-19*
migration trends 16-17, 20, 22-23
statistics:
definitions 153-159
reporting on 177-178, 189-192, 194-195
suburbs 134-140, 223
surveys 161-164

T-V

teachers 81-82
TIGER file 219-220
unmarried couples 34
urban population 135

W

water, and population growth 26-27
whites:
education 72, 76-77*

health 149
household types 39
income 110
out-of-wedlock births 39, 47
women:
family heads 35-36, 39
health 149
income 111
labor force participation 86-88, 224
marriage and economic status 48-50
poverty 105

X-Z

young adults:
delayed family formation 38, 47
yuppies 120

Photo by Christine Dunn

William Dunn is a contributing editor of *American Demographics* magazine, a Dow Jones monthly business magazine. His reports on demographic trends have also appeared in *Nation's Business.*

He began writing about demographics in 1977 at *The Detroit News,* one of the first reporters in the country to cover population trends as a regular beat. From 1986 to 1990, he was the demographics writer for *USA Today* and the Gannett News Service.

His articles on a variety of other topics have been published in numerous major publications, including *The New York Times, The Los Angeles Times, The Boston Globe, Us,* and *Publishers Weekly.*

Dunn, who lives in Chevy Chase, Maryland, with his wife, Christine, is at work on another book to be published by American Demographics Books in the spring of 1993.

Also From American Demographics Books

Capturing Customers: How to Target the Hottest Markets of the '90s
Peter Francese and Rebecca Piirto
Explains how to integrate psychographic information with media preference data, demographic data, and geographic information. This perspective allows you to fully understand who your customers are and how to market to them most effectively. In a highly competitive, information-driven business environment, marketing efficiency is the key to success.

Beyond Mind Games:
The Marketing Power of Psychographics
Rebecca Piirto
The first book that details what psychographics is, where it came from, and how you can use it. Anecdotal examples of applied psychographic research make this one of the most interesting, revealing, and enjoyable books in the field of marketing.

The Seasons of Business: The Marketer's Guide to Consumer Behavior
Judith Waldrop
A unique guide to seasonal marketing that examines, for every month, the primary marketing events, participation in sports and leisure activities, health-care issues, and personal attitudes. Learn which demographic groups are the principal players and which consumer concerns are most pressing.

Desktop Marketing:
Lessons from America's Best
Richard K. Thomas and Russell J. Kirchner
Dozens of case studies show you how top corporations in all types of industries use today's technology to find tomorrow's customers.

The Insider's Guide to Demographic Know-How: How to Find, Analyze, and Use Information About Your Customers
Diane Crispell
Using her behind-the-scenes knowledge of the data industry, the editor of the award-winning newsletter, *The Numbers News*, shows you how to find and analyze the data you need to make important decisions—and do it at the most economical price. Features a directory listing over 600 sources of data and related services.

The Almanac of Consumer Markets:
The Official Guide to the Demographics of American Consumers
Margaret K. Ambry, Ph.D.
Organized by age group, this ground-breaking reference profiles American consumers by variables separating buyers from nonbuyers—education, income, health, household type, and much more—and highlights the demographic changes that will be creating new markets in the 1990s.

American Demographics magazine
The most authoritative information about consumer change and how it affects your business. This monthly magazine is your guide to understanding today's marketplace and the consumer information industry.

The Numbers News
A monthly newsletter that gives you a jump on the future, with information on important trends such as the aging of the population, increasing ethnic diversity, and the fragmenting of household types. A behind-the-scenes news section provides informed coverage of census reports, new products, and data sources, to give you the marketing advantage you need.

Books and publications may be ordered by calling 800-828-1133.
For more information write to:

AMERICAN
DEMOGRAPHICS BOOKS.

P.O. Box 68, Ithaca, NY 14851